Give Your Child a Superior Mind

A PROGRAM FOR THE PRESCHOOL CHILD BY

Siegfried and Therese Engelmann

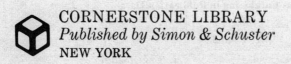

CORNERSTONE LIBRARY
Published by Simon & Schuster
NEW YORK

This Cornerstone Library edition is a revised
edition of the original hardcover book
published by Simon & Schuster

Manufactured in the United States of America
10 9 8 7 6 5

Library of Congress Cataloging in Publication Data

Engelmann, Siegfried.
    Give your child a superior mind.

    1. Education, Preschool—1945-   I. Engelmann,
Therese, joint author.   II. Title.
LB1140.E5   1981   372′.21   80-27527

ISBN 0-346-12532-4

Contents

4: WHAT YOU MUST KNOW 72

PART TWO: The Preschool Curriculum

7: THREE YEARS TO FOUR YEARS 136

8: FOUR YEARS TO FIVE YEARS 188

PART ONE

CHAPTER I

Issues

THIS BOOK PRESENTS a detailed program for teaching academic skills—reading, language, arithmetic—to your preschool child, an endeavor that may seem intimidating to you. There are three reasons for teaching academic skills to your preschool child. These are:

1. If your child learns these skills as a preschooler, your child will be smarter than the average child and will be in a position to learn new skills at a faster rate.

2. The schools are not well designed to teach every child academic skills. If you leave the teaching to the schools, your child may be a school failure and may learn to hate school and academic work.

3. Perhaps most important, teaching your child is a very nice and natural thing to do. The most basic relationship among humans is the transmission of knowledge from parent to child. Parents teach other important skills, such as dressing and eating. They direct the child's activities. Academic skills are important, and the child will be engaged in them for a lifetime. When the skills are taught in a home-teaching situation, the child is shown that the parent is interested in these skills and that they are part of the parent-child relationship.

Teaching your child is not easy, but it is probably not as difficult as you imagine. Initially, your child may balk, just as the child may have balked about getting dressed in some situations or following some of the other rules that you had established. Even though teaching academic skills requires some preparation, a schedule, and a commitment, it can be a very rewarding part of the day, a basis for the most intimate kind of sharing.

Regarding your ability to teach: If you can teach your child how to dress, you should be able to teach academic skills. Follow the same format of helping the child and not expecting the child to do everything at once.

Regarding your child's ability to learn: Even if your child gives no sign of being exceptionally bright, your child can learn to read and learn to perform arithmetic operations before entering the first grade. Furthermore, if you work with your child, your child will become very smart.

THE PHYSICAL ENVIRONMENT— THE FIRST TEACHER

The child's rate of early learning is limited by practical considerations. Before learning more sophisticated skills, the child must learn the basic ones. The environment for infants is usually quite similar, because children must learn the same skills. A child raised in Nebraska makes the same babbling sounds as a baby in Peru. These children learn to walk at about the same age and they learn basic hand-eye operations at about the same age. The most potent environment conceivable could not seriously accelerate their performance through infancy because the physical environment is teaching them at a very high rate. The physical environment gives them feedback as to whether they are moving their hands appropriately. The physical environment teaches the behaviors associated with walking. Failure to follow these rules leads to punishment. If the child does not maintain an appropriate center of balance when trying to walk, the physical environment will be very consistent. If the child tries to walk inappropriately seventy-eight times, the physical environment will punish the child seventy-eight times.

Plop. The environment is not moved by sympathy or tears. It does not care how charming the infant is or how good the child has been at doing some other things. The seventy-eighth trial is met with the same response the others received—plop.

For the physical environment to be an effective teacher of infants, very little conscious manipulation by adults is needed. If the child has freedom to attempt to do things, the child's wired-in tendencies to explore, imitate, and create changes in the environment will interact with the environment and produce good learning. During this learning, the environment plays the role of an overbearing authoritative agent that constantly monitors the child, lavishly correcting any errors the child makes and reinforcing the child for appropriate behaviors. The reinforcement takes the form of permission. If the child appropriately observes the rules of maintaining balance, the environment permits the child to walk.

When the overbearing physical environment is stripped of authority and transformed into a more gentle thing, learning becomes severely retarded. Imagine a place that is designed to handcuff the physical environment, a monotonous place, with no great range of things to see or hear, with nothing very hard or very soft, very loud or very subtle. Put infants on their backs in shallow cribs, make a rule that we never turn them over, rarely pick them up (even when we feed them or change them) and give them the barest human contact. Attendants will not talk to them. In such a place, the physical environment would be handcuffed.

This description refers to a real place, a foundling home in Teheran, described by Wayne Dennis in *Journal of Genetic Psychology* (1960). Only 14 percent of the children were able to crawl *at the age of one to two years*. Only 42 percent of them could sit alone at this age. And only 15 percent of them could walk alone *at the age of three to four years*!

15

THE SOCIAL ENVIRONMENT

The physical environment effectively teaches the first skills the child must master. But it stops dramatically at this point. It does not teach the mental skills the child is expected to learn—language concepts, reading and arithmetic skills, and social skills. These skills are far beyond the domain of the physical environment. Consider the physical environment's responses to a child's attempt at reading the word *mat*. Let's assume that the child wants to read the word accurately and that the child calls the word "egg." Would the physical environment throw the child to the ground or perhaps prevent the child from saying the word? No. Would the environment provide the child with any information that the response is inappropriate? No. The environment that had been so typical when the child was engaged in learning to walk, ride a bike, open doors, and put on clothing is now mute. It does not respond because these incredible mental operations are not part of the physical environment. They don't exist in the same way that walking or opening a door exists.

By observing the physical environment, we discover what an effective teaching environment must do. If the physical environment is successful at teaching physical skills, it seems reasonable to believe that an environment modelled after it would be effective for teaching mental skills. The difference would be that human agents would have to perform feedback and correction functions that the physical environment performs for physical skills. When the child attempts to open a door, the physical environment "corrects" the child. Only a certain set of behaviors will lead to an open door. The physical environment rejects all others. (If the child tries to push on the door without first turning the knob, the door does not open.)

An effective environment for mental skills would provide similar feedback. Just as the physical environment rejects inappropriate attempts to open the door, the effective social environment would have to reject inappropriate attempts to read a word. The social environment should not be nasty, but it should recognize that there is no natural environment for learning cognitive skills. This environment is a creation. If it does not make demands that are beyond the child's capacity and if it monitors and corrects the child's initial attempts to perform on new learning activities, it will work, which means that it will be capable of teaching a wider variety of skills, and it will teach more during a given period of time.

Once we view the environment for cognitive skills as an unnatural contrivance, we can appreciate the notion that we should design it carefully. We should design communications that are effective and unambiguous, design practice so that it is productive, and design interactions so that they reinforce or "turn on" the child.

IS INTELLIGENCE INHERITED?

The premise that kids get smarter if we teach them more during a given time period makes sense rationally, but it goes against the grain of child-development philosophies that stress the individual nature of each child. It may also go against the grain of our own observations. The most cursory survey of humans within a community reveals that they differ on every measurable trait or characteristic. Just as their heights and weights vary, their sexual appetites vary, their performances on IQ tests vary, and their interests vary. Some are mentally quick; others are phlegmatic. Certainly these differences are not entirely determined by the environment that these different people encountered.

These differences are real, and they would certainly persist in the face of any socialization or environmental forces. If snowflakes are uniquely individual, something that is a million times as complicated—such as the human—will certainly exhibit individual differences. The question is not so much whether these differences exist, but how they compare with the differences that we observe when we go from one group to another. For instance, if we had a group composed of one hundred people from the United States and one person from the Australian bush, we would probably discover two distinct populations. There would be some variation among the people from the United States, but this variation would be small compared to the difference between any person from the United States group and the person from the bush. Yes, there will always be variation within a given environment. Two children growing up in the same home will be different children. But within-group variation is small compared to what we can do by changing the environment drastically. Through drastic changes we can alter the content and the rate of learning.

Children with Identical Inheritance

If the assertions that we have made about the environment are valid, we would be able to see great differences in the same child who is raised in drastically different environments. Unfortunately, we cannot readily raise the same child over and over in different settings to observe the outcome. Which brings us to the identical twins. Identical twins grow from the same egg and therefore have precisely the same set of genes. They are like clones. Typically, a pair of identical twins grows up together wearing the same clothes, doing the same things, and achieving the same IQ (which is somewhat lower than that of non-twins). But what happens when they are separated at birth, with each member of the pair raised in a drastically different environment? Although there have been no studies in which the environments have been designed to maximize the intellectual potential of separated twins, there have been studies that involve twins who had been separated shortly after birth. In 1937, Newman, Freeman, and Holzinger reported on nineteen pairs of separated twins. Of these, five sets went to environments that differed considerably in the mental skills that were taught. One twin from each set received at least four years more formal schooling than his sibling. When these twins were tested later in life, the twin who had received the greater amount of formal education averaged sixteen points higher in IQ than his less fortunate sibling. (Sixteen points can be the difference between a person who has an average IQ and one whose IQ places him in the upper 5 percent of the population.) The set of twins who had grown up in the least similar environments showed the greatest difference in IQ—*a difference of twenty-four points.*

Although the studies by Newman, Freeman, and Holzinger were consistent with most of the other studies of separated twins, the works of British psychologist Cyril Burt, who held the chair of psychology at London's University College and who had been knighted by King George VI, presented voluminous data that showed a different trend. Burt's studies showed no difference in the IQ's of separated twins regardless of their circumstances. In fact, the differences and the IQ's were sometimes the same down to the numbers beyond the decimal point. In 1976 Burt's work, which was both appealing to traditional education and was considered unimpeachable, was discovered to be largely fraudulent. Investigators were not able to find the raw data from which Burt's summaries derived, and the field investigators who had co-authored the later twin studies with Burt appeared to be perfectly fictitious people. They did not exist on the University records and none of Burt's eighteen closest colleagues had any precise knowledge of these two field investigators.

Interestingly enough, the Newman, Freeman, and Holzinger study has been historically interpreted by educators as demonstrating that identical inheritance leads to identical intelligence. In fact, the human organism that would behave as depicted in Burt's fictitious portrait would be far different from the one we know. It would learn in spite of its environment. Regardless of what the environment presented, the organism would learn something else, as if the content of what is learned is predesigned. Fortunately, humans don't behave this way. They learn what the environment teaches.

THE PHILOSOPHY OF THE SCHOOLS

The traditional educational establishment wants to believe the message that Burt's studies conveyed—that intelligence is wired not merely as a potential but as a predesigned outcome. Why does the traditional establishment espouse this position, particularly since it seems to run counter to the basic objective of the schools? The answer seems to be that the schools do not want to assume any form of accountability for student performance. The schools would be excused from such responsibility if the schools' role was not important in making children smart or successful (as measured by achievement performance). Therefore, the schools are quick to endorse the idea that the child is responsible for learning or for not learning. Certainly with older children, this position seems reasonable. But when we consider young children and beginning skills, the position is objectionable. If these children are to learn the basic skills, the schools must provide instruction that will teach, clear communication of concepts, feedback, and reinforcement for appropriate performance. The schools, in other words, must structure the teaching situations carefully enough to assure that the teaching happens. Instruction should take place whether or not the children are eminently well prepared. The record book, however, shows that the schools are virtually incapable of teaching children who are not well-prepared. The history of Title I programs shows that the incredible amounts of money put into the schools for these programs produced no difference in the performance of poor children.

More typically, the school provides institutional remedies

for instructional problems. If poor children are not being taught well in schools, the system uses the bus to solve the problem. While bussing may be justified for non-instructional reasons, it will not go far to solve the instructional problem of poor children.

The schools do not fail with all children. However, even when working with easy-to-teach children who are well-prepared and ready for instruction by all readiness measures, the schools often manage to fail. And in this failure, we see what is perhaps the epitome of Burt's fatalism. The schools adorn the child who fails with the label "specific learning disability" or simply, "learning disability." Although this label is extremely popular in most school districts, it seems to exist without its logical counterpart, the label of "specific teaching disability," which should go to the schools. If we take a moderate position, we would have to assume that the schools should be at fault for the child's failure at least occasionally. Since the schools are so thoroughly imbued with the idea that what happens to the child is not actually an effect of instruction, the schools assume that if the child has the learning or performance problem, the child is the cause of the problem. The possibility that the teaching (or lack of it) is at fault does not become a serious consideration. So foreign is the idea that the school is at fault that the label of "specific learning disability" is used. This label implies that although the child was ready to learn a skill like reading according to readiness measures and IQ measures, the child failed. But whose fault is that failure? The child's. The child possesses a very tricky flaw that could not be detected by these other instruments.

If you have a preschool child, the dominant philosophy of schools carries a possible warning for you. Possibly, the schools will fail with your child. Incompetent teachers exist in most schools. They harm children and leave serious scars, not only on sensitive learning mechanisms but on self images.

A few years ago, we were alerted to a first-grade classroom in a middle-class school that had an appalling reading

21

record. At the end of the school year, sixteen children in the classroom could not read. All sixteen were judged (by the school diagnosis but not by the parents) as "not ready," "immature," or "dyslexic." During the summer following the first-grade year, we worked with some children from the classroom. All learned to read. Learning to read was not the hardest part for these children. A far more difficult task was for them to learn that they were not dummies.

This classroom presented an extreme case; however, in many middle-class first grades, one-fourth or more of the children fail to learn to read. These children have the skills necessary to read. They are simply victims of circumstance. They become confused about what the teacher is trying to teach. The teacher does not work with them enough to receive information about their problems or confusions. The confusions grow into habits. Now the teacher observes the problem and observes that these children do not respond to attempts to "correct" the problem.

Every aspect of the schools suggests that they are not professionally capable of teaching effectively. The people who have supervisory positions in the schools typically have no exceptional knowledge of how to teach or how to train. The training that the schools provide through preservice and inservice programs is typically ineffective. The training that teachers receive in colleges of education often fails to teach fundamental procedures of structuring the environment so that effective teaching takes place.

The notion that the formal teaching relationship should be handled by the schools while the parents should simply maintain a good relationship with children makes two assumptions. The first is that the schools know more about teaching than you do. The second is that the format of instruction provided in the typical classroom is based on solid data. Both assumptions are unfounded. The typical beginning reading programs used in the schools are "sight-word programs," sometimes referred to as "look-and-guess" programs. In various comparative studies, these programs always produce results inferior to the more linguistically- or phonetically-based programs. The phonic programs teach children how the various letters go together and make up the word. The sight-word programs don't demonstrate the relationship between spelling and the pronunciation of the word. They teach words as wholes or units without reference to the parts or letters. Jeanne Chall of Harvard and other investigators have observed that schools rarely (if ever) use data when making selections about programs. The decisions are most frequently emotional.

Math programs, science programs, social-studies programs—all follow the pattern of the beginning reading programs. The most widely endorsed and frequently purchased programs usually produce the poorest achievement. The academic incompetence of the schools does not imply that there are no competent teachers or administrators in a school. Often a typical school will have some impressive teachers. The problem is not so much with the individuals, but with the system. It is designed around a philosophy that was functional when our country was young and the job of the schools was to sort out people so that most of them failed and turned from the mental pursuits to manual ones. At one time, the sorting function of the schools was functional and appropriate philosophies surfaced to justify the failures. The simplest form of justification came from philosophies like Burt's. If the child who fails would fail under any circumstances, the school is completely exonerated for failing the child. The child, after all, is lacking. This philosophy is designed to make the elite believe in themselves. It is not well designed to promote excellent teaching.

In summary, the intelligence of children suggests that they will learn if the environment effectively teaches. The schools are not designed to provide effective teaching. The next question is, "Can the parent effectively provide academic instruction?" The answer is, "Probably." Consider a typical school situation. If there's a child who is having special problems and if an aide is available, the aide works with the child. The aide may have no more idea about what to do than the teacher does or than you do. You should be able to do a significantly better job than either aide or teacher if:

1. You use a better program.
2. You work with the child in a setting that calls for a fairly high rate of response from the child and that provides feedback.

Studies of program success in school indicate that "on-task" time is highly correlated with program effectiveness. Even if you work for no more than fifteen minutes a day, your child will probably receive more direct instruction than the schools would provide. Since you will be working with one child, you'll be able to observe problems and correct them immediately. You'll learn to anticipate them and buttress against them. In a school situation such individualized, responsive instruction is quite difficult to achieve.

FACTS ABOUT TEACHING PRESCHOOLERS

We began working on academic skills with young children in 1958. We have seen a generation of them grow up. And observing them has confirmed the adage that as the twig is bent, so grows the tree. Although these young adults are individuals and are quite different from each other in many ways, they share a few common features. They are unusually skilled in specific academic pursuits. The children who completed the arithmetic program outlined in this book are extremely talented in arithmetic, although they received very little special teaching after they entered public school. Two former students received a fairly extensive program in absolute pitch. We taught them to identify notes played on a musical instrument. As adults, they retain this talent, although one of them has very little involvement with music.

A preschool academic program is not a panacea. It merely directs the twig in a particular direction by reinforcing some skills and by prompting particular mental organizations—awareness of specific discriminations or details. It does not automatically make children superior in social situations that involve their peers. To become facile with peers, children should associate with peers and learn the rules of that particular game. Without such exposure, the children will have no opportunity to learn the subtle cues that indicate when to kid around and when to shut up and the vast set of taboos that characterize social situations (how close you stand to another person, how long you look at his face, how loudly you talk, which gestures you use, and so forth). If children receive no training in these areas, the children will grow up with incredible social deficiencies. The deficiencies will be no larger than they would be if the children had received no intensive academic work as preschoolers; however, you must recognize that the academic program is not a substitute for social learning. The academic program must be something that is *added* to the child's activities, not a substitute for other activities.

Since 1964, we have been involved with programs that teach young children (first through the University of Illinois; later through the University of Oregon). In one of the larger projects, the University of Oregon provided a most successful demonstration with disadvantaged children in kindergarten through third grade. This program involved over ten thousand children in communities across the United States. Other studies have dealt with disadvantaged preschoolers, young children with low IQ's (under 85), deaf children, and gifted preschoolers. In Oregon, we have operated a learning center since 1970. We have specialized in problems and in so doing have probably had as much experience with young children as anybody. We have never seen a young child who could not be taught to read within a reasonable period of time (such as a school year). We have never seen a "dyslexic" child. We have never seen a child who had normal skills who could not be taught arithmetic or other academic skills. A somewhat hackneyed-sounding motto tells it the way it is: The children are capable of learning if we are capable of teaching.

Do Preschoolers Learn Faster than School-Age Children?

No, and it's a myth that they do. They learn more slowly. Expect them to be slow. Remember that if the capacity of humans were judged on the rate of their initial learning, humans would be the dumbest of all animals. Chimpanzees, squirrels, dogs, and goats all learn initial skills at a faster rate than humans. Typically, girls learn faster than boys. Naturally, there is a range of variation among girls and boys; however, the average girl baby will talk better and sooner, will learn faster, and will adapt better to changes in situations. We had three boys followed by our only daughter. We kept careful logs of their performance, and we were extremely proud of our boys' progress. If our children had come in the opposite order (with the girl first), we might have wondered what was wrong with the boys. At the age of three years, our boys were very, very average. They were beginning to produce three-word utterances, such as, "Go with Mommie?" At the same age, the girl was producing sentences such as, "Can I wear my blue coat when I go to the store with you, Mommie?"

Quicker learning makes for more rapid progress because complex skills are composed of simpler skills. Although faster learning is an obvious advantage, a slow start does not mean that the child is slow or that the child is incapable of learning as much as the child who is initially faster. The child's learning rate will increase with each new related skill. When we are required to learn generically new skills, our initial performance is very slow. This fact was dramatized in a new learning experiment conducted by Oregon Research Institute. The subjects in this experiment were required to identify spoken words that were transformed into patterns of tactual vibration and that were presented to the forearms, not the ears. The purpose of this experiment was to demonstrate how people learn generically new skills—those skills that are highly different from virtually anything they have previously learned. The subjects in this experiment were bright young adults. The task was to learn to identify twelve tactually-presented words. The number of trials required by the average subject was about 2,000—dramatically confirming the difficulty of the task.

Two subjects in this experiment had received an intensive preschool education. As preschoolers, these boys had been slow. (In fact, they were developmentally slow—not walking until after fourteen months; not talking until after eighteen months.) As young adults, however, these boys learned the tactually-presented words in far fewer trials than the other subjects, even though the other subjects were very bright.

The effects of the early instruction these young men had received were apparent in the tactual learning experiment. These young men outperformed their peers by a large margin. One mastered the twelve words in seven hundred trials, about one-third the number of trials required by the averaged subject. This rate of new learning would not have been predicted by the boy's behavior when he was two years old. His preschool instruction, however, taught him more than facts. It taught him how to learn. By the time he was five, he was extremely smart. As a young adult, he retained not only information, but that important ability to learn new skills.

In summary, children are ready to learn academic skills when they are quite young; their initial learning may be slow, but we should not become upset over initially slow learning. The pattern will change dramatically with practice.

Will Early Reading and Academic Work Injure the Child?

Somehow, the age of six-and-a-half became the American age at which formal education is begun. Somehow, this age became the so-called "age of readiness." Unfortunately, the notion of readiness is circular. A six-and-a-half-year-old child is quite easy to teach, far easier to teach than a three-year-old. The six-and-a-half-year-old learns faster, generalizes more readily, and knows more, which means that it is easier to communicate with this child. If our criterion for teaching children is the ease with which we can teach, we should wait until the child has a mental age of six-and-a-half. Better yet, why not wait until the child's mental age is ten or fourteen?

If we view the problem differently, however, we see that the gains a child achieves during the preschool years gives the child a real head start. If the child who receives early instruction has mastered more skills by the age of six than the average six-year-old, the child with the preschool instruction is ahead in two ways: the child knows more and the child is capable of learning additional skills more rapidly. If both receive "average" opportunities beyond this age, the child who received early stimulation should continue to maintain a lead over the average child.

There is no evidence that early reading will injure the eyes, that early learning will put a lid on the child's capacity to learn, or that the early focus on academic activities will distort the child's personality in any way. Certainly you can overdo a good thing, turning it into a charade that could injure the child. But spending twenty minutes a day on academic skills will certainly not warp the child's psyche.

It could be argued that if the child reads extremely small print and spends hours each day in this activity, the eyes will become egg-shaped. However, most of what the child will read is presented in very large print. The print is not excessively close to the child. And it is hard to imagine how looking at the printed page for short periods of time would be any more damaging to the eyes than looking at a picture book, a jigsaw puzzle, or the display of an electronic game.

The biggest possible harm that could come from early reading is early failure. But if you use a program that keeps pace with the child's capabilities and that develops skills in steps that are manageable for the child, early academic experience will instill confidence and the knowledge that "I can do it."

Will the Early Learning Create a Strain on the Parent-Child Relationship?

The program that we suggest will work, but it is not magic. If you have trouble managing children (getting them to do what you want them to do) you will have a strained relationship whether or not you teach academic skills. The reason is that the child, not you, controls most situations. The child trains *you* to be solicitous, to bribe, and to avoid situations that are not palatable to the child. Here is the formula for managing children in academic situations:

1. Make the rules of the situation very clear. Tell them what you want them to do and possibly what sort of reward they will receive for doing it the right way.

2. Set the stage for praising the children. When children perform, you will praise them. The praise is much more potent or reinforcing, however, if you set the stage so that the children will probably perform *beyond your expectations*. Therefore, state your expectations so they are less than you believe can be achieved. For instance, if you think that the child may make one mistake in reading a group of letters, you tell the child: "These letters are very hard. If you can read them without making more than three mistakes, you will do a very good job." If you think that the child should remember something that you had worked on, such as the name of a dinosaur, tell the child: "This is a hard name. I remember it because I'm super-smart. But it's so hard, you probably don't remember it."

3. Act surprised and pleased if the child exceeds your expressed expectations. "Wow, I didn't know you knew your letters that well . . ."; "I thought I was the only one who could remember the name of stegasaurus." Remember, it's

29

far more reinforcing to exceed somebody's expectations—to really show them—than it is to meet expectations.

These rules are simple in principle, but require practice before you become fluent at applying them. So practice. You will find that you can nicely apply variations of the techniques to non-academic situations. For example, if you're going to go on a trip and you suspect that the child will become restless after about 30 minutes in the car, state your expectation that the child will understandably become restless after about 30 minutes. "This is a long trip, and I know how hard it will be to sit quietly. I'll bet if you try hard, you can do it almost all the way from here to the highway." If the child exceeds this expectation, you respond with surprise: "Look at that, you're still sitting still and we're already on the highway!"

Don't over-use the technique or it will become a hollow ploy. Remember, however, that the most important reinforcer you can use is praise. If you are pleased with what the child has done and if the accomplishment is not something that the child perceives as something that is obviously simple, your child will work very hard for your praise. Do not give it so freely that it means nothing. If you praise for every trivial thing the child does, your praise for real accomplishments has very little credibility.

In some situations, you may use tangible rewards. You may give a monetary reward for every lesson the child completes (with the understanding that the child works well during the lesson). Or you may reward the child with something like smiling-face stamps, washable "tatoos," or other symbols that children like. These rewards are reasonable, and issuing them is not bribery. Bribery occurs when you "negotiate" after a problem has occurred. If you set up the rules for earning smiling faces or pictures of animals before the lesson, you're not bribing. You're giving the child a salary for working hard. Whether the child earns the salary is basically the child's decision. And the rules for the behaviors that lead to the salary are clear.

Working on academic skills with a preschooler is counter to much of what you have read and heard about children. Unfortunately, these fatalistic philosophies are not consonant with what we know about children and how they learn. Children respond to the environment. Their capacity to learn and the content of what they learn depends on what the environment teaches. IQ correlates with just about every available measure of the environment's activity level, from the age of the parents (with older parents producing smarter kids) to the per-capita number of telephones in the state where the child is raised. It correlates with the value of the property, the size of the community, and with what the parents do. These facts about the environment suggest that the environment is flexible and that we can mold it to be more effective in maximizing the capacity of our children. Instead of relying on the traditional environment that is rich in learning opportunities for the child, we can take the environment a step further and mold it into a purposeful instrument that teaches and that guarantees your child will have a superior mind.

CHAPTER II

The Story
of Genius Builders

IN *Genetic Studies of Genius*, Catharine Morris Cox gives brief biographies of three hundred historical "geniuses." On the basis of performance and skills exhibited by these three hundred geniuses during their childhoods, it is possible to estimate IQ scores, and Dr. Cox makes what seems to be reasonable and honest estimates. The classifications begin with the geniuses in the 100–110 IQ range (Copernicus, Sir Francis Drake, Michael Faraday, and others) and continue upward, through the 110–120 group (Oliver Cromwell, Andrew Jackson); 120–130 (Haydn, J. S. Bach); 130–140 (Rousseau, John Calvin); 140–150 (Hobbes, Kepler); 150–160 (David Hume, Tennyson); 160–170 (William Pitt, Alexander Pope); 170–180 (Voltaire, Coleridge); 180–190 (Bentham, Goethe); and finally, 190–200 (one entry: John Stuart Mill).

We do not agree that there is any great significance in the classification of "geniuses" according to childhood IQ, because obviously Sir Isaac Newton, with his estimated 130 IQ is at least a full cut above Thomas Babington Macaulay or Hugo Grotius with their 180 IQ's. However, it might be interesting to examine the relationship between the early training of these geniuses and their degree of "giftedness." If our interpretation of the active environment is correct, there should be a strong relationship. There *is* just such a relationship. As you progress through the book from "IQ 100" to John Stuart Mill, you come across a number of references to home tutoring and intensive early training. And the closer you get to Mill the more frequently these references occur. The trend becomes so clear from IQ 180 onward that only a true exponent of the fixed capacity theory could fail to see it.

We will let Dr. Cox (who is not sympathetic with the environmentalist's interpretation of IQ) speak for herself, with an excerpt from each of the cases listed as having a childhood IQ of 180 or more.

Jeremy Bentham (jurist and philosopher): "When he was 3 his father bought a Latin grammar and other books to begin his classical education. The Greek alphabet he learned on his father's knee, using Lily's *Grammar* and the Greek Testament as the two principal instruments of instruction."

Thomas Babington Macaulay (English historian, poet, statesman): " 'Still the merest child,' he was sent, reluctantly on his part, to his first school. . . . Before the age of 7, Thomas wrote a compendium of universal history, which his mother describes as 'a tolerably connected view of the leading events from the Creation to the present time, filling about a quire of paper.' "

Blaise Pascal (French geometrician, philosopher-writer): "When Blaise was 3, his father began to devote all of his time to the education of his children. The boy never attended school and had no other teacher than his parent. When young Pascal was 8, the family moved to Paris and the father began a systematic course of training, the rigor and originality of which can be likened only to the discipline of John Stuart Mill."

Johann Wolfgang von Goethe (German poet): "From the age of 3 until he was 6, Goethe attended a day nursery or kindergarten, and here, according to tradition, he learned to read. His father had already begun to tell the little lad and his sister the history of the town. . . . Goethe's father early recognized his son's unusual ability, and friends of the family enthusiastically mapped out careers suited to such rare talents."

Hugo Grotius (Dutch jurist, founder of the science of international law) : "Hugo remained at home in the care of his parents until he was 8 or 9, and was instructed by them in the rudiments of Christian doctrine and impressed with sound principles of morality and honor. Before he was 7, the foundations of his knowledge of the Latin and Greek languages were laid by his tutor, 'an excellent man.' "

Gottfried Wilhelm Leibnitz (German philosopher and mathematician) : "Leibnitz was brought up in a studious and scientific atmosphere; he enjoyed an education very unusual in the period of German decline in which his early years were passed. His father, when teaching him to read, made every effort to instil in him the love of history, both biblical and secular. After his father's death, which occurred when the boy was 6, his mother devoted herself to his education and, in order that his formal training might be of the best, sent him to the Nicolai School in Leipzig."

John Stuart Mill (English philosopher, writer, logician and economist) : "Until he was 14, Mill was educated at home by his father. He began to learn Greek at 3; and from then to his 9th year he studied Greek classics, making daily reports of his reading. At the same time under his father's direction he read innumerable historical works."

Every single genius at the top end of the IQ scale received intensive early training. Every single one was subjected to an extremely active environment, not one that folded its hands and waited for the child to "mature" but one that went after him and *trained* him when he was still of preschool age.

Perhaps it seems that these men were atypical because of the feats they accomplished early in life. How could a nor-

mal child ever learn Greek at 3, as John Stuart Mill did?
Mill throws some light on the issue in his *Autobiography*.

> I have no remembrance of the time when I began to
> learn Greek. I have been told that it was when I was three
> years old. My earliest recollection on the subject is that of
> committing to memory what my father termed Vocables,
> being lists of common Greek words, with their significa-
> tion in English, which he wrote out for me on cards. Of
> grammar, until some years later, I learned no more than
> the inflexions of the nouns and verbs, but after a course of
> Vocables, proceeded at once to translation; and I faintly
> remember going through Aesop's fables, the first Greek
> book which I read . . . What he [my father] was himself
> willing to undergo for the sake of my instruction, may be
> judged from the fact that I went through the whole process
> of preparing my Greek lessons in the same room and at the
> same table at which he was writing: and as in those days
> Greek and English lexicons were not, and I could make no
> more use of a Greek and Latin lexicon than could be made
> without having yet begun to learn Latin, I was forced to
> have recourse to him for the meaning of every word which
> I did not know. This incessant interruption, he, one of the
> most impatient of men, submitted to, and wrote under that
> interruption several volumes of his History and all else
> that he had to write during those years.
>
> The only thing besides Greek that I learnt as a lesson
> in this part of my childhood [before 8] was arithmetic:
> this also my father taught me: It was the task of the eve-
> nings, and I well remember its disagreeableness. But the
> lessons were only a part of the daily instruction I received.
> Much of it consisted in the books I read by myself, and
> my father's discourses to me, chiefly during our walks.

From Mill's account you receive the picture of a boy—not
a machine that learned Greek at 3 and Latin at 8. Granted
his performance is good, but notice the characteristics of
this environment, evident from Mill's quote. The environment works throughout the child's waking hours; it takes
pains to ensure that the child has learned his lessons; it
carefully reduces the possibility of mistakes; it establishes
a clear pattern for using what is learned; it forces the child

when necessary; it establishes firm models for him to follow. This is an environment that will succeed with *any* healthy infant. Yes, if we could play a little game with history and switch the real John Stuart Mill with some unfortunate infant from the slums of London, the history books wouldn't change very much. The unfortunate would become a Mill.

It was no secret that John Mill was a "manufactured" genius, yet, partly because of Darwin, most people who lived in Mill's day were not convinced that such genius-building was possible.

To understand the situation, we must turn back two hundred years to John Locke, the English philosopher who took the first important step in emancipating man from the Old Testament conception of the human being as a thin veneer of goodness through which bleed the sins of Eve and Cain. Locke proposed that man's mind is something like a blank slate when he is born, a slate on which society would write. Many people violently disagreed with Locke, but they had no powerful weapon with which to fight him.

Locke was followed by a series of great philosophers—Berkeley, David Hume (who showed that man is not chained to God's will and that there is no way to know about God even if there is a God), Jeremy Bentham (great political and social reformer), and James Mill (John Stuart Mill's father).

John Stuart Mill was at the end of this chain, and in some respects he was its culmination, the proof that man could be molded. His life, his training, his intellectual heritage set him up as a symbol of the widespread reforms in education, law and politics. But his was not a unique case.

Before the stage is completely set, another strand of the story must be woven. To pick it up we have to go to the Continent six years before John Stuart Mill was born. Here we find Karl Witte, an Austrian clergyman, expressing his views on education to a group of local instructors. Karl is complaining that traditional education places too much emphasis on natural aptitude. The local instructors do not share Witte's views. They favor the idea that it's impossible to change a person's capacity to learn.

Finally, Witte—a little rednecked—says these words, "Now I naturally must keep quiet, for there are thirteen or fourteen of you against me. But I hope to prove to you in fact that I am right. If God grants me a son, and if he, in your own opinion, is not to be called stupid—which Heaven forfend—I have long ago decided to educate him to be a superior man, without knowing in advance what his aptitudes may be."

Witte keeps his word. A son is born in 1800, and his education begins from the cradle. His wife thinks her husband's efforts are a waste of time. She thinks that the boy is dull. The members of the instructors' circle are amused by the proceedings. But suddenly, the snickering stops. What had been a slow infant and a normal 4-year-old has become an exceptional 6-year-old; and then an almost astonishing 9-year-old.

Most of those in the old instructor's circle are saying that the child's mental superiority had been evident from birth. But not all of them. Here is part of a letter from a friend, dated June 3, 1810 (when young Karl was almost 10):

Honored friend:

You have kept your word! Your Karl has become what you promised before his birth he would become, nay, he has done even better. When, ten years ago, you declared to me ecstatically in the presence of our deceased friend Glaubitz that you were hoping soon to be a father and that you fervently wished to be the father of a healthy son, you added the unforgettable words, If my son will be healthily organized, I am determined to educate him to a superior man.

I then contradicted you, saying that the success of your favorite plan did not depend alone on the health of the boy you were expecting, but more especially on his natural aptitudes. . . . I continued to express my doubts, but Glaubitz assured me that you had already transformed a boy in Switzerland in a short time into a more than common man, although he had been given up by his former educators as almost stupid. I then promised you that I would delay my judgement until your boy should someday appear himself and speak for or against your assertion. Here he is, your boy. I see him in manly maturity, with childlike innocence and goodness in a rare union—a charming picture of ennobled humanity! O lead me into a room filled with such men, and I shall deem myself to be removed from earth and in company of higher spirits!

It seems safe to conclude that the friend was impressed. And according to other sources, his enthusiasm was not unfounded. Young Karl entered Leipzig at 9. He received his Ph.D. at 14, his Doctor of Laws degree at 16. He was immediately appointed to the teaching staff of the University of Berlin. At 23 he became a full professor at the University of Breslau, and he remained there for the rest of his life, building a reputation as a teacher, writer and scholar.

Before Karl was 20 years old, his father had written a book detailing the boy's training. It contained over a thousand pages of almost unreadable, monotonous detail. However, some people read it and some believed. One seems to have been a mathematics master at a Belfast academy, James Thomson. Although he subjected all *four* of his children to an active Witte-type environment, his oldest two sons were the ones who received the intensive treatment. And they became gifted. By the time they were 10 and 12, they were admitted as regular university students at Glasgow. "No brain can stand it!" the critics shouted, but the two Thomson boys went ahead, distinguishing themselves in school and then later in life—James becoming an authority on engineering; his younger brother, William, one of the nineteenth century's greatest physicists, Lord Kelvin.

One of the more prevalent beliefs about early education in the days of the Thomson brothers, Mill, and Witte was that it would sap a child's vital energies and strain his brain. Mill lived to be 67 years old, and although his life was not a model of psychological adjustment (since he suffered a "nervous depression" as a young man) he was productive to the end. James Thomson lived to be 70 years old. He, too, was productive until the end of his life. Karl Witte and Lord Kelvin both lived to be 83 years old and both were productive until their last days. But the issue about early education had been settled long before any of them died. It had been settled in 1859.

That was the year of Darwin. The theories of the day had been shot through with the optimism of reform. Even the theories of evolution had been optimistic. They held that animals could transmit acquired characteristics. If a giraffe stretched his neck hard enough, it would become longer, and this long-necked tendency would be transmitted to the giraffe's offspring. And then Darwin stepped onto the stage. The conflict between optimism and fatalism was quick, the outcome decisive. The basis of this conflict can be studied in the two most important works published in 1859—John Stuart Mill's *On Liberty* and Charles Darwin's *The Origin of Species by Means of Natural Selection or, The Preservation of Favored Races in the Struggle for Life*. (Almost ironically, in the same year—1859—John Dewey was born.)

There it was—the weapon. Psychologists, anthropologists, geneticists and miscellaneousists had their proof. The giraffe didn't get his long neck by reaching, by exercising; *he inherited it*. So it is with intelligence. The mind cannot be stretched any more than the giraffe's neck can. Intelligence is inherited! The emphasis should therefore be on eugenics, on selective breeding. Forget about Mill, Witte, and the Thompson brothers. Forget about the effect of intensive early training. Instead, dig up genealogical facts; draw family trees. Find proof like the Jukes family with its umpteen generations of degenerates. Find genetically illustrious personages like Sir Heneage Finch (who had in his family tree the Earl of Aylesford, Daniel, 2d Earl of Nottingham, Thomas Twisden, and, of course, Heneage Legge.)

Today, our still current—but seriously threatened—beliefs about intelligence are not merely tinted with Darwinism; they are saturated with it. Binet, Piaget, John Dewey and practically all other important educational philosophers start from the unquestioned premise that man drops from the womb with a fixed capacity. The whole idea behind IQ testing rests on this assumption. The entire philosophy under which your children are educated hinges on it.

The belief in intensive early education was lost in the wake of Darwinism, but it sputtered again at the beginning of this century. A volume of Karl Witte's works had been gathering dust in the Treasure Room of Harvard University Library—the only copy in the United States. It came to the attention of a handful of people in the Harvard and Tufts circle. Several of them were enthusiastic enough to give it a try. One was Dr. A. A. Berle, Professor of Applied Christianity at Tufts College. He educated his children according to Witte's principles. His daughter Lina matriculated into Radcliffe at 15; his son Adolf (who later became a renowned lawyer) entered Harvard at 13. Said Dr. Berle, "If this result had been secured with one child, the usual plea of 'unusual child' might possibly be raised. But it is unthinkable that there should be four 'prodigies' in one family!"

Another to try the Karl Witte approach was Leo Wiener, who later edited and translated Karl Witte's book into English: *The Education of Karl Witte*. Professor Wiener explains his philosophy of educating his children: ". . . I have sought to train them in effective thinking and to give wholesome food for the strengthening of the intellect. And I have always tried to present this food in an appetizing way —that is, to make the studies to which I wished them to devote themselves really interesting. It is the things in which children are most interested that they most readily learn."

His son Norbert had a different evaluation of his father's cuisine. He writes in his autobiography, *Ex-Prodigy: My Childhood and Youth,* "Algebra was never hard for me, although my father's way of teaching it was scarcely conducive to peace of mind. Every mistake had to be corrected as it was made. He would begin the discussion in an easy, conversational tone. This lasted exactly until I made the first mathematical mistake. Then the gentle and loving father was replaced by the avenger of the blood. The first warning he gave me of my unconscious delinquency was a very sharp and aspirated 'What!' and if I did not follow this by coming to heel at once, he would admonish me, 'Now do this again!' By this time I was weeping and terrified. Almost inevitably I persisted in sin, or what was worse, corrected an admissible statement into a blunder. Then the last shreds of my father's temper were torn, and he addressed me in a phraseology which seemed to me even more violent than it was because I was not aware that it was a free translation from the German."

Professor Wiener robbed his son of a great deal, but he provided an intellectually active environment, and Norbert (although he had a shredded self image) responded accordingly. He entered Tufts at 10, graduated at 14, and received his Ph.D. from Harvard at 18. He continued his studies at Cornell, Columbia, Cambridge, Göttingen and Copenhagen, and became the father of cybernetics, the great-uncle of communication and system theories. He died in 1964.

Some astonishing successes were achieved during the early 1900s. Unfortunately, the movement was, for the most part, in the hands of "eccentrics." Some of the environments that were provided taxed the limits to which children could be pushed emotionally.

Leta Hollingworth, in her book *Children Above 180 IQ,* reports on a woman who became so engrossed in educating her child that "she often accompanied him to school, sometimes registered for courses along with him, or herself took courses calculated to make her more useful in his train-ing . . . During E.'s college career the two were often seen together on the campus."

Winifred Sackville Stoner educated her daughter in a relatively active environment. The daughter published a book of verse at 7. The mother wrote several books on edu-cation. In one of them, *Natural Education,* she provides some of the most interesting and entertaining arguments found in the literature. She tries to discredit Montessori with the folowing: "Doctor Montessori speaks quite iron-ically of 'foolish fairy tales,' but if there are no fairies, then we mortals must have killed them with our cruel doubts. Fairies will not dwell with those who have lost faith in them. But I can not see how any one doubts fairies' existence when he stands by a sleeping baby's couch and watches the smiles playing on his rosy lips. Surely the imaginative fairy hovers about the babe and whispers stories which make him smile."

In another place Mrs. Stoner uses the case-history method to demonstrate the value of early education. "Fitzgerald Villiers-Stuart, the 7-year-old author of *The Biography of a Brownie,* and Byron Cade, the remarkable young pool player, are all examples of the early development of innate tendencies."

Henry Olerich, another early training advocate, selected an orphaned infant "to test in a practical way a new theory of education which we believe to be much superior to any system heretofore used." The 8-month-old girl he selected was "an average one in good health. . . . She was, however, somewhat pale and sickly . . ." At 3 years of age she was de-scribed by *Pedagogical Seminary* as "advertised by some as the most advanced juvenile scholar on record. She has been exhibited in many American cities . . ."

We don't know what happened to Viola after her early ac-complishments. Olerich doesn't mention her in his later writings, probably because he became interested in prob-lems of greater magnitude. In his preface to *The Story of the World a Thousand Years Hence* (a 177-page book published over twenty years later by the Olerich Publishing Company) he has this modest statement about the value of his present contribution. "It [the book] clearly points out how every man, woman, and child can live a free, easy, independent, happy life financially, industrially, domestically, socially and parentally. It clearly and definitely presents the first real glimpse of ideal civilization, a real heaven on earth, and is, therefore, the most important message ever delivered to struggling humanity."

The exponents of the movement were eccentric, but they succeeded in making their children gifted. At one time, shortly before World War I, there were three handmade prodigies at Harvard. One of them was William Sidis, the son of Dr. Boris Sidis. The father seemed to be insensitive to his boy as anything but a kind of exhibit. Years later, the advocates of fixed capacity cried that the father had stretched the son's mind too far and that it had snapped. Certainly something happened, but was it an overstretched mind or an emotional reaction?

Norbert Wiener gives a partial answer. "Young Sidis, who was then eleven, was obviously a brilliant and interesting child. His interest was primarily in mathematics. I well remember the day at the Harvard Mathematics Club in which G. C. Evans, now the retired head of the department of mathematics of the University of California and Sidis' lifelong friend, sponsored the boy in a talk on the four-dimensional regular figures. The talk would have done credit to a first- or second-year graduate student of any age . . . The papers had a field day when, after one or two years of limited success at Harvard, Sidis received a job at the new Rice Institute in Houston, Texas, under the sponsorship of his friend Evans. He failed to show the maturity and tact needed to make good at this impossible task. Later on, when he carried a banner in some radical procession and was locked up for it, the papers were even more delighted.

43

"Sidis broke down after this episode. He developed a resentment against his family so bitter that he would not even attend the funeral of his father ...

"I saw him many years afterward, when he used to haunt the halls of the Massachusetts Institute of Technology. His intellectual career was behind him. He asked for nothing more than a job at which he might earn his bread and butter as a routine computer, and the chance to indulge his simple amusement of collecting streetcar transfers from all over the world. He avoided publicity as he would the plague."

The active environment succeeded with William Sidis. However, it was presented in an impossible emotional setting. William fought back with his most powerful weapon—rejection of his father and himself. But the advocates of laissez-faire education didn't see it that way. They began the chant of "overstretched mind." Textbooks on abnormal psychology contained a brief reminder of the streetcar-transfer–collecting unfortunate from M.I.T., and the issue was closed. Good people, the authorities agreed, do not push their children.

But even while the Sidis episode was unfolding, another interesting case was reported, the case of Martha. Martha learned to read at a very young age. As an older child, she achieved an IQ of 150. However, Martha is of primary interest not because of her performance but that of *her brothers*. She had two older brothers. The oldest, according to Lewis M. Terman, "has the highest IQ I have found among California children ... This boy was given a course in intensive mind culture similar to that employed in the case of Martha ... There is one other child in the family, a boy two years younger than John. This boy is making an average record in the third grade and seems to be little if any more advanced in intelligence than the average child of his age. *This boy enjoyed no special instruction like that given the other two children for the reason that the father at the time was fully occupied by professional duties.*" [Italics ours.]

After the failure of William Sidis, parents still taught their preschool children, but seldom admitted it. They would often say, "Imagine little George learning to read all by himself! We didn't even know about it." Unfortunately, the theorists of the day were only too eager to believe these comments, because they needed support for the idea that gifted children are genetically different from normal children. Accordingly, the authors of the California study concluded, "Nearly half of the gifted children learned to read before starting school . . . Most of these learned to read with little or no formal instruction."

Nearly forty years later, a response came from Dolores Durkin, who investigated the spontaneous early reader. She writes, "Parents sometimes say of their preschool child: 'He learned to read all by himself.' Data on these 49 early readers indicate that *none of them learned without some kind of help*." [Italics ours.]

Score one point against the notion that the gifted child is a genetic phenomenon. Return to the California Study and score a few more.

1. The children in the study showed no exceptional early development. In fact the parents did not first notice that their children were gifted *until they were $3\frac{1}{2}$ years old*. That these children were not gifted from birth is rather difficult to explain genetically.

2. A healthy majority of the subjects who had siblings were first-born. A similar tendency is seen among historical geniuses. There is no way to explain this tendency genetically, because the genes cannot know in advance whether the present effort is to be the first born, the fifth, or merely a nice try. The only explanation that makes sense is that the first-born child is the one who is in most direct communication with adults, who is charged with the greatest amount of responsibility, and who is therefore subjected to the most active environment.

3. The parents of these gifted children were probably

quite a bit more pushy than they claimed to be. Over 70 per cent of them indicated that they "allowed the child to go at his own pace." But consider: most of the subjects received private tutoring and spent an average of six hours a week working on their outside lessons. This is a pretty good indication that the parents encouraged their children a bit more than they admitted.

The genetic interpretation of giftedness and intelligence is a myth, supported by an almost unbelievable collection of folklore. It is a cruel joke, but it is not funny when you consider that your child is the victim.

CHAPTER III

The Theory

THE LEARNING PROCESS—A STEP AT A TIME

REDUCE YOUR VOCABULARY to several hundred of the simplest words, and step into a world of bizarre shapes and sounds. Put a familiar figure—a mother perhaps—in the scene. Now try to pay attention. You can tell by the sound of her voice that she's trying to teach you something. But what? She's walking and saying, "Fast." She's telling you about the room. The room. Now she's walking again, but she looks different. Mad maybe. No, not mad. She tells you about the room again. "Fast," she says. Or is it about her? You thought it was called "walking," not "fast."

Oh well. "Fast," you say.

She smiles. "Slow," she says. But she's *still walking*. Something's not right. You'd like to go out and play. Instead you search the room for the slow. It must be around someplace. You're confused.

There are two elements in any learning situation, a teacher and a learner. In the preceding chapter, we looked at the teacher's most obvious characteristics. Now we are looking at the learner.

One hundred per cent of all healthy children who have parents interested enough to try teaching such concepts as *fast-slow* learn these concepts. So we know that the child will learn what his mother is trying to teach. But how? How does he find that invisible quality we call "fast." Many learning theories would have you believe that the young child operates on a concrete level, that he digests concrete sensory impressions and somehow spits them out again as a concept. But how can this process lead him to *fast-slow?*

It can't. *Fast-slow* is not a thing, and it doesn't actually describe things. It describes actions—and actions aren't things. So *fast-slow* is at least two rungs up the ladder of abstraction from the concrete thing.

Yet the child learns to understand *fast-slow.* The concepts and skills in his repertoire bring him within range of it. They let him know that his mother is trying to teach him something. They tell him to direct his attention to her. They provide the root concepts to which *fast-slow* will attach, the words that describe motion and those that describe objects. "See, *mother* is *walking* fast." "The *train* is *moving* fast." "The *turtle crawls* slowly." This is as far as the concepts in the child's repertoire take him. He must travel the rest of the way alone in one jump. There are no halfway steps. There is nothing between what he knows and what he must learn. In a year, he will deal with similar concepts through analogy, noting the similarity of certain concepts to *fast-slow.* But for the present, he must leap and hope.

LEARNING AND EVOLUTION

The human infant comes into the world with nothing but a few primitive reflexes, his sense organs—and his brain. When the infant matures, he will be the smartest animal on earth. This is a fact. It is also a fact that no other animal is born as vulnerable as is man. Other animals have instincts that tell them when to become afraid, when to fly north, when to fight, when to mate—and how. These animals start with more information than man and end with less.

The lower they are on the phylogenetic ladder, the more they start with and the less they are capable of learning. A frog whose optic nerves are crossed, so that the image that should be coming to the brain from the left eye comes from the right, will never learn to adjust. If he wants to strike at an insect to the right, he'll move left—a hundred times, a thousand times. Virtually all of his knowledge is wired in. There is a report of a human, on the other hand, who had *an entire cerebral hemisphere removed* and still attained an IQ of 115.

Man must be prepared to learn from any of a thousand teachers. While instinctive knowledge might serve him well in some situations, he would be at a disadvantage in most others. He is therefore born with nothing that interferes with *any teacher*. His brain is nonspecialized.

And here we see a parallel between the learning process and the evolution of life forms. Nonspecialized life forms are able to achieve the greatest evolutionary development; nonspecialized brains are capable of achieving the greatest thought development. The price man pays for his oversized, nonspecialized brain is slow initial learning. To understand why this is true, think of the brain as a pegboard on which your opponent places a single peg. You don't know where the peg is, because you are blindfolded. Still blindfolded, you try to put your peg next to his. You keep trying and trying until you succeed. Obviously, the difficulty of this game depends on the size of the pegboard. If it is small, your task is not difficult. If it's the size of Rhode Island, you are in trouble.

The pegboard inside man's head is tremendously large. A newborn horse learns to walk in less than two hours, a dog in less than eighty. The human infant requires over six thousand hours to learn to *crawl*. Yet, the physical environment presents the same basic problem to all animals. All must learn to keep their center of balance in a certain relationship to their supporting limbs, keep the appropriate limbs rigid. A human obviously has a greater ultimate capacity than a horse, yet the horse outperforms the human on *initial learning* tasks. Furthermore, the relationship between ultimate capacity and initial learning speed can be seen up and down the phylogenetic ladder. The organism with the greatest ultimate capacity is the one with the biggest cortex (the biggest pegboard) and the one that is slowest during the initial learning stages.

Isn't it possible that this relationship also holds within a species? Isn't it possible that a healthy child who is slow during his first two or three years is actually a child with a bigger pegboard and therefore a greater ultimate capacity? The advocates of fixed intelligence say no. They maintain that since IQ is genetically fixed, the fast-learning infant will be the fast-learning adult. There is little evidence to support this position, and it is just as reasonable to take the opposite stand. Actually, the most sensible conclusion seems to be that any healthy infant, fast or slow, has the potential necessary to become "gifted." Remember, if you judge the capacity of a human—any human—on the basis of his *initial learning speed,* you would have to conclude that horses should ride men and dogs should master them.

LEARNING AS EVOLUTION

Historically, the theory of evolution has been opposed to the theory that intelligence can be molded. Strangely enough, however, the two theories are not necessarily incompatible. If we study the principles of evolution in relation to *the learning process itself* and not to the native capacity of the learner, it becomes evident that learning is actually a kind of evolutionary process closely paralleling the evolution of life-forms in at least four ways:

1. Both evolution and learning move in fixed steps. In evolution, there is no halfway step between a mutation that

provides protective coloring and one that does not. In learning there is no halfway step between the concept *ball* and the higher order concept, *red ball*.

2. The driving force of both evolution and learning is sheer trial and error. For every new form of species that survives, there are thousands that die off. Similarly, for every acceptable idea the mind creates, thousand fail. Trial and error has to be the driving force of learning, because the child cannot look into the future. He has no way of knowing in advance how the environment will react to a given idea. The only—the *only*—way he can find out is to try out an idea and note the reaction of the environment. Remember, the child comes into the world prepared to survive in virtually any intellectual environment. This means that since he cannot look ahead, he must produce the basic responses demanded by virtually every environment. He must produce the sounds he would need to learn virtually every language in the repertoire of man. Only in this way will he be assured of producing the sounds of the particular language he is expected to learn. Similarly, he must experiment with a host of rudimentary ideas to assure that he will stumble on the ones considered necessary by his particular environment.

3. Both evolution of life forms and learning are characterized by a process that can be described as "natural selection." The natural selection of ideas is quite similar to the selection of life forms. Those that are not consistent with the environment's very narrow demands are rejected. We like to think that some environments are "intellectually liberal." Actually, they are not. Even the most liberal environment doesn't allow the child to think that all men with deep voices are "Daddy," that all letters are "a," or that there can be any appreciable deviation from the required concepts. Environments that are quite liberal have been created artificially by placing subjects on soft beds in surroundings that are almost devoid of sights and sounds. Subjects

who are placed in such environments for prolonged periods, show significant signs of mental and emotional disintegration—sometimes becoming haunted by zany hallucinations.

4. Both evolutionary changes and the learning process are generally irreversible.

We pictured the mind earlier as a kind of pegboard. Actually it's more like a dark catacomb of caves. When the child comes into the world, these are unmapped. An incoming sensory impression is free to wander through them, pausing from time to time to mark a spot that seems appropriate. And then it continues, wandering aimlessly through the dark echoing chambers. Slowly, the structure of the mind changes. As the infant matures the chambers become illuminated. The points at which incoming impressions most frequently pause become linked together to form a modest rail system that meanders through the caverns. The system is awkward at first. Collisions of impressions and ideas are frequent. Movement is slow and is achieved only through great effort. The tracks are not firmly rooted and cannot stand up under heavy loads. The child learns more about his world, and the rail system becomes improved. The rails become shinier, faster. The paths are more direct. A newly installed set of switches keeps impulses zipping along on a precise schedule. What had been accomplished through the greatest effort is now achieved automatically. Once these tracks are laid, once this system is established, the mind is relatively fixed in its potential and limitations. It is possible to tear up the tracks and re-lay them, but the original tracks were laid on a perfectly flat, smooth surface. When the system is torn up, large chunks of the surface come with it. Any replacement system must therefore be laid over extremely rough terrain. This system can never achieve the speed or efficiency of the original. There is a certain note of finality about the track-laying process.

The function of a preschool education is not so much to

teach the child specific facts as it is to direct his track-laying efforts and help him build the kind of system that will require the least amount of rebuilding. The highest evolutionary development is possible only if the system is smooth and properly directed. A preschool education assures such direction. It is insurance against the development of complicated but cumbersome systems somewhat analogous to giant sloths or brontosaurs.

RULES, RULES, RULES

To look at learning from another angle, let's go to the town of Doom, which is located in the flood plain of a great dammed river. The dam is weak and will soon break. The mayor of Doom is not particularly concerned, however, because the citizens of Doom are the most completely logical and obedient people in the world. So he forms a committee of the most logical of all. "Now, boys," he says, "follow my instructions to the letter. Determine what the condition of the dam is, and draw all the logical conclusions you can. I want your report in two weeks." The members of the committee go out obediently with clipboards, slide rules, callipers and geiger counters. Two weeks later, they submit their report, a voluminous thing that tells about the structure of the dam, its weaknesses and so forth. The report concludes, "The dam will break within two months, in which case an estimated ninety to one hundred per cent of the population of Doom will be killed. Immediate evacuation could save one hundred per cent of the lives, however."

Three days later the dam breaks and ninety to one hundred per cent of the population of Doom is drowned. Why? Simply because there is no logical connection between the statement "Immediate evacuation could save one hundred per cent of the lives," and the command, "EVACUATE." The command is not implicit in the statement. It follows

53

from personal motives. The committee was given the verb *is*. All strictly logical conclusions therefore had to be expressed with this verb. But the command "evacuate" does not depend on the verb *is*. It uses the verb *do*, the language of action, which never can be derived from *is*.

The mind of man, according to traditional learning theory, functions in a manner similar to the committee in Doom: it is supposed to deal in information received through sensory impressions. And yet, if this theory is correct—if the mind deals in information—how can it act in the way we know it acts? Assume that a ball conveys the impression of ballness or roundness, or whatever. This "ballness" comes into the mind as a kind of visual fact, or an expression of what *is*. If the mind is to use this information, it must use the language that is given, namely that of visual facts. Any conclusions must be expressed in this language as an *is* statement. *The incoming impression therefore can never become linked with the word "ball" because obviously the word "ball" is not in the language of a visual fact,* just as the command "EVACUATE!" can never derive from *is* statements. To link the visual fact with the word, the mind would have to use action language.

This point is not easy to see, but it is extremely important and worth mulling over for a few minutes. The language of the mind must use the verb *do,* and the verb *do* is not contained in any sensory impressions. At best, sensory impressions can create a certain feeling of pleasure or pain; beyond that, nothing—no necessary information about what the organism should do about it. A ball is capable of communicating an infinite number of concepts. It contains enough information to form links with any concept in the repertoire of human experience. In addition to "ballness" the ball, that innocent little plaything, is porosity, buoyancy, inertia, gravity, inches, miles, pounds, ounces, beauty, nonmetallic, nonconical, non-Mr. Jones, and on and on forever. But none of this information *has to be* derived from ball. A certain feeling on the retina, a certain taste and smell—these are the only necessary derivations. Any further refinement is a creation of the mind.

One of the fundamental canons of traditional education is that children learn from concrete things and progress from the concrete to the abstract. This notion would have a strong appeal if the mind could deal with things directly. *But the mind deals only with rules about things.* Rules are abstract notations. So the mind does not move from the concrete to the abstract but from the abstract to the more abstract. From the beginning, the child learns rules. He learns to track objects by making up rules about moving his eyes. Nothing concrete here. The rules apply to all objects, not a particular, concrete few. He learns to walk by making up rules about his center of balance. He doesn't merely learn to walk on a certain floor in a certain concrete situation. He learns to walk on any flat surface. He learns to talk by making up rules about controlling his voice. He learns the concept "chair" by making up a rule that tells him how to identify, classify and use the concept. At no place along the way does he deal directly with concrete things. It is a serious mistake to think that he does.

Learning Involves the Entire Child

The instructor has drawn three lines on the board. The one in the middle is noticeably longer than the other two. The instructor now starts around the class, asking, "Which of these lines is the longest?"

"The one on the left," says the first young man.

"The one on the left," says the next, and the next. All members of the class except Peter are shills and are in on the trick. Finally, the instructor comes to Peter.

"What about it? Which of these lines is the longest?" Peter is a litle surprised at what a big production the instructor is making about something so obvious. "The one on the left," he says. And he actually believes it. Peter does not see what is on the board. He sees what his classmates said they saw.

Not everybody reacts as Peter does in this experiment. But everybody is governed by the same need that prompted him to rework the raw data he received. This is the need to live in a predictable world.

All thinking and learning are motivated. A thought is information expressed in the action language of *do*. In imposing the notion of *do* man imposes *himself* on every thought. Thoughts are not foreign objects wandering around in the brain. They are creations, born out of a great deal of trial and error. They exist for the simple reason that they serve the thinker in making sense out of jumbled impressions that constantly bombard him. They make his world more predictable and orderly, less full of surprises and contradictions. They represent a massive personal investment. Their creator will not easily give them up. If you tilt his world or warp the mirror in which he sees himself, he will go to great extremes to preserve cherished rules. He may fight back, with rage and fear. He may kill or go insane. Or, he may find a much easier solution—resolving the conflict as Peter did by "seeing" the left line as the longest one.

A reaction similar to Peter's was observed in concentration camps during World War II. Inmates who had been subjected to brutal punishment resolved the horrible inconsistency of their predicament by believing that the guards and officials were perfectly justified in their brutality. By accepting this idea, life once again was sensible.

A similar reaction is seen among young children who cripple themselves merely to prove that their parents are correct. These are children who have been told they are stupid. "Why aren't you more like your sister? Why did she inherit all the brains in this family?" The child deals with himself in much the same ways he deals with other objects and relations. He makes up appropriate rules. In making up the self rules, he starts with the premise that his father is always right. If the father says he is stupid, he must be stupid. And he proceeds to prove it to himself by being deliberately stupid.

A trained observer can quickly spot a child who has been led to believe that he is stupid. The child will manage to give the wrong response even if the task is relatively easy for him. When he is asked a question he tenses up because he *knows* what is going to happen. He knows that the wrong answer will slip out, and that he won't be able to hold it back. He pauses and his eyes dart. He fights down several words; then he says the wrong answer and he seems almost relieved. "I don't know that," he says. "I keep forgetting."

A child of 5 with a distorted self-image can be rehabilitated. He can gain confidence and achieve reasonable adjustment, but it takes time and the rehabilitated child will never be as quick as an uncrippled child.

A wide variety of teaching methods can achieve reasonable results. Some of these are very permissive and "child centered." Others are quite directed and stern. Some use teaching machines, others rely on teachers. But they all have one thing in common. They help the child to believe that he *is* capable and *can* succeed. Unless the learning task is presented in this way, a long-range learning program will fail.

Conversely, a teacher can make up for a host of mistakes by enlisting the child's total resources, and getting him involved in the learning situation. Dorothy's case history is typical. When we gave Dorothy her initial reading lesson, she was in first grade, rapidly becoming a candidate for the remedial group. She came from a large working-class family. She was quiet and shy. While her mother had not yet completely destroyed Dorothy's image of herself, she was working at it. "I'm afraid she's going to be like the oldest, Henry. Never could seem to catch on to reading." Dorothy had received no grade on her first report card because "There was nothing to grade," her teacher said. "No response."

Six weeks later, Dorothy had been promoted out of the slow reading group. Her mother was now dragging Dorothy around the neighborhood, reading book in hand. "You ought to hear this young lady read!" she would announce. And unless you were pretty quick on your feet, you *would* hear her read. And she wasn't bad. In fact, the results achieved with Dorothy were phenomenal. But these results had far less to do with the method we used to teach reading than the method we used to teach *Dorothy*. The secret formula was the *pride* we instilled in her. We spent most of the early lessons convincing her that she was intelligent. At first she resisted. But soon she grew to like the idea that *we* thought she was smart. She wouldn't let us down. She would work hard so that we would not find out the truth. She worked as hard as anyone we have ever seen. Then it seemed as if she realized one day that she was actually doing the things she wanted us to think she could do. She could read. She *was* smart. Before long, even her mother admitted it. Dorothy was saved. All it took to save her was the truth. Dorothy was intelligent. All healthy children are.

The platitude, "Learning involves the entire child," is true. The child makes up rules about everything in his world, including himself. Self rules are particularly important because they deal with the competence of the rule-maker. They influence his entire output of rules.

In making up self rules, the child tries to see his reflection in the environment. And he thinks he succeeds, because he does see something out there. He doesn't know that he is actually looking at a model of himself. He doesn't know that this model may be only a hideous caricature. He sees it and treats it in the same way he treats all other things in his world. He makes up rules that seem to conform to what he sees. If he sees a miserable failure, a child who can't please, can't succeed, he will make up the appropriate rules and he'll respect them.

The human animal is the only one on earth so intelligent that it can actually *learn* to be stupid.

How Specific Are the Rules?

In 1935 Dr. H. W. Nissen was testing West African natives who failed miserably on simple visual-perception tests such as the form-board test. The object is to fit the appropriate block into the appropriate hole (the square block in the square hole, and so forth). Despite the terrible performance of the natives, however, Dr. Nissen was reluctant to conclude that these natives were actually inferior in visual perception. Why? Simply because Dr. Nissen himself was quite a source of entertainment for the villagers. Even the very old native women could see signs in the bush that completely escaped him.

The notion of general visual perception is an illusion. We don't merely learn to *see*. We learn to see specific things. The tennis player sees certain motions of his opponent that tell him where the ball will go; the adult reader sees whole words; Dr. Nissen's natives see signs in the bush.

To get an idea of how detailed, how specific the rules are for learning to see, come back to the early 1930s. The operation for removing congenital cataracts has been perfected only recently and it provides a rare opportunity for studying exactly what is involved in seeing. The operation enables adults with congenital cataracts to see for the first time. These adults can tell us what they're experiencing. They can follow instructions.

The investigator enters the hospital room, greets the patient, and places a cube of sugar on the table in front of him. The patient studies it and says, "Sugar cube." The investigator then picks up the sugar cube, places it in his other hand and asks, "Can you tell what this is in my hand?"

The patient strains. Finally, he says, "Sugar cube."

The investigator now suspends the cube from a string. "Can you tell me what this is?"

The patient squints. He cocks his head one way and then the other. After perhaps a minute, he says, "I don't know what it is."

The investigator turns a colored light on in the room and again places the sugar cube on the table. "Can you tell me what this is?"

"No."

This patient received his sight *eleven months ago* and he is still unable to identify something as visually simple as a cube in any but the most familiar visual circumstances.

Let's visit another patient. This one has received two weeks of intensive training in distinguishing a square from a triangle. Most learning theories assume these are simple configurations that are perceived as wholes. Let's see.

The investigator presents a card with a triangle on it. "Can you tell me what this is?" he asks.

The patient nods his head, "One." He pauses and nods again. "Two." He repeats the procedure. "Three. It's a triangle."

The investigator asks, "Can't you identify it without counting the corners? Look at it."

"No, I'm sorry."

A simple configuration? No. A triangle is the sum of many specific rules that tell about the triangle, and about the different ways it can be distorted by changing its position or the setting in which it appears.

Man's complex abilities are the product of his complex experiences. This axiom holds for any complex ability. Man has the capacity to remember, but what he remembers is strongly influenced by his experiences. Consider Silas and Clem, two fictitious characters who demonstrate the influence of experience on memories. Silas is a city boy, a first-class sissy. He is an only child and is not allowed to play with other boys, because his disposition is far too sensitive. He is "encouraged" to do a great deal of reading and to be very quiet at home and in school. He has an IQ of 136 and has never received a mark lower than A— or a bad mark in deportment. Clem is a country boy. He spends most of his time with his two older brothers. He's helped his dad overhaul the truck and the tractor, and he helped build the new barn. Clem is a joker in school. He plays the class clown and he's good at it. He sings in the church choir. He has an IQ of 92.

An examination of their IQ tests shows that Silas scores much higher than Clem on "memory items." Can we conclude that Silas has the superior memory? Certainly, as far as a kind of verbal learning is concerned. But an IQ test provides a pretty narrow definition of "memory." Let's broaden it somewhat.

First, let's see which boy can remember the most about spoken German after a month's training. This is a test of memory on verbal items. Yet Clem wins.

Now let's see which boy is best at learning and remembering the lyrics of a song he has never heard before. Clem wins again.

Next, a test to see who is best at remembering a tune. Clem wins (this time by default, because Silas can't carry a tune).

A test to see who is better at remembering a route that leads to a log cabin way back in the woods. Clem finds the cabin after only one trial. Silas gets lost after eight.

The next test involves learning three smutty jokes. Clem, the class clown, wins again.

Finally, the boys are tested to see who can remember most about the relationship of the parts in an electric motor. The motor is disassembled and the boys are quizzed about the various parts. Clem wins by a country mile.

All of these tests clearly involve "memory." Yet each one is relatively independent of the others. Telephone operators score high on those IQ questions that measure the ability to repeat a series of numbers, "2 5 6 3 4 8 0 1." However, idiot savants (severely retarded children who have developed a strange set of rules about language) exhibit almost fantastic rote "memories." It would not be unusual for one to repeat these numbers, in order: 2 8 5 7 3 4 0 1 6 3 7 3 2. Or perhaps he'll recite them in *reverse order*. Yet, this same individual may not be able to remember a three-word sentence that is repeated a dozen times. The point is this: there is no such thing as "memory" or "perception" or "learning speed" apart from specific tasks. And a child's performance on a given task is predictable if you know something about the *experiences* he has had. He doesn't merely *learn;* he learns specific facts and relations.

The Illusion of General Learning

In addition to specific fact-type learning, there seems to be a more general "intuitive learning." However, this is an illusion, much like the illusion that all motives are conscious.

The feeling of intuition is actually nothing more than the by-product of a very sloppy learning situation. It can be induced merely by presenting a concept in such a way that the learner must spend an unnecessary amount of time trying to learn it. The intuitive feeling can be eliminated by improving the presentation, thereby reducing the amount of time required to learn the concept. Since most of a person's basic concepts were acquired in a rather sloppy learning situation, these concepts demonstrate the point nicely. People generally cannot do a very good job of defining such concepts as *behind, fast, same*—concepts from which very important conclusions and deductions derive. In fact, people will rarely admit that they use certain definitions of these words, even after it has been demonstrated that these definitions are absolutely essential to the understanding of the concepts. These people have an illusion of what the concepts mean; and this illusion interferes with the intelligent use of the concept. It is difficult to draw conclusions from something if you aren't sure what it is that you're drawing from.

Let's go back to the child who is trying to learn *fast-slow*, and see how this illusion gets started. He is sending out many possible explanations: some have to do with the light coming through the window, others with the dress his mother is wearing, others with his posture and feeling. In the midst of this activity, he sends out the core rule, the rule for *fast-slow* that works. It tells him to "say 'fast' if he covers the distance in less time."

But the child does not limit himself to this rule. Instead he fuses *all* of the hypotheses that are going on at the time into one molten tangle. Why not? The environment didn't indicate that these other ideas were unfit. So everything that hasn't been rejected gets used. The resulting rule may contain an awareness of an itchy shoulder blade, a command for the child to bob his head, a dark unconscious equation about anger and "fast," a feeling of soft light, a pattern of color that appears on the mother's dress, a few isolated words, and somewhere in the scramble the core rule. This rule works. *But it doesn't work as well as a more streamlined rule would,* simply because this rule has too many unnecessary parts.

Here's what happens to the child who has learned a sloppy rule for *fast-slow* when he tries to learn the concept *acceleration*. His mind starts manufacturing thoughts. It knows that *acceleration* is blood-kin to *fast-slow*, but that's all it knows. It doesn't know which part of *fast-slow* acceleration is related to. So it has to test all of the parts. It has to manufacture thoughts that relate acceleration to the yellow flower pattern, to the soft light, and to every other part of the original rule. It doesn't know ahead of time that acceleration is related to the distance-time part of the original rule. The more parts there are to the original rule, the longer the testing process will take. The longer the testing process takes, the more *irrelevant rules* the mind will have made up. Those that aren't rejected by the environment will become attached to the concept *acceleration*.

The cycle is self-perpetuating. Rules with many irrelevant parts beget rules with many irrelevant parts. Sloppy learning begets sloppy learning.

Transfer and Generalization: The Lazy Man's Way to Learn

Not everything the mind learns is direct learning. There is also the kind of learning that is called "transfer" or "generalization." The child transfers or generalizes when he does such things as putting an *ed* ending on past-tense verbs. He has somehow generalized the *ed* principle.

Learning theorists generally regard transfer and generalization as "nonspecific" phenomena. What transfers is supposed to be some kind of vague strategy.

There is one rather crushing drawback to this position. How can a child's behavior be quite specific if what he's using is "nonspecific?" Look at the child. He doesn't put *ed* endings on nouns. He doesn't say, "I sitted in the chaired." He may say, "I sitted," but not "in the chaired." And he always puts it on the end of verbs, never at the beginning: "I edsit in the chair."

If what transferred were nonspecific, he'd have no basis for using it, and his behavior would be completely accidental and unpredictable. When the child transfers or generalizes, he's actually using the same approach he uses when he makes up new rules, with one exception. He doesn't make up anything new. Instead, he takes a part of a rule, without the slightest revision, and plugs it into a new situation. Sometimes the process works, in which case it is a terrific time-saver. Other times, the result is something like the word "sitted."

Nobody has to teach a child to transfer or generalize. The trick is to direct him, to provide the rules that will lead to the most productive generalizations and transferences. The more irrelevant details that are fused into the core rule, the more possible directions in which generalization can go. However, the environment specifies only a few acceptable directions. Any deviation from these directions merely consumes time and contributes to a system that is awkward and slow in dealing with intellectual tasks. The greater the deviation, the slower the system—the slower the child.

Meaning What?

The teacher points to the picture of sheep. "See? Here are three sheep. One . . . two . . . three. Now look what happens when we add two more sheep. We have *five* sheep." The teacher believes that she has done a good thing. She has taken horrible addition and explained it in terms of something the child can comprehend—sheep. She has taken an abstract meaningless notion and transformed it into the concrete. She has made the experience meaningful for the child.

Or has she?

What kind of "meaning" is she trying to implant? Is she trying to clarify the core of the concept, or is she trying to show specific relations? Probably a little of both. Primarily, however, she is trying to instill the *illusion* of meaning. She is trying to make the experience meaningful in the same way she feels its meaning. Unfortunately her feelings have little place in content education because they have no public significance. She is dealing with something that is quite specific, but it is hidden in a morass of personal meaning. She believes that this formless meaning is an essential part of what she's trying to teach, but she is wrong.

When the teacher tries to make material meaningful in this sense, she is contributing *nothing* to the understanding of the concept. In fact, she's helping to teach the child to learn a clumsy concept. The real meaning of the concept she's trying to convey is the core meaning. Although this type of meaning is not generally recognized by educators, it is the one of primary importance in any learning situation. The core meaning is simply the essential part of the total meaning stripped of irrelevants.

Core meanings don't exist in vacuums. They are different for different tasks. The only way to find the core meaning is to start with a specific task, such as addition. Then play a game of "Can we do without you?" Take the most obvious parts of the total meaning and ask yourself, "Can we teach addition without referring to sheep? Can we teach addition without referring to cows?" And so forth. Every time you answer "yes," you have eliminated a part of the total meaning from the core meaning. Every time you say "no," you have found a part of the total meaning that is essential to the understanding of addition. This means that addition can be comprehended without understanding how addition relates specifically to sheep. You can teach addition in terms of sheep, but you'll be teaching a relationship that is not essential to the understanding of addition.

All of those concepts that *cannot* be eliminated through the "Can we do without you?" game are essential to the understanding of addition. No matter how much they are obscured under the crust of irrelevant detail and "oblique" meanings, they are *essential*. Without them, there can be *no* understanding of addition! As you will see in later sections they do not resemble the concepts normally considered as necessary prerequisites to addition. Instead they bear a striking resemblance to the logical structure of addition. The concepts that are essential to the explanation are a great deal like the concepts the theoretical mathematician uses.

Language, the Concept Carrier

The usual interpretation of language holds that words are the only source of meaning. Not so. Statements have a meaning that goes far beyond the meaning of the individual words. Statements are actually formulas for understanding the patterns in the environment's repertoire of concepts. These formulas allow the child to draw conclusions about ten little Indian boys or a forest full of pixies without having to assemble these objects.

The idea that the statements in the language have a meaning all their own may be a little hard to swallow. The following demonstration may soften it up a bit. Consider this argument:

All elephants have a trunk.

Farouk is an elephant.

Therefore Farouk has a trunk.

Obviously, you don't have to assemble a pack of pachyderms to determine the validity of the conclusion. It's true. But why? Its truth doesn't stem from the individual words and it doesn't necessarily stem from the "form" of the argument (although logicians would give quite a battle on this point). It stems from the basic assumptions of these statements. The conclusion is true because the argument expresses a truth about the structure of the physical world. In other words, it is true because it is true. And it is true regardless of what words you plug into it. It is true even when the words have no significance at all.

All fertwerts have youps.

Clarence is a fertwert.

Therefore Clarence has a youp.

The conclusion follows. You know that if the concepts

fertwerts and *youps* meant something consistent with the statements, the conclusion would have to be true.

This truth certainly does not come from the words. Therefore it must somehow come from the basic assumptions of language.

The average reasonably advantaged child learns at least *one hundred* of these formulas *by the time he's 6!* And he uses them. The child in the extremely active environment learns them in a more precise manner and uses them in a broader range of situations. He therefore becomes more adept at drawing conclusions and making up productive analogies. Language is premised on a set of assumptions that link statements to events in the physical world, so obviously the child who has a broader knowledge of language formulas can draw a greater range of conclusions with a great deal less effort. Language is symbolic, not merely in its concepts, but in its operations. It enables the child to perform in seconds what it would take a languageless being days or perhaps centuries to achieve.

An Active Environment, a Cleaner Learning Program

Earlier we mentioned that the primary role of the active environment was not so much to teach specific facts but to guarantee that the child's mental rail system was progressing in the right directions and wouldn't have to be torn up.

Now we can expand on this idea. During the infant's initial learning, the active social environment is almost helpless in directing learning. The child must start with raw feelings and make sense out of them, and no power can simplify the job, reduce the amount of chance in the learning situation, or provide a shortcut. The child must grind away in all directions until he works out the right combination of rules. But every time the infant learns something, the direction of the next step becomes more clearly defined. When the 14-month-old infant wants to learn to say "bye-bye," he no longer has to grind away in all directions, just one. "Bye-bye" has to grow out of the rule for making the voice behave. All thought-manufacturing efforts must therefore be concentrated in this direction. Learning takes place faster.

With each step the potential of the social environment to influence the child becomes stronger. This doesn't mean that the social environment will necessarily exercise its influence; it merely means that the potential is there. Some environments never flex their muscles and take advantage of the child's increasing ability to receive. The active environment does, however.

It works in two ways.

1. It pushes the child forward whenever possible. The human race required thousands of years to move up from the caves without outside assistance. The child doesn't have that much time. If he is left on his own, he may never learn the concepts he will need, and the chances are overwhelming that the concepts he learns will be so tangled with irrelevant detail that they will be quite clumsy in generating related concepts.

2. The active environment also assures cleaner rules by presenting concepts in a cleaner manner. The presentation is designed to *isolate* the concept from the irrelevant aspects of the situation. Illustration: The teacher in the active environment does not simply walk across the floor when trying to teach *fast*. She carefully rules out as many areas of possible misunderstanding as she can. She shows that *fast* is not another word for "mother" or for "walking" by showing that fast can be used *in connection* with these words. "See? Mother's *walking*. Mother's *walking fast*." Now she takes a toy car and scoots it across the floor to show that fast is more than a property of mother. "This car is moving, *fast*." She has isolated the concept by showing that it doesn't belong to mothers, or walking, or cars. The child can now pinpoint his rule production. He will spend less time learning *fast-slow*

and his total rule will contain fewer irrelevant details. By presenting a greater number of rules, and by presenting them in a cleaner manner, the active environment reduces the number of dead-end rails the mind will lay. It limits the direction of the mind's output and provides the mind with the kind of track-laying tools that will serve it throughout its existence. This is the active environment's primary role in increasing the child's capacity to learn.

Summing Up

Understanding the theoretical side of learning is not difficult if you start out with the unyielding premise that there is no magic in the world. Face the fact that not one shred of what the child learns is or can be given to him. No outside power can provide him with specific *facts* and specific *assumptions* about a specific interpretation of a specific environment. He must somehow provide the interpretation, the specifics.

Once you accept this position, then you can direct your efforts to explaining learning phenomena in the most unmagical manner possible. Yes, the working of the mind is cryptic on the neurological and electrochemical levels. Yes, sometimes it is even confusing on the behavioral level. But a great deal of this confusion can be stripped away if you realize what has to be. A child has to deal with rules of action and only rules of action. He has to deal with specifics. These specifics have to tell him both about his environment and himself.

The environment has to bear the responsibility for the kind of rules the child makes up. It presents the raw material from which the child must build his rules, and it rejects rules that aren't adequate.

The differences in environmental presentations has to account for the range of differences observed in the human animal throughout the world. The environment has to be empowered with the capacity to transform the "universal baby" into a Trukese or an upper-class American, into a moron or a genius. A child is the product of what he learns. His intelligence, capacity and range of skills reflect his environment—his teachers.

CHAPTER IV

What You
Must Know

FROM WHAT IS KNOWN about the nature of the
child and the nature of the learning situation, we can arrive
at rules that create the proper intellectual climate for the
child, both during lesson periods and during the rest of the
day. These rules are important. Familiarize yourself with
them before you start working with your child.

Recognize the Fact That the Concepts the Child Learns
Before His Fifth Birthday Are Among the Most
Difficult He'll Ever Encounter

Evidence that the normal child is potentially gifted is offered by the concepts he learns during his preschool years.
He learns such extremely relative, abstract relations as *me*
and *you*. "When I talk about me, I refer to either me, myself,
or I. When others talk about the same entity, they refer to
he, himself, him, you, or George Hansen." Here's another:
"When you face me, your left is my right, but your up is my
up." There is nothing trivial about these concepts. For the
equipment the child has when he tackles them, they are as
difficult as any concept he'll ever encounter. Don't ever mini-
mize them. Don't ever assume that they are easy.

Recognize the Importance of Rote Learning

If a child is to learn a complex skill, he must move in essential steps. Each step is not merely interesting or important, but absolutely necessary. What follows depends on it. So it must be learned; it must be taught. Sometimes it can be taught by analogy; sometimes by context. But in many instances it must be treated as a raw irreducible element, in which case it has to be taught by sheer rote. Educators are generally anti-rote. But their position is inconsistent and stems from a failure to realize that certain steps are essential prerequisites to a concept. They think that the child can "get the general idea." He can't. He learns only specifics. Please note: We are not advocating a memorization approach. We advocate the fastest, most productive way of climbing the ladder of abstraction. If certain rote elements are *essential,* we advocate teaching them. If, on the other hand, they are unessential (like the hordes of multiplication and division facts teachers feed children in a school mathematics program) we suggest not teaching them.

Recognize the Importance of Language

The child can take the words and formulas of language and construct rules from them. Language is the quickest and most certain way to teach the higher abstractions a child should learn.

Recognize That the World of Concepts Does Not Have a Completely Consistent Pattern

An impatient father is trying to teach his extremely talented 5-year-old son how to tell time. The father instructs the child to refer to the right side of the clockface as the "after side" and the left side as the "before side." The child can't seem to keep them straight. After his fourth or fifth mistake, the father blows up. "Damn it," he says. "How many times do I have to tell you? THE RIGHT SIDE IS THE AFTER SIDE!" He continues in this vein for several minutes. When he's finished, the child, who is in tears, gingerly touches the left side of the clockface and says in a high, strained voice, "But Dad, this is the clock's right side." It all makes sense to the father now. But his insight comes a little late. People have a right side to their face. Why shouldn't a clock have a right side to its face?

This is not a singular example. A child's incorrect rules aren't the reflection of an inferior mind or native slowness. Usually these rules are quite intelligent. They stem from specific confusion about how far a rule should be extended.

Recognize That the Child's Rules Can Always Be Inferred and Expressed in Words

The child isn't going to wave a flag and say, "Look, I'm extending the notion of reversal to something that can't be reversed." But his behavior will give him away. A teacher should be primed to make inferences from his behavior, not about what a stupid kid he is, but about the specific areas in which he is confused. As you will see in the following sections, these inferences are not too difficult to draw if you know what you're looking for and if you start out with the idea that a child's mistakes can be expressed in words and boiled down into a simple statement of his rule.

Present Minimum Necessary Rules

The child can turn verbal statements into rules just as you can change his rules into verbal statements. That's because

74

the cores of the thought and the verbally stated concept are identical. To the teacher this means that she can present stripped-down streamlined concepts, reduced to their logical core. She can present them as a series of statements. The child can take these and transform them into streamlined near-minimum rules, free of irrelevant detail and yet perfectly adequate for the tasks that will follow.

All skills can be taught from verbal rule-type statements, whether these skills deal with learning to judge the trajectory of an oncoming ball, learning to stand on your head, or learning to solve a problem in solid geometry. But they apply especially to verbal, symbolic learning. And when skills are taught this way, as minimum essential cores, they are handier. They are better deductive tools. They lead to the generation of cleaner ideas. They simplify future learning.

Try to Appreciate the Meaning a Concept Has for a Child

One of the most disastrous mistakes educators make is in assuming that a child who does not "understand" something in the way they understand it has no understanding at all. They assume that a child does not fully understand the notion of "time" until the child has had a great variety of time experiences. This mistake is the result of confusing the "felt meaningfulness" of a situation with the core meaning. Do not make this mistake. Remember that a child can have a very narrow understanding of "time" and still deal effectively with certain time problems. The core meaning derives from specific tasks, not from amorphous feeling. Granted, the ultimate goal of education is to provide the child with a very broad understanding of concepts. But this goal should be achieved through ordering different tasks and building the core meaning in planned stages.

Recognize the Threat of the Learning Situation

Look at learning from the child's point of view. One day he identifies the letter *K* and you praise him. A few days later, he says "K" and you nod. A few days later he says "K" and you reply, "Yes, but what *sound* does it make?" What has happened? He said it just as well as he ever had, but now, for some reason, the answer won't do. When you ask a child to learn, you're asking him to abandon responses that are known and experiment with ones that are unknown. You are asking him to change his world when he would rather dig his nails into it and hang on. The potential rewards for his sacrifice are praise and a strong sense of accomplishment.

The promise of rewards must overbalance the inevitable threat of the learning situation. Until it does, the child will not be an eager learner. He cannot apreciate the rewards of learning until he's experienced them. Therefore, you must see him through the phase of initial resistance. You must *push him*. Only about one out of ten children would learn much if the decision to learn or not to learn rested with them. They would go along with the learning situation until they felt threatened. Then they would decide that learning was not for them after all. Despite the common-sense assumption offered by many educators, children are not good judges of what they can learn or when they are ready to learn it.

Stick to a Regular Teaching Schedule

Children of 2 or 3 years are fairly rigid in their behavior. Their rigidity is simply a defense against a world that's too full of surprises and squashed expectations. A rigid schedule lets them know precisely what's going to happen next. As they grow older, they usually realize that their rigid behavior slows them down, just as their security blanket held them back when they wanted to play outdoors. So they relax their rigid hold. You should encourage them to do just that.

You should be on guard for signs of over-rigidity, but you should also make use of the child's rigid tendencies. Make lessons a rigid part of his daily schedule and you will not only reduce the threat of the learning situation; you will make the lessons a necessary part of the child's day.

When the child begins formal instruction, have lessons at least five days a week, at a special time (such as immediately after breakfast) in a special place. As the child gets older, become a little more flexible about the place and time.

Keep Your Explanations Short and Simple

Remember that the child's knowledge of the world is fragile and skeletal. He understands things only in terms of this bony framework. It's a drastic mistake to assume that he knows much more.

He cannot follow you when you go into more than a two- or three-sentence elaboration on a subject, because when you start to elaborate, you're no longer talking in terms of familiar rules, or you're no longer talking about these rules in a familiar manner. Explanations make much more sense when they're reduced to a simple statement about a single issue. You will probably discover that when your child makes persistent mistakes, you are presenting more than one task for him to learn. It may seem to you that there is only one, but if you examine your explanation, you'll see that you probably weren't talking in simple statements, but complex ones that required learning more than one skill.

Isolate the Concept You're Presenting

Here is the general formula for making presentations that *should* allow the child to take one clean, quick step:

1. Consider how you can present the concept in its simplest form. Use the fewest number of props, the shortest explanation, the simplest situation. Reduce the variables and you reduce the number of possible blind alleys.

2. Anticipate the possible wrong interpretations the child can make. If there are four elements in your demonstration, there are at least four possible kinds of mistakes. Try to find them. After you have worked with the child you will be able to make pretty good guesses about the possible areas of difficulty.

3. Rule out all of the blind alleys but one. If you're teaching *fast-slow*, for instance, use the procedure we mentioned earlier to rule out the possiblity that the concept has to do with anything but an object in motion, and rule out the possibility that the concept belongs to a particular object in motion.

4. When you find that the child is going down a blind alley, correct his mistake immediately, and try to infer the kind of rule he must be using. You can't always rule out blind alleys beforehand—in fact, you'll be doing well if you can rule them out half of the time. Usually there is only one rule that can account for his mistakes. Use whatever is handy to create a contradiction between his rule and the one you want to get across. Show him that his rule can't survive. Do it gracefully, but dramatically.

We are talking in rather abstract terms here. But in the following sections we will present many examples of how the formula applies to specific learning tasks. Remember the general formula, however. You will have many occasions to apply it.

Require Complete Responses for Statements that Involve Units of Measurement

For most verbal exchanges, partial-statement responses are both acceptable and desirable. When you teach discriminations that involve measurement units or numbers, it's a good idea to require the child to make a complete statement. The complete statement assures that the child is not confusing the numbers with some other numbers:

"What is your address?" "My address is 1224 Tulip Drive."

"When is your birthday?" "My birthday is November 4th."

"How many inches are in a foot?" "There are twelve inches in a foot."

If the child has no trouble with these (and similar) measurement discriminations, drop the full-statement requirement. If the child tends to confuse the number of days in the week with the number of weeks in the month, retain the full statements until the errors have diminished.

Require the Maximum Number of Responses

Misconceptions are the worst flaws a teaching program can have. They are symptoms of an entire association track that must be uprooted and replaced. If the misconception has been used for any length of time, the uprooting becomes extremely difficult. And the rerouted system will have to be laid over scars. It will never be as smooth as the original.

Private tutoring is far superior to the classroom in reducing the number of misconceptions a child develops, and private tutoring produces noticeable IQ gains, not uncommonly fifteen to twenty-five points after a year of such tutoring, regardless of the method used. These gains are not solely the result of reduced misconceptions, but the reduction of misconceptions plays a vital role.

Take advantage of the tutoring situation by requiring the

maximum number of responses. Remember the child's correct responses will reinforce rules he is learning.

"There are seven days in a week. Say it . . ."

"There are seven days in a week."

"Very good. Are there thirty days in a week?"

"No."

"How do you know? You know because there are *seven* days in a week. Are there 360 days in a week?"

"No."

"How do you know? Because . . ."

"There are seven days in a week."

"Very good."

Recognize the Effects of Stress on Learning

When a rule works for a child, he invests emotion and part of himself in it. It becomes a predictive tool that he relies on. The more he relies on it, the more self he has invested in it. Fundamental rules, such as "Falling from a high place results in hurts" are never questioned. They are too loaded with "self."

Rules that are being learned don't normally have a great deal of self-investment in them. The child hasn't learned to rely on them yet. But when stress is introduced, the situation changes. Emotion and feelings of self become attached to new rules. Since these rules are loaded with "self," the child confuses them with rules that he has learned to rely on.

The net result of this process is that the child in a stress situation tends to repeat the same mistakes, over and over. The more vehemently you try to extinguish the incorrect response, the more persistently he will hang onto it. When he behaves in this manner he is not being willful or stupid. He is giving the response that seems correct to him, the response that is loaded with self and should therefore work.

Try to avoid stress in the learning situation. Keep the number of incorrect responses down. And always try to correct a child's responses in a way that will introduce the least amount of stress.

"Seven days in a *month?* I know what happened here. You remembered two statements at once. Let's see if we can straighten them out. How many days are in a *week?*"

"Seven days in a week."

"Sure. So there can't be seven days in a month. There are thirty days in a month. Say it . . ."

This approach is much better from a learning standpoint than the more natural and traditional "NO!" approach. Failure words (such as *no*) slow down learning by increasing stress. Use them sparingly.

Never end the lesson on a sour note. There will be times when your patience will run short and stress will enter the learning situation. When these situations occur, remember to provide a solution for the child. Show him that he can work his way through stress situations. This is important. Always end the lesson on a pleasant note, even if it has been a complete flop. Just as the last thing you eat usually leaves the most vivid taste in your mouth after a meal, the last part of the lesson is the most vivid for the child. So always make sure that the child leaves the learning situation with a sense of mastery—not failure and bewilderment.

Allow the Child to Learn a Full Range of Abstractions

Introductory explanations on any subject should deal with the raw core—no flourishes and nuances, just the bare rudiments in the simplest, most dramatic manner possible. As the child progresses—as he begins to put some meat on the bony skeleton of original rules—explanations can become more casual, more relaxed. Ultimately, the child should learn to handle abstractions on all levels, from the precise approach used for beginners to the very casual inarticulate approach used for graduate students. The child who learns to handle explanations on only a few levels is in trouble.

Actually, you won't have to worry too much about introducing the more casual approaches. This comes naturally. You will probably find it much more difficult working out the precise explanations tailored for the beginner.

Teach the Child a Set of Rules That Works

This is the primary aim of any educational program. But to achieve it, you've got to extend the teaching situation far past those few minutes each day that are devoted to formal teaching. If the child is to have a workable set of rules, he has to know more than how to read on a third grade level or how to solve algebra problems. He has to understand his place in the family and in the universe of the neighborhood. The image that he learns at home should fit. He should see himself not as a member of royalty, but as a child—a smart child but nevertheless a child. He should understand quite firmly that he is not the pivotal point of the universe. He should see the ways in which he's like other children.

If he sees himself as others outside the family will see him, if he knows what to expect, he won't be disappointed or hurt when he ventures outside the family circle. He will have a set of rules that work.

1. *Be consistent yet human.* There has been a great deal of emphasis on parental consistency in child rearing. It has stemmed from the findings that children who are subjected to grossly inconsistent behavior become severely disturbed. This is quite true. A certain amount of consistency is necessary. However, it does not follow that parents should try to behave in an ultra-consistent manner. Ultra-consistency, in fact, encourages the child to learn an oversimplified set of rules about the world, because ultra-consistency allows him to live in a world that is artificially predictable. What he learns in the home will not serve him outside the home when he faces the irrational, subtle, unpredictable side of humanity.

During lessons, be patient, consistent and predictable. At

other times, be pretty much yourself, and try to be reasonably consistent.

2. *Don't lie to the child.* "Mommy? Why do I have this belly button?"

"Oh, darling! *Must* you ask such questions!"

There are many ways to lie. This mother has just demonstrated one of them. She indicated through her social evasion that the child's question is not a proper one. This is a lie.

Lies should be avoided whenever possible for the simple reason that they lead the child to learn unproductive rules. When he learns that great areas of life should not be questioned, he's learning one of the most unproductive rules imaginable. For a child to develop creatively and not merely mechanically, he should know that anything, *anything*, in the world of thought can be questioned. This doesn't mean that he should be allowed to spout questions in an incontinent stream or that he should use them as a transparent device to interrupt your conversations with other adults. He should understand the restrictions on question-asking, but he should know that any question is legitimate.

3. *Don't over-answer questions.* Don't try to turn questions of policy into something reasonable.

"Why do I have to take a nap?"

The mother answers with reasons. "Naps are good for growing children, and I think you'll be grouchy if you don't take one."

"But what if I don't want to take a nap?"

This is a question of policy. She should give the most accurate policy reason. "You have to because I say so and I'm the boss. When you grow up, you can be boss. But until then, you'll have to do what I say. To bed."

These frank statements make a lot more sense to a child than an argument that never seems to strike a reasonable, plausible note. Satisfy the child's need to know, but don't over-answer with windy explanations and don't conceal the real answer with rationalizations.

4. *Don't be afraid to show your ignorance.* If you set yourself up as an idol, you will just encourage the child to learn a set of rules about you that he'll have to unlearn—painfully —when he's older. Let him know that everybody makes mistakes. A child will ask many questions that will be beyond you. "Why do seeds grow up?" "What's this thing on the washing machine for?" "Why does Daddy have whiskers?"

If you don't know, there's only one answer: "I don't know." The answer to some questions may be found in reference books. If so, you may want to look up the answer with the child, thus demonstrating that even very smart mothers and fathers learn new things.

5. *Give the child plenty of free time.* We've stressed the point that the most active environment is the one that produces the greatest learning gains. Please don't interpret this to mean that you should ride herd on your child all day long. Mothers who do this aren't actually providing an environment with greater vistas of learning. They're sifting many dimensions out of a rich environment and funneling everything through an oversimplified, artificial medium— Mother. They're robbing the child of a great part of his education.

Let the child work out rules for handling life, not simply the child-mother phase of it. Let him learn from wagons and skates, from taking the role of the bad guy in a game of cowboys and Indians, from watching stones form rings on a puddle of water, from trying to make up rhymes, from watching ants in the grass, and from being teased by older children.

Formal lessons should not consume more than one to one and a half hours of the child's day. In the remaining time, he should be free to think, to play, to be a child.

6. *Help your child develop a positive (but realistic) image of himself.* We've mentioned this point before, several times. But it warrants another reminder. Rig the learning situation so that the child feels that he has succeeded, that he is smart.

And tell him he's smart. *Never* tell him he's stupid; *never* make adverse comparisons with other children. And *never* allow his brothers or sisters to suggest that he's stupid.

7. *Help the child to develop desirable personality characteristics.* Harold charges into the kitchen. "I want a cookie," he announces.

"Sorry," his mother says, "that's not the way to ask for it."

"Please!" Harold says.

"No, not in that tone of voice."

Harold flashes a frozen grin. "May I please have a cookie?"

She hands him a cookie.

"I can do a trick," he says. He motions for her to bend over. Then he hugs her and kisses her on the cheek. She gives him another cookie, and he runs outside.

Harold's mother has a rule: Only one cookie in the afternoon. But this rule is not like the one about taking a nap or crossing the street. This rule is made to be broken. Harold's mother uses it to encourage Harold to develop desirable personality characteristics. She is showing him that *some* rules (and only *some*) can be broken with "charm."

Teaching, when it is stripped of its mysticism and sentimentality, is the cold, hard business of reinforcing desirable responses and extinguishing undesirable ones. No parent wants to look at teaching his child with such a calculating eye—few parents can. But the fact remains that the parent has to mold the child. Part of this molding process involves the child's personality and general approach to the world. A parent who thinks he's saving his child a portion of pain or anguish is completely misguided if his child learns that he can punish people merely by thrusting out his lower lip and stalking off to a corner. In the big wide world, nobody will care. The parent, therefore, should not allow the child to learn such rules.

Encourage persistence. "You are a hard trier. You just

keep on being that way, and you'll be able to do anything you wish." When the child works on a job to completion, let him know that he's done well. Reward him. Perseverance is probably the most valuable intellectual asset any human can have. Also reward humor, kindness and other personality traits you think are valuable.

Do not reward crying, pouting and irritating baby-like behavior.

8. *Help the child to develop physical as well as mental skills.* Granted, physical skills don't have a very direct relationship to mental skills. But there is an important relationship. If the child's physical skills are not up to par, he will not be equipped to associate with children his own age. So he will retreat to the soft predictability of the home. And he will slip further and further behind. The further he slips, the less he has in common with his peers and the less he wants to associate with them.

A child must learn a great deal from his peers. He must learn how to argue, how to play, how to pretend, how to belong. He must learn conventions and taboos, status symbols and subtle cues. If he doesn't learn much of this from his peers, he isn't going to learn it.

Teach your child to throw a ball and turn somersaults. Roughhouse with him, and see to it that he plays with other children. Physicall skills are helpful in assuring acceptance from the child's peers. So they occupy an important position in any learning program.

Recognize Your Limitations

Most parents can be very effective teachers even if they blunder through their presentations, spend too many words on explanations, fail to interpret mistakes properly, and are generally weak in the technical aspects of teaching. They can compensate for a host of blunders by showing the child that they are on his side, even when the going is tough. But some parents cannot compensate for their mistakes because they cannot demonstrate to the child that they are on his side. They lose perspective, usually in one of two ways. Either they start to become a part of the child or they treat him as a kind of enemy who must be brought under control. The parents who become a part of the child can't let the child alone. They intrude into every facet of the child's existence. They must know everything the child does and must share every experience. They can't let go. They smother the child.

The parents who think of their child as an enemy can't control themselves very well during the teaching session because they think that the child is being willful when he makes a mistake. So they scold him and punish him for his mistakes. They produce an unsure, unhappy child.

Neither type of parent can help himself. Probably both could benefit from psychiatric help. If you find yourself becoming too involved or too hateful, don't teach, or if you do, teach on a more limited basis than we suggest in this book. Try to find out why you feel the way you do. The theory that rational understanding can cure behavioral patterns is grossly overestimated, but if you have an idea of why you act the way you do, you will have a base to start working from. Then you can begin to develop a new outlook. It takes time and work, but it can be done.

The Grand Principle

Give your child an active and realistic environment, not one that's stereotyped and oversimplified, not one that neglects important skills or intellectual dimensions, not one that encourages patterns of behavior that won't work outside the home. Give him an environment in which he learns who he is, what his role is, an environment in which he learns that he is loved, in which he becomes outfitted with all of the equipment—both physical and mental—necessary to meet the challenge of life.

PART TWO

PART TWO

The Preschool Curriculum

ON THE FOLLOWING PAGES is a fairly detailed description of what to teach the preschool child and how to teach him, a program designed to give you the information you'll need to be effective. This program is based on the "minimum-essential" concept. Its goal is to teach the greatest number of concepts and applications with the fewest number of rules and conventions. Therefore, teaching techniques are "extended" wherever possible. What this means, simply, is that if two methods of presenting a new concept work about equally well and one method has been used before, that one will be used again.

Naturally, you can deviate from the suggested presentation plan if you wish. We make no claim that this program is the ultimate achievement in preschool education. However, if you plan to deviate from it, please check ahead in the book to make sure that you are not bypassing concepts or methods that will be extended later. Space limitations prevent us from explaining the logic behind each element and the manner in which it will be extended.

The curriculum is divided into four parts, each part covering a specific age. These are: birth to 18 months; 18 months to 3 years; 3 years to 4 years; 4 years to 5 years. While there is a crude basis in developmental characteristics for this division, it was adopted primarily for convenience.

It is easier to discuss the child's learning program year by year or stage by stage than it is subject by subject. The periods are arbitrary. There are no sharp lines in development.

Some progress norms are indicated throughout the training program. The primary purpose of these is to give you a *rough* idea of what to expect. They are designed to show you that some concepts, although they seem easy, require a great deal of time. Teaching counting to a 3-year-old, for instance, requires not a few days or weeks but almost a *year*. Don't pay any attention to the norms unless you train your child according to the method outlined. You can't work with a child twice a week and expect him to perform according to a five-day-a-week standard. And don't be surprised if your child deviates from these norms. The biggest differences should occur in subjects that are "sloppy" in their deductive structure, such as reading. In extremely slick deductive subjects, such as arithmetic, the child should stay fairly close to the norms throughout (except perhaps at the beginning).

CHAPTER V

Birth to Eighteen Months

THE AVERAGE 18-MONTH-OLD INFANT has a vocabulary of about ten distinct words and a dozen others that don't quite make the grade. He is able to obey a few verbal commands, such as "Wave bye-bye," and he is socially responsive. The baby raised in a carefully controlled, active environment speaks a few more words and obeys a wider range of commands. However, the gains of the active environment are meager and represent a meager return in terms of the investment, the additional amount of time spent with the child.

Why spend it, then? Three reasons:

1. The child doesn't merely learn spoken words and responses to commands during this period. He learns what he is, where he is, and most important, who cares. He learns basic attitudes. Will he be cautious in approaching the world, afraid to try new things—or daring? The roots of his approach grow out of this period.

2. The child isn't the only one who learns. The teacher does also. She learns about her pupil. She watches him grow, and she observes him. She notes how much exposure he requires to learn such simple tasks as grasping a rattle. She

thereby gains an appreciation of what he must go through to master more complex tasks. She practices teaching, and she learns tricks for holding attention. She interprets his responses, and she begins to appreciate how the world must look to him. What she learns during this period is as important as what the child learns.

3. Small gains during this period snowball into larger gains in following periods. If a preschool education is measured according to the amount of time required to teach given skills, one would have to conclude that preschool educations are worthless. Traditional learning theorists fell into serious error on this point. They said, "Look, a seven-year-old kid can learn to read in far less time than a four-year-old kid. So let's wait until he's seven." *This reasoning rests on the idea that the child is not learning anything in the interim that will interfere with his ability to become a good reader.* The absolute level of performance is what is primarily important. If you can elevate the child to a high level of performance by the time he's 5 years old, he will be gifted, and the amount of time spent on various tasks doesn't matter too much.

Actually, we can't evaluate the meager gains of the active environment during the first eighteen months. But they are gains, and the maxim of the preschool education is that small gains become greatly magnified as the child matures. A small gain means that the child is pointing in the proper direction and that he is one step closer to the absolute level of performance he should achieve before he's 5.

The active environment concentrates on four major areas of learning during the child's first eighteen months.

1. It helps the child develop a positive image of himself and his world.

2. It provides plenty of sensory stimulation.

3. It provides adequate physical stimulation.

4. It teaches the necessary ground rules of language.

Help the Child Develop a Positive Image of Himself and His World

Love your baby, and let him know that you love him. Love is the handmaiden of education; it is a source—a most important source—of motivation. When the child is older, you will present learning situations that are potentially threatening to his security. But this threat is counterbalanced if he goes into the learning situation with somebody who radiates a sense of security strong enough to see him over the rough spots.

Emotional experiences are very important to the baby. If you play a record of obscure music every time you feed the infant, he will prefer that piece over other equally obscure pieces when he is tested later in life. (And as you might expect, he will not remember having heard the piece before.) We're not suggesting that a mother is no more than a piece of obscure music, but the same principle holds. She will influence his attitudes and capacity to learn more than any other person in the world, whether she teaches formal subjects or not. She will paint his emotions and help focus his eyes on what is "important."

She is his most logical teacher. She will be a much better teacher if the child learns to associate her with pleasant experiences.

So give him those experiences. Have fun with him. Pamper him. Show him he's an important person. Behave the way the typical loving parent should behave, and you'll teach the child some of the broadest and most useful facts of life he'll ever learn.

Provide Plenty of Sensory Stimulation

Parent to child: "Okay, now when you want to look at something close, you sort of cross your eyes a little more.

95

Here, watch me. . . . Now it's your turn." Obviously, the child isn't going to learn to focus his eyes from this kind of experience. You can't reach him directly because he hasn't yet learned the rules necessary for communication. But you can reach him indirectly by providing lots of interesting things to look at, feel, taste, smell. Open his various "windows" of feeling, his sense organs. Bombard him with sensory experiences.

1. Acquaint him with a range of experiences. Create different moods. Let him explore both hard corners and soft pillows. Hang rattles over his crib. Move him from scene to scene. Change his position—prop him up, lay him on his belly, put him on his back, carry him.

2. Make sure that the intensity of the sensory experience changes from time to time. To bombard the child doesn't mean to have seven parts of the environment competing for his attention. It means to have ten one time, and one the next. People who work in factories with a high noise level develop a functional deafness. You don't want the baby to do that. So keep the sensory experiences from being mere noise. Do this by changing pace.

3. Maintain a reasonably high noise level, even when the child is sleeping. At this age he can learn quite easily to sleep with the radio on—and ability to sleep in noisy surroundings teaches the child how to concentrate under noisy conditions. Both sleeping and concentrating on a mental task require a blotting out of the surroundings. If you suspend all activity and tiptoe around the house when the baby is napping, you're not doing him a favor.

Provide Adequate Physical Stimulation

Early physical stimulation helps muscles grow properly. Provide it by massaging the newborn infant's limbs every other day or so. Also tickle him. When he gets older, play roughhouse games in which he hangs and uses different muscles. The infant who strains a great deal will have better muscle development when he is older. This is the principle on which isometric exercises are based. (The placid baby should be helped with physical stimulation more than the physically active baby.)

Teach the Necessary Ground Rules of Language

An 18-month-old baby touches a ball and says, "Ball." This task seems to stand at the bottom of the ladder of abstraction. But it is not. It is the product of much learning.

Although you cannot do much to teach language directly to the infant, you can present language so that he learns its basic assumptions. And you can present tasks that enable the infant to learn a great deal about language before he actually begins speaking.

1. Teach the child to point to objects. You can point to things in an infant's surroundings for hours and he won't know what you're trying to do, because he's looking at one tangled nothing. But if you touch *him*, and name the part of the body you're touching, he can *feel* the significance of what you're doing. Although he probably won't distill the correct concept from your presentation, he'll have the scope narrowed considerably. Name the parts of his body while you are changing him. "This is your *hand*. *Hand*. I'll hold it up here where you can see it. *Hand*. And this is your foot. Here it is down here . . . *Foot*."

After the child is a year or a little older, have *him* point to various parts of his body on command. "Can you touch your foot? *Touch* your *foot*." Show him how. Take his hand and touch his foot. "There. You're touching your foot."

Soon the child will have the idea that language is supposed to point things out. Extend the pointing tasks accordingly. Give him the name of any object he points to.

"I'm taking off your waterproofs. Off they come. Oh, you're pointing to your *waterproofs*. Good."

Extend his knowledge of his body to your body.

"Can you point to *my* nose? Good . . ."

Next, extend pointing to the breakfast table, the bathtub and so forth. "Can you point to your *spoon?* Your dish? Can you point to the wall? . . . the ceiling? Good boy."

Always reinforce a correct answer with a word of praise. Handle mistakes gracefully. If he touches your mouth instead of your nose (which he will probably do) say something like this: "Oh, I see. You want to show me my *mouth*. Yes, *mouth*. That's good. But can you show me my *nose?* My nose? You want me to show you? Here it is . . . nose. I found it."

2. Acquaint the child with the expressive qualities of language. Use different inflections to indicate different moods. Don't use baby language, because it leads to a dead end. Instead, use regular words and an expressive tone. By changing inflections and moods you point out to the child that talking is not mere noise. It is related to things that are happening.

3. Teach the child that actions can always be translated into words. The culturally deprived child does not understand this maxim. As a result, he sees no contradiction in pushing down on a bar and saying, "I'm pushing up." He doesn't understand that this action is generating the statement "Pushing down," and that his conclusion must be consistent with this statement. He can't reason effectively with language because he can't see how language is related to the physical world.

This relationship can be taught very easily during the infant's first eighteen months (although the education does not end at eighteen months). Teach the infant that words can be transformed into actions and that actions can be transformed into words. Teach the first transformation by having him follow orders. In addition to pointing at various things, teach him "bring me," "kiss," "bye-bye" and so forth. The second transformation is achieved by describing what the child is doing, so that he learns that his actions can be transformed into words. "Oh, you're bringing me a book. That's the girl. Give Daddy a big kiss." "Look at that boy knock down blocks . . . and pick them up . . . and *throw* them at his moth—"

Show him that you've got words for every action.

4. Define the purpose of language. You are a model for the baby. You define the language for him. Is it something sparse and sterile? Is it so much chatter and noise? His conclusions will be based pretty much on your behavior. Ideally, he should learn that language is a *human activity*, something that people should do. He should learn that it is purposeful activity, and that it is an attempt to reach other people. He will learn this if you use language as it should be used, with inflections, and moods, familiar words and actions. Talk to the child; he'll listen and learn.

Caution. This period of childhood is the most difficult for parents. Babies come through it in fine condition. It is far more telling on the parents. The baby cries and they want to know why. Unfortunately the baby can't tell them, so their imaginations run wild. Before the baby is 1½ years old, they have probably worn out one copy of Dr. Spock and have their second copy well on its way.

To worry is natural. But try not to worry too much about his development. Individual differences among infants are great, because of neurological factors and because of sheer chance. The baby who happens to figure out the correct fundamental rules will be a long way ahead of the baby who doesn't. To speak about averages during this period is dangerous. The average baby walks at about 13 months, but the variation in performance is tremendous. Girl babies are usually ahead of boys in all early development—from grasping to talking. But a given girl may be considerably behind a given boy. Don't worry about slowness unless the child's departure from the norms is quite drastic. If you're in doubt, consult your doctor. Probably the best book for gauging the development of the infant is the Gesell Institute book entitled *Child Behavior*. The explanations of development are thoroughly ridiculous, but the norms and charts on behavior to 2 or 2½ years are very good.

CHAPTER VI

Eighteen to Thirty-six Months

THE 9-MONTH-OLD INFANT learned concepts that are to be found in any physical environment. The 18-month-old infant is reaching for concepts that aren't as obvious and aren't presented with the heavy-handed forcefulness of the physical environment. They are abstract, human and subtle. Most of them hinge on what the child has already learned about language.

The infant in an active environment enters the 18-to-36-month period not distinguishable from any other normal, healthy infant, and he leaves it virtually the same way. He achieves slight gains, but again, the immediate return on one's investment will be slight, although it will be definite. At 3, your child will be definitely ahead of the average 3-year-old in some important ways. Specifically, he'll understand more about basic relations and actions; he'll be able to identify various objects and the letters in the alphabet; and he'll know how to count.

NAMING OBJECTS

AN OBJECT IS A THING—any kind of thing from an elephant to a plastic truck. And the general rules for handling objects are the same for both elephants and plastic trucks. This is one of the first patterns of rules the child learns, and he would like nothing better than to reduce everything in his world to objects so that he could use these rules for everything. Unfortunately, he must now learn concepts that deal not with *things* but with *something about* things.

When you presented objects during the child's first eighteen months, you generally followed this procedure:

Isolate the object.

Name the object.

Require the child to point to the object.

As he becomes more verbal, you should expand this procedure:

Isolate the object.

Name the object.

Require the child to repeat the name.

Require the child to point to the object.

Require the child to name the object as you point.

By changing the rules in this way, you are making the total learning task much more difficult. It is far, far more difficult for the child to produce the appropriate name than it is to point to the appropriate thing when you give him the name.

Familiarize yourself with these steps. They are necessary for a smooth, sound presentation. If the child has trouble with one step, return to the preceding step. If the child has trouble naming a flower, require him to point to the object:

"Can you find a flower? . . . Good. Can you find another one? . . . Good. You found *flowers*. What did you find?"

"Soller."

"Yes, flower. Good boy."

The child will not burst into language. His development will be gradual before 2 years and than rather fast (averaging probably better than four new words a day). He will have a tendency to overgeneralize words. Overgeneralization is necessary to determine the scope of a given concept. It is necessary for testing the limits of the concept. He might want to call all brightly colored things flowers, for instance. Be careful about how you treat overgeneralizations. "Yes, it *does* look like a flower, doesn't it? But we call it a *scarf*."

NAMES FOR PARTS OF THE BODY

By the time the child is 2, he should be able to locate (with some lapses) hair, head, face, nose, ears, eyes, mouth, tongue, teeth, chin, neck, shoulders, arms, elbows, wrists, hands, fingers, thumbs, back, chest, abdomen (belly), navel, legs, knees, ankles, feet and toes.

At two, the emphasis changes from *locating* to *naming*. When you ask the child to name a body part, make sure that he's had practice in saying the name and that he's familiar with the part you're referring to. Play a game with him. First have a quick round of Can You *Find* Your (or My) . . . Hair, Nose, etc. Have the child repeat the name of the part as he locates it. Then play a game of Can You *Name* This Part. Point to the same parts the child has just located. "What is this called?"

"Hair."

"Good boy."

Don't get too clinical. Have fun with the child. If naming objects becomes a chore, forget about it for a day or two. In general, however, continue to make use of changing and bathing times to teach the child about his body.

Then let him show off what he has learned. Showing off can be overdone, but if used properly, it provides the child with an important demonstration about the value of what he has learned. During the performance make sure that the audience responds appropriately. It is a shattering experience for a child to perform for a father who merely nods several times before returning to his evening paper.

NAMES OF OBJECTS THE CHILD COMES IN CONTACT WITH REGULARLY

The procedure for presenting these is the same as that for teaching names of body parts. You will probably already have started by the time he is 18 months old.

Teach at the most logical time. When he's eating, talk about the names of food, the implements and so forth. (Don't ruin the meal by making it a quiz, however.) When he's playing with different objects, teach the names of those objects.

The teaching should occur in a pleasant context. For instance, you are dressing the child, and you're talking to him, "Give me your arm. That's it. Put it through the sleeve. Now let's button the shirt." Identify familiar objects. "This is a button, isn't it? Button." Have him repeat the name if he will. Later ask him to name the object. "What's this thing called? Do you remember?"

By the time he is 26 months old, he should be able to *locate* most of the articles he comes in contact with every day— toothbrush, spoon, cup, bib, shoes, shirt, pants, potty, toaster, refrigerator, rug, car, truck, walls, ceiling, chair and many more. He should also be able to *name* some of them.

After 26 months, put more emphasis on identification. In teaching objects that the child has never seen before, make verbal responses a part of the learning.

1. The first task is that of repeating the name of the object.

"This is called a shovel. That's a hard one to say. You want to try it? Shov-ul."

"Subul."

"Pretty good. Listen again. Shov-ul. Shov-ul. Hear the shhh. Shovel."

"Shubul."

"Yes, shovel. Good boy."

2. The next task is *locating*. This comes later, after he has come in contact with shovels on several occasions. "Look at all those tools in Daddy's shed. Can you show me which of them is a shovel? . . . That's the one. Shovel. Say it . . ."

3. The final task is *identification*. It comes still later. "What's that thing called?"

LEARNING NAMES OF ANIMALS

When a child learns the name of an animal from real life, he is dealing with an object, and he learns it just as he learns about any other object. When he learns about the animal from a book, however, the task is more abstract. Some primitive people are completely incapable of recognizing a photograph of a familiar person. They can't *see* anything because they can't translate a two-dimensional representation into a three-dimensional object.

We suggest teaching about animals from a book. This is a meaningful experience (despite the reservations of educators). The purpose of books is not to duplicate reality, but to extend it.

Since this task involves a translation, additional steps must be added to the presentation.

1. Isolate the object in the book.

2. Name it.

3. Require the child to repeat the name.

4. *Relate the book object to the objects in the world.*

5. Require the child to point to the book object.

6. Require the child to name the book object to which you point.

7. *Require the child to relate the book object to the objects in the world.*

Buy a well-illustrated book of animals, preferably one that shows baby animals with their parents. Children like to know that they are part of the baby community.

Make the task an enjoyable activity that occurs three or four times a week. Animal sessions can start when the child is about 2 years old. "Do you know what we're going to do tonight after supper? We're going to take this book and look at some of the anmials in it—big animals and baby animals."

Introduce each animal by going through the first four steps noted above. As part of isolating the object, point out each animal's distinguishing characteristics. A child of this age can't see the differences between a bear and a beaver. They are both brown things. Show him how they're different. "See this big funny tail. *Splat.* He can hit the water with it." Point out the stripes of the tiger, the mane of the lion, the neck of the giraffe, the trunk of the elephant, etc.

Relate the book object to objects in the world by *putting the child in the picture* and by *taking the object out of the picture and putting it in the room with the child*. Be dramatic. "Look at this elephant. If you were standing in this picture, next to this elephant, do you know how big you would be? I'll mark it with this pencil. . . . There. You wouldn't even come up to his knee! And do you know how big that elephant would be if we put him in this room? He would be up to the ceiling and he would fill this whole room. His head would be way over there and his tail way over there."

After the child has studied the various animals in the book for about two weeks, he should be ready to *name* some of them. Set him up by reminding him of the distinguishing characteristics of each. "Look at this animal. Oh, he's big. And he's got a big trunk and big floppy ears. He's so big he'd fill this room if he were here. Do you remember the name of this big animal?"

Later, require the child to tell you something about the relationship between the book object and the animal in real life. "What's the name of this animal with the big claws and brown coat and the little tail? . . . Yes, a bear. If we had a bear in this room, how big would he be? . . . Would he be this big? . . . *This* big?"

Before he is 3 years old, the child should know the names of the animals in his book. Now is the time to take him on a field trip, perhaps to a zoo or a farm, and give him a chance to show off and use what he has learned. Let him find out that what he has learned from a book can open a whole new vista of experiences. This is a valuable lesson.

THE NAMES FOR LETTERS IN THE ALPHABET

The rules for learning to identify the letter F are very similar to the rules for learning any other object—chair, house, elephant. But learning *all* of the letters in the alphabet makes this task more difficult than any of the others the child has yet tackled. In learning to identify animals, the child has been confronted with a few animals that were similar, but not with twenty-six of them, with no feathers or stripes, spots or colors to distinguish them. All of the marks we call letters are black on white, with only slight differences. The task is a great deal like learning to identify 26 chimpanzees. In order to master the letters of the alphabet, you must become critically aware of the *differences* between them, of the *details* that define each.

The materials you'll need for teaching letters are:

1. A book
2. A set of capital letters
3. A chalkboard

The book should be large and colorful, and each page

should show the capital and lowercase version of a letter. You can make a set of letters on cardboard cards (about 3 inches x 3 inches) or you can buy a set of plastic letters or letter cards at the dime store. String these in alphabetical order on the wall of the child's room. The chalkboard should be fairly large (30 inches x 20 inches). You will use this piece of equipment throughout the child's education, so get one that will still be usable in three years.

Lessons should be daily and should start when the child is about 30 months old. By this time, he will have developed a reasonable set of verbal rules and will have had experience with book learning. Lessons should come at a fixed time every day, preferably right after breakfast. The child is fresh at this time, and he is usually not engaged in some other activity. Lessons should last no longer than five minutes. The pace should be reasonably fast, and the child should be required to respond frequently.

The tasks should be presented in the usual order:

Isolate the letter.

Name it.

Have the child repeat the name.

Have the child locate the letter.

Have the child name the letter.

Introduce the letters by telling the child, "We're going to learn the *names* of the letters in the alphabet." It is important to refer to the letter *names*. Later the child will learn that letters also make sounds.

During the first two or three lessons, let the child become familiar with the book. He'll pay more attention to the objects pictured on each page than to the letters. Identify the objects in the pictures. "Well, this looks like a ball, but it's really an apple. See the stem?" Next point out the letter. "Look here. This is a letter. And the name of this letter is A."

"Leaf."

"Yes, that's a leaf coming out of the apple's stem. But look at this thing. This is A. Can you say A?"

"A."

"Good."

Do not indicate that "A is for apple." A is not for apple and it should never be presented in this manner because the relationship is obvious only to those who know how to read and can see that the first letter in the word apple is an A. For the beginner, "A is for apple" is a false rule, and the potential source of a basic misunderstanding.

After the child has had a chance to become familiar with the book (2 or 3 five-minute sessions) begin concentrating more on the letters. The child, understandably, will want to remain with the familiar objects in the book, the eggs and the umbrellas. Pull him away from these but not in a threatening manner. Acknowledge the egg and assure the child that his response is correct before moving on to the letter E.

Go over four or five letters during each session. Then briefly review them and spend the remaining time looking at what the child wants to look at in the book. Begin the next lesson where you left off the time before and study four or five more letters. Review from the beginning of the book. Once every week or so, start from the beginning and run through all of the letters.

Get the child used to the term letter. "Is there a letter on this page? . . . Yes, there it is." Next name the letter. "That's the letter C." Now point out its characteristics. "Give me your hand. We'll trace it. The C starts here and goes around, and around, and around until it *stops* here. It stops and leaves a space here. That's the letter C. Can you say C? . . . Good."

Briefly, here are the most important characteristics of each letter:

A—Stands on two legs that come to a point at the top; bar in the middle.

B—Upright line with two humps coming out of it.

C—One smooth curved line with a space.

D—Upright line with *one* big hump coming out of it.

E—Upright line with bar at top, bar in the middle, bar at the bottom.

F—One leg and bar at top; bar in the middle.

G—Smooth curved line with space and shelf at bottom of space.

H—Two legs with crossbar in middle; no point.

I—One leg.

J—Hooked leg.

K—Two legs with bar leaning out.

L—Leg with bar at bottom.

M—Two legs; point in middle; point down.

N—Two legs, with a slide in between.

O—Smooth curved line; no opening.

P—One leg with small hump at the top.

Q—Smooth curved line with no opening; tail at bottom.

R—Two legs; small hump at top.

S—Small curve at top and small curve at bottom.

T—One leg and bar across the top.

U—Two legs up in the air; curved bottom.

V—Two legs up in the air; pointed bottom.

W—Two legs up in the air; point in middle; point up.

X—Two crossed legs.

Y—One leg with two bars reaching out.

Z—Slanted leg with bar at bottom and bar at top.

The child can easily confuse a letter with any of those that have similar characteristics. He can easily confuse a U with a V (since both have two upside-down legs), an X with a K (since both have two legs and something else leaning out), an R and a B (since both have a straight line with a hump at the top). Certain letters are more commonly confused, however. Anticipate trouble with these, and spend more time pointing out the special characteristics that define each one.

110

A and H: Both have a bar; their names are similar. Point out that the A comes to a point at the top.

C and G: They have similar sounding names; G has a shelf.

E and F: E stands on a bar; F doesn't. (Note: Do not point out that one has two bars while the other has three; "two" and "three" mean nothing to the child. Point out how the additional bar makes the figure look different.)

J and G: They have similar sounding names. The confusion between these will be increased after the child learns that the J makes the sound that would be reasonably associated with the G.

M and W: They are practically identical except for their position. The child doesn't know that the position changes the letter into something else. To him it's the same letter, regardless of its position. Point out that when the legs are in the air, it's a W.

M and N: They sound similar, and they are usually presented closely together. Point out that M has a point and N has a slide.

O and Q and Sometimes C and G: All are similar in shape. Point out that O is perfectly smooth, while Q has a tail and C and G have an opening.

R and B and Sometimes P: Bottoms are different. Dramatize these differences by starting with P on your chalkboard, then change it into an R and finally a B.

K and X and Sometimes Z: All seem to form an angular crisscross pattern. Point out the crossing in the X, no crossing in the K or the Z. Practice tracing these letters to show the difference in construction.

V and Y: They have similar shapes. Point out the long leg on Y.

After going through the alphabet book once, start from the beginning and put emphasis on *locating* the letters. Name each letter and point out the distinguishing characteristics; then ask the child to find the letter in the sentence that usually appears at the bottom of the page—"A IS FOR APPLE."

"Look at all of these letters down here. Can you find an A? Remember, it has a point at the top and a bar in the middle and it stands on both legs just as you do." Take four or five letters for each session, then briefly review them at the end of the lesson.

After going through the entire book in this manner, switch emphasis to *identifying* the letters. The child will make mistakes, but don't panic. Mistakes should be avoided whenever possible, but sometimes, especially during the early stages of learning, making mistakes is about the only way a child can get a valid estimate of how much he actually knows. Sometimes everything seems quite sensible until he has to produce a certain response. (This particular experience is not limited to early childhood.)

Prepare the child for each letter by reviewing its characteristics, just as you do with the animals. "See this letter? It stands on both legs; it has a crossbar in the middle and a point at the top. What letter is it?"

If the child has trouble, help him out. "This is an A. Can you say that? . . . Good."

Present four or five letters during each session. This should take no more than two or three minutes. Spend the rest of the time *locating* various letters.

Continue in this manner until the child knows all of the

capital letters perfectly (two or three months). String up the plastic letters or letter cards in his room; put them where he can reach them. Before naps, go over them. "Okay, I'm going to point to a couple of these letters. See if you can name them. . . . This one, with the crossbar at the top and one leg . . . T. Good."

This type of exercise is good because it weans the child from the context cues of the book. When he learns the U in the book, he learns that the umbrella is on the page and the truck is on the facing page. These cues are helpful at first, but he shouldn't learn to rely on them; they're not a part of the letter code.

By the time the child is 34 months old, he should know his capital letters perfectly. At this time, stage a field trip—the reward, the demonstration that what he has learned is useful. "We're going for a drive and we're going to read the names of letters on signs. Let him read STOP, RR, A&P, GOLDEN'S DEPARTMENT STORE, CHICKEN.

"See? There are letters everywhere, and you can read them!"

LOWERCASE LETTERS

In one sense, learning lowercase letters is much simpler than learning the uppercase counterparts. In another sense, it's much more difficult. The child already knows half of the lowercase letters, because they obviously are reduced versions of the big letters: c, j, k, o, p, s, u, v, w, x, y, z. Close behind are four letters that are similar to their uppercase mates: f, i, m and t.

More difficult are the remaining letters—a, b, d, e, g, h, l, n, q and r. They must be learned pretty much from scratch. Also, there is something more than mere object identification involved in four of these letters; b, p, d and q are so named because each assumes a certain position. They are actually the same "object" in different poses. The child has had a taste of this concept with M and W, but b, p, d, q are so much more difficult that he may not fully master them for a year or more.

1. Introduce the lowercase letters by telling the child that for every big letter he has learned, there is a *small* one. Refer to the book. "Look. Here's big A and small a. Here's big B and here's small b."

2. Then concentrate on the *irregular* small letters: a, b, d, e, f, g, h, i, l, m, n, q, r and t. Point out that these letters are different from their big ones. "These are hard ones. The small h doesn't look anything like the big H, does it? No, we just have to learn these." Point out the distinguishing characteristics of each letter.

a—Has a big curved hood.

b—Can be made into a B by adding the upper hump. It has one upright line with a hump at the bottom and changes into B when another hump is put on top.

d—Upright line with a hump at the bottom facing this way ←.

e—Smooth curved line with opening and crossbar.

f—One leg with hook at the top and crossbar.

g—One egg on top of another egg.

h—One long leg and one short one. Short one curves.

i—One leg with dot over it.

l—One long leg (looks like big I).

m—Leg in the middle and on each side, humps on top.

n—Leg on each side, hump on top.

q—Long leg with hump at *top*. Hump faces this way ←.

r—Leg with curved arm.

t—Hooked leg with crossbar.

Trace each letter and make sure that the child refers to it as a *small* letter, a small b or a small k—not merely as a, b or k. This convention will avoid a great deal of confusion later on.

3. After introducing the letters, go through the book again. This time cover up the big letter with a piece of paper or your hand, and ask the child to locate the small letter. "Can you find the small g?" After he finds the appropriate letter, have him repeat the name and note the distinguishing characteristics. "Yes, you can tell this is small g because it has one egg right on top of another egg. That's small g." Cover eight to ten letters during a session.

4. Now move to your chalkboard. Print four small letters on it—a, b, e, f. Don't introduce b and d together, and be careful about printing small a and small g. Don't print them this way: *a, g*. Print them this way: a, g. Ask the child to locate each of the four letters. This task is far more difficult than the preceding one because it forces the child to work without the benefit of any of the context cues he had in the book. Even when the big letters were covered, the illustrations and other marks on the book provided him with a number of cues for figuring out a given small letter. Now the only cues he has are the distinguishing characteristics of each letter. Remind him of them. "Okay, I want you to find small e. What do we know about small e? It curves around something like an o and it has a crossbar, hasn't it?" Take his hand and point to the first letter. "Does this one curve around? . . . A little, but does it have a straight crossbar? No, so it can't be small e." Move to the next letter, and to the next. Repeat the same four letters every day in different orders until the child can identify them accurately (probably two to four sessions). Then move on to another four. Continue through all of the irregular letters this way.

5. Finally, switch the emphasis from locating to identifying. Present four letters at a time and ask the child to identify them in turn:

m   n   q   r

Point to the first letter and ask, "What's the name of this small letter?" If the child has trouble, remind him of the distinguishing characteristics. "It stands on two legs. It looks a little like a big letter you know." Expect the child to have some trouble identifying b, d, p and q. Help him out on these. "This one looks like a small p but it's facing the wrong way. What letter is this?" Present four letters during each session until the child can accurately identify all of them except b, d, p and q.

6. Give the child practice in working with b and d. Show him how you can make a small b from a big B. "Remember, small b and big B face the same way. In fact, if you take the top hump away from a big B, you've got a small B. Watch . . ."

By the time the child is 3 years old, he should be able to identify all of the small letters except b, d, p and q.

QUALITIES, ACTIONS, GEOMETRIC SHAPES, AND RELATIONS

THE SAME BASIC RULES APPLY to learning the name for any object. Unfortunately, objects are not the only things that have names. There are names for the movement of an object and for the links between two or more objects. Some of these non-objects are pretty easy to learn; some are tough. The child has no trouble learning the color red, but he may scratch his head over the notion of *between*.

Teach the easy non-objects first and the harder ones later. Use the same basic approach as you did for teaching objects:

Isolate the element (which is somewhat more difficult to do).

Name it.

Have the child repeat the name.

Have the child locate the element.

Have the child name the element.

Color: Begin before the child is 18 months, on a once-in-a-while schedule. Isolate the notion by presenting two identical objects (such as balls or blocks) of different colors. Acknowledge that you are presenting objects. "Blocks." Now point to one of them. "Red block. Red." Now present something else—a book or a piece of paper—that is red. "Red book. Red." Finally, present something that is not red. Ask the question, "Is this red? No, this is *not* red." Present only one color at a time, and concentrate on the most vivid colors—red, yellow, blue, white, black.

Most children pick up the notion of color quite readily from this casual presentation. However, some don't, in which case the concept must be more carefully isolated. This can be done by presenting a sheet of white paper and changing its color by placing colored cellophane over it. First, identify the paper. "This is paper. This is white paper." Then, cover it with blue cellophane. "This is blue." Follow with a red sheet of cellophane and say, "This is not blue." The notion of color can be isolated even more dramatically by coloring clear water with food dye, thus actually creating color as the child watches. If the child has trouble with color, it is important to work with only one color at a time. After demonstrating blue in the ways suggested above, make crayon marks of different shapes on paper and identify these as either blue or not blue. "Is this mark blue? No, this mark is not blue." As the child learns to make the distinction between blue and not blue, introduce yellow and not yellow. Follow with red and not red. If your child is a boy and has trouble with red (confusing it with brown and green), he may be color blind. Have him examined by a physician. The possibility of color blindness in girls is slight.

The child should know all of the more obvious colors thoroughly by the time he's 3.

Light-Dark: Again this is a visually easy task, and the rules are not too different from those that involve the thing itself. To isolate the notions light and dark, start with an illuminated room. Identify it as an object first. "Room." Now shut off the light. "Dark room." Turn the light back on. "Light room." Now show the child that the qualities *light* and *dark* can attach themselves to any object. Take a familiar object and identify it. "Ball." Turn out the light and put the child's hand on the ball. "Ball. Dark ball." Now turn the light back on. "Light ball." Repeat with several other objects. Light-dark exercises fit in nicely at bedtime.

Hot-Cold: This is another quality that is obvious. Teach hot-cold as you did color. (The fact that you use the same approach tells the child that the concept is of the same order; he therefore looks for the same kind of thing—namely a quality that can attach to different objects.) Fill a glass with fairly hot water. "Water . . . hot." Now cold water. "Water . . . cold." Repeat with another object to liberate the concept from water. "Pan . . . hot" (but not too hot). "Pan . . . cold."

ACTION WORDS

An action, like a quality, is attached to a single object in its simplest form. "Ball. Ball rolls." You have to look beyond the thing itself to find the action, but you don't have to look very far.

To demonstrate actions, isolate the action concept in the way you isolated the concepts of hot-cold and light-dark.

Demonstrate the action, "jump." The equipment you'll need consists of two people who can jump. Identify each. "Mommy . . . Daddy . . ." "Mommy . . . jump." You've shown that Mommy is Mommy, whether she's standing still or engaged in jumping. Next, indicate that "jump" is not merely something that happens only to Mommy when she entertains. "Daddy . . . jump. Daddy . . . jump."

Most actions do not need to be demonstrated. Actions, like qualities, are obvious. The child naturally picks up a general feeling for them. The 18-month-old youngster is familiar with a smile, a clap, a "bye-bye" and a splash as action-type events. He also knows that the command "NO!" means assume a state of suspended animation. And his knowledge of actions will probably parallel his ability to get around, growing with such words as fall down, hurt, walk, touch, jump, eat, see, bite and so forth. The chances are you'll have to demonstrate only a few of the action concepts he'll learn between 18 and 36 months, and these are easy. Just remember the basic format. Take the object to which the action will attach and identify it. Put it in the action state. Then introduce another object to eliminate the possibility that the action applies only to the first one. Done.

ACTION WORDS OF THE SENSES

There is a group of actions that are not so obvious. These are the actions associated with the senses: the acts of seeing, hearing, touching and smelling. The best way to isolate these is to deprive the child temporarily of a sensory sensation. The child should be 30 months old before these concepts are presented.

Sight: Most children use the word *see*, but only as a general term to indicate anything of interest. To them it may well mean, "look at this." To isolate the act of seeing, place a familiar object such as a ball in front of the child. Identify it and acknowledge any familiar qualities it may have. "Ball . . . red ball . . . big red ball." Now say, "See the big red ball? Yes, you see the big red ball." Place your hands over the child's eyes. "See the big red ball? *No*, you do not see the big red ball." Repeat with several other familiar objects.

Hearing: Same procedure. Present a familiar sound, perhaps the music from a record player (not too loud). Identify the sound in all the detail the child understands. "Do you hear 'Mary Had a Little Lamb'? Yes, you hear 'Mary Had a Little Lamb.'" Now cover the child's ears. (Experiment on yourself first to make sure that by covering your ears you can eliminate the sound of the player.) After a few seconds, uncover the ears and repeat the question. "Did you hear 'Mary Had a Little Lamb' when I had my hands over your ears? No, you did not." Repeat with several other familiar sounds and noises, including your own voice. Manipulating the volume on a TV set is another good way to provide a hearing demonstration.

Touch: Same procedure. This demonstration should follow those for sight and hearing, so that by the time you present touch the child has the general idea of what you're driving at. Take a familiar object, preferably something with a soft texture—a stuffed animal perhaps. Identify it. "This is Peter Rabbit, isn't it?" Now place Peter behind the child, within reach but out of sight. "Are you touching Peter Rabbit now? No, you are not touching Peter Rabbit now." Take his hand and put it on the rabbit. "Are you touching Peter Rabbit now? Yes, you are touching Peter Rabbit now." Repeat with another familiar object. Then show that touch doesn't apply only to some kind of behind-the-back activity. Do this by having the child touch things while he's looking at them.

Smell: This is difficult to demonstrate, partly because the child has rather poor powers of olfactory discrimination and partly because it's hard to get him to imitate the act of smelling, of inhaling. If he catches on to this part of the riddle, the rest comes pretty easy. If he doesn't, he'll try to smell with his mouth open or he'll get the idea that "smell" means "try to blow the petals off the flowers."

Probably the best method to teach "smell" is to encourage the child to imitate you when you smell something. Give the impression that smelling is fun. Sniff a rose and then exclaim, "Ahhhh. I smelled the flower. Watch me. I'll do it again . . . Ahh, that's fun." Then give him a chance to try. Even if he doesn't do it properly, he'll have fun and you'll have a few laughs from his attempts.

He'll catch on in time.

GEOMETRIC SHAPES

To put a round peg in a round hole you've got to abstract something from both the peg and the hole, the notion of roundness. The roundness is a kind of quality that attaches to the peg and the hole, but it looks different on the peg than on the hole. Roundness is not an obvious quality like hot or red.

To teach geometric shapes, you have to teach both faces of the shape, the peg face and the hole face. The basic procedure is the same as it was for other qualities. Use one of the educational coordination boards which have holes of different shapes and corresponding blocks. These blocks are sections of the various forms. The round block is actually a cylinder, much like a piece sawed from a broom handle. The triangular block is like a section cut from a triangular broom handle. And so forth. The shapes that must be abstracted from these blocks are visible only on the ends of the blocks, not on the long, horizontal sides. Point out these shapes when the child is about 28 months old.

First, identify the block in all the detail he understands. Then turn it on end and *trace the quality you want him to learn*. "Triangle. A red wood block in the shape of a *tri-*

angle. Can you say triangle?" Now introduce the distinguishing characteristics of a triangle. Do this by placing the block horizontally on the floor (so that the triangular shape is visible on each end). "See? A triangle has a big bottom and a point at the top. Now watch. I'll roll it over on its side, and look! It still has a big bottom and a point at the top. I'll roll it again. It still has a big bottom and a point at the top." (Note: This explanation does not rely on the fact that triangles have three corners. Later, this notion should be introduced, but it means nothing to the child who can't count.) Introduce the other geometrical shapes in the same manner.

The Circular Block: Is round on the end. No matter how you roll it, it still looks the same.

The Square Block: Has a big bottom and a top that's just as big. No matter how you roll it, it retains this shape. (Later, the four-corner idea should be introduced.)

The Rectangular Block: Something like a square, but when it is rolled, the end does not always look the same. Sometimes it's taller; sometimes shorter.

The child will learn to identify the blocks quickly. But in spite of your demonstrations, his judgments probably will be based on such equations as "Triangle = red block. Square = green block."

After the child can identify the blocks reasonably well, point out that the holes in the board have the same qualities as the blocks. The circular hole is like the letter O. The oval is like a lopsided O, like an egg. The square has a big bottom and a top as big, and the triangle (if you stand in the proper position) has a large bottom and a small top.

Again, he'll use shorthand equations for remembering which hole is which. "Triangle = one next to the chimney of the house."

Use the chalkboard to wean the child from his spurious equations. Draw the shapes on the board and ask him to *locate* them. Remind him of the defining characteristics of each. "Find the triangle. Remember, it has a big bottom and a point at the top." As soon as he is able to locate the figures accurately (which shouldn't take more than several two-minute sessions), ask him to identify them. Remember: If he falters, remind him of the cues. "It's big down here, isn't it? . . . and it's not so big up here at all. In fact, it comes to a point, doesn't it? What shape is big down here, and has a point up here? Big on the bottom with a point at the top."

Don't keep him guessing too long, however. The longer he's in doubt, the more he's considering false rules.

Teach geometrical shapes on a casual basis, with perhaps one session a week. By the time the child is 3, he should be able to identify the various shapes and have a fair understanding of how they attach to various objects.

POSITION RELATIONS

In the next two sections on relations we include all of the concepts that have to do with position (behind, under, next to) and all of the comparative words (bigger, hotter, faster). These concepts logically fall in the same class because the rules for all of them are similar in form. All (except *between*) can be reduced to the comparison of two objects according to some kind of standard. All can be reduced to the same statement form, "Object A is _____ Object B." Put any preposition or comparative words in the blank and the statement makes sense. Object A is *behind* Object B. Object A is *bigger than* Object B. The child must learn more than the words *behind* or *bigger than* because these words make sense only when they are in a statement. You can't talk about the bigger than. Nor can you refer to a single object as having the quality of bigger than or be-hindness. Only when you consider two objects and the speci-fied relationship do words like *behind* or *bigger than* make any sense. These concepts cannot be comprehended apart from statements.

Since the various relations can be expressed with the same statement form, you can use the same basic learning set to teach all of them. The major element that will change from task to task is the particular relation word you're presently demonstrating.

"The ball is *in* the box."

"The ball is *behind* the box."

"The ball is *bigger than* the box."

The child can catch onto the game rather quickly, because it's obvious which element in the statement is describing the difference seen in each presentation.

Introduce relation some time after the child is 2½ years old. Begin with the prepositions *in, on, next to, behind, over, under, around* and *between*. For your demonstrations use the same objects, three or four familiar toys and two containers capable of holding the toys.

In: Demonstrate the concept with a container and toy. First identify the objects. "This is a pail, yellow . . . and red. This is a block. What letter is on the block? What color is this?" Now demonstrate the relation. "Watch. The block is *in* the pail. Say it . . ." Follow up with a rhetorical ques-tion. "Is the block in the pail? Yes, it's in the pail." Remove it. "Is the block in the pail now? No." Replace it. "*In* the pail." Remove it. "Not in the pail." Repeat the demonstra-tion with another container and another toy (a wastebas-ket and ball perhaps) to demonstrate that the concept *in* does not belong exclusively to blocks and pails. After the initial demonstration, have the child *locate* the concept by telling when the block is in the pail and when it is not. "Is the block in the pail now? Is it in the pail now?" Finally,

124

have him *identify* the concept. Place the ball in the pail and say, "Where is the ball? It is . . ."

On: Turn the pail over and place the block on top of it. "The block is *on* the pail. Is the block *on* the pail? Yes." Remove the block. "Is the block on the pail now? No. The block is not on the pail." Demonstrate *on* with another set of objects. Have the child first locate and then, when he's ready, identify the concept.

Next to: Place the block next to the pail. "The ball is *next to* the pail. Is the ball *next to* the pail?" Remove it, and continue as you did with the other concepts. *Next to* has two meanings. In one sense it means at the side of (not the front, not the back, but the side) ; in the broader sense it means near. Teach it in the latter sense. Later you can refine it by showing that the block is not strictly "next to" the pail when it is in front and behind.

Behind: This is a more difficult concept because it hinges on a viewpoint. If we come up behind a boy who is crouched behind a trash can, we can say that he's hiding behind the can, even though he's in plain view. He's *behind,* because we assume the viewpoint of someone standing on the other side of the trash can. Teach the concept by starting with this viewpoint. Place the block behind the bucket, so that it's not in the child's view. "The block is *behind* the pail." Now move the block to a different position. "The block is *not behind* the pail." Move the block so that it is once more out of the child's view. "The block is *behind* the bucket." Repeat with other familiar objects.

Over: There is an *over* that implies action and a stationary *over.* Teach both. Start with the stationary *over.* Hold the block over the bucket. "The block is *over* the bucket." Use the regular procedure, starting with locating the concept, and then proceeding to identifying it. Stress the verbal pattern. After he has learned the stationary *over*, show him the action *over*. Begin by demonstrating that the block can "move." Hold it in your hand and move it about. "The block is moving." Stop. "Now it's not moving . . . now it's moving again." Once you establish the idea that the block can move, move the block over the pail, and say, "The block is moving over the pail." To reduce the possibility that the child will have trouble when you introduce *under*, demonstrate that the pail can go over the block as well as the block can go over the pail. Help him get used to noting that the *one on top is the one that is over*. That's the one you *start with* in your statement. "The pail is [now you refer to the object beneath it] *over the block*."

The child should catch on very quickly, once he understands the general format of the different relations.

Under: As with *over*, there is an *under* that implies action and another one that is static. Suspend the pail from a doorknob or the like. Place the block under it. "The block is *under* the pail. Say it . . . Is the block *over* the pail? No, the block is *under* the pail." Teach in the usual manner. Then introduce the notion that the block can *move under* the pail. Slide the block along the floor. "The block is moving under the pail . . ." Reverse the objects so that the child learns to look for the position rather than particular objects. *Over* and *under* are more difficult than most of the other relations.

Around: Demonstrate *around* by circling the pail with the block. "The block is moving *around* the pail. "Now stop the block. "Is the block moving *around* the pail now? No. Here it goes again. What is the block doing? Good. Moving *around* the pail."

Between: Unlike the other relations, *between* involves three objects. The subject object must be in such a position that a straight line drawn from the second object to the third would pass through the subject object. Then you would say, "The subject object is *between* the second object and the third object." The subject object can be either moving or stationary. Teach it both ways. First, place the block between the pail and another familiar object. Demonstrate that any object can go in the middle. That is the one that is always *between* the others. After the child learns the static *between*, the *moving between* should require no more than a quick demonstration.

There are other words that show position—*against, through, in front of,* and so forth. Teach these in the same way you presented the other position words.

You probably won't have to teach all of the position concepts we outlined here. Perhaps half of them. Once the child catches on to the format, he should be able to handle them on his own. Your rule for teaching them should be this: Teach when the occasion arises. Keep the pail and block reasonably handy. When the child encounters a new concept such as *over*, take a few minutes to demonstrate it *if it's reasonably convenient for both you and the child to take time out for a demonstration*. If not, wait until later.

By the time the child is 3, he should know all of the position words.

COMPARATIVE WORDS

There are certain words used to compare two or more objects by a set standard. Take two or more elephants and compare them by the standard of size and you'll find yourself talking about "small" elephants. The smallness is not in terms of any absolute standard. It has meaning only in terms of the elephants you are comparing. The child of 18 to 36 months encounters three very important sets of comparative concepts—*big-little, fast-slow* and *tall-short*.

Big-Little: Demonstrate with three objects of the same class—three blocks or three balls or three containers. They should be of different sizes. Identify each in detail. Then set the medium-sized object and the small object together. Point out that in this setting the medium-sized object is *big*, while the other is *small*. "See? This one is big." If you are dealing with containers, demonstrate the difference in size by covering the small container with the other. Show that it won't work the other way.

The notion of *big* becomes reasonably obvious in this setting. The child can see bigness as a quality. The object that is taking up more space is the one you call big. So far so good. Now substitute the large object for the small one, so that you're dealing with the large and the medium-sized object. Point out that the large one is "big." The other is now "small." The child is forced to conclude that the bigness couldn't have been anything accidentally connected to the medium-sized object. Rather it must have to do with some kind of comparison. Introduce the large and the small objects together and show that the comparison holds. The child should catch on to the notion of *big-small* without much difficulty. Make sure that the objects are obviously different-sized. If they're not he will become quite confused.

Fast-Slow: Demonstrate *fast-slow* by once more using two objects of the same class, two trucks or two vehicles of any kind. Move one of them faster than the other. Have the child first watch the one that is going faster. "I'm going to move both of these cars across the floor. You tell me which one is going *fast*. Here we go. Which is the fast one? Of course! *It got there first* . . ." After he can locate the concept *fast* by pointing out the fast car, have him identify the concept. "Tell me about this car. Watch it go past the other one. What do we call a car like that? Of course! *Fast*." Finally, introduce the idea that the other car is slow. Use the same procedure. Instruct the child to work from what he knows. *"Find the fast one.* Yes. And the other one *must be slow."*

Tall-Short: This concept refers only to objects that are standing. A tree is tall, but once it's felled it becomes long. To demonstrate *tall-short*, use three objects of the same class—three people, three block buildings, three plants. First, compare the middle-sized one to the short one, concluding that the middle-sized one is tall (or taller). Next, compare the tallest object with the middle-sized object. "Now this one is the tallest one." Finally, compare the tallest one with the shortest one. Follow the same general procedure outlined for presenting *big-little*. After the child understands the concept *tall*, point out that the other object being compared is *short*.

COUNTING

THERE IS A KIND OF COUNTING that involves nothing more than saying sounds in a certain order—much like reciting a poem. "One, two, three, four, five." There is also a kind of counting that involves coordinating this poem with a hand movement: every time you make one of the sounds, you touch one of the objects in front of you. Then there's a kind of counting in which you have to understand that the last sound you make tells you something not only about the last object you touched but about *all* of the objects you've touched so far. When you count to ten, you have ten objects. Of the different kinds of counting, some are easier than others. You can teach the child at least one kind by the time he's 3—the recitation counting. You may even start on one of the other methods, but don't make the mistake of thinking that simply because the child can say, "One, two, three, four, five . . . ten" he should be able to bring you three blocks from a pile of ten or count out the number of blocks in the pile. These tasks are miles removed from his recitation.

During the 24- to 36-month period, teach the child to recite the numbers by making counting a part of the bedtime ritual. Begin by counting to five. "Now I'm going to turn out the light on the count of five. Ready? One . . . two . . . three . . . four . . . *five*." Next, have the child say each number after you. "Say it." Then, after several weeks, let him solo, saying the entire series at once. Recite it first so that it is fresh in his mind. "Now it's your turn to say it all by yourself . . ."

After he can handle the first five numbers, introduce the second five. Always start counting from *one*. Use the same procedure. "I'm going to turn the light off on the count of ten. Ready? Here we go . . ." The child should learn to count to ten by the time he is 30 months.

RIGHT-LEFT

THIS IS ONE of the most difficult concepts imaginable. It assumes that the world changes in one dimension according to your position. This is a rather strange notion. If you want to see how strange, lie on your right side in a hammock. The heavens are left and the earth is right. Turn over and the heavens are right and the earth is left. Stand in one spot and note all the landmarks as right or left; now stand on your head (facing the same direction you were facing when standing upright) and you have magically reversed every element in the surroundings from right to left and from left to right.

The fundamental viewpoint of right-left begins with the absolute element, the one that doesn't change—*the me*, the person in the center of the right-left grid.

Since the fundamental viewpoint involves a knowledge that one side of your body is different from the other and that each side has a name, the most logical method to teach *right-left* is to dramatize this difference first.

Teach *right-left* when you're dressing the child. Use the terms. When you want the child's left foot, ask for it. "Give me your left foot." Help him develop a fundamental association for right and left by following this policy. *Always squeeze his right hand or foot when you say "right." Never squeeze his left hand or foot when you say "left."*

"We're going to put your shirt on now. Give me your right hand." Point to it. "Right." Squeeze it. "Now your left hand. Left hand." Point to it. Do not squeeze.

When he nears his third birthday, you may want to teach him to shake hands. "Remember, we always shake hands with our *right* [squeeze it] hand. Let's shake." Don't expect him to learn quickly. He has two hands and both look and feel quite alike to him. He has no hint. The purpose of squeezing the right hand is to create such a hint. But it takes time, perhaps *a year or more.*

Note: Never use the word "right" to indicate that the child is correct. Say "Good," "Fine," "That's it," or something other than "Right." You'll prevent a great deal of confusion by adopting this convention. There's nothing more pathetic than to hear a child ask, "Is this my left shoe?" and receive the answer, "Right." Or——

"I'll start reading at the left side of the page."

"Right."

STORIES

BEDTIME STORIES have a definite educational value in addition to their obvious entertainment function. They acquaint the child with the basic conventions of our language; they present new ideas, and they contain the elements necessary in any account of what happened—the answers to the questions *who, what, where, when* and *why*.

Read to the child. Read as much as you wish. And when you read, show the child how the pictures of the book depict a part of the story. "Read" the picture by interpreting the *details* in the illustrations. This takes practice, and it's not as easy as it may sound. Test yourself the next time you look at a cartoon or other picture that tells a story. Ask yourself, "Which *details* in the picture are telling the story?" Find them.

When interpreting pictures, first identify the objects and characters; then draw conclusions. "How do we know Jack is outdoors? Because he's climbing a tree, and trees grow outdoors. Is Jack happy? Is he smiling? No, he's not happy at all, is he?"

Television is a good source of stories. But television can be overdone a lot easier than reading can. Very few mothers can sit down and read to a child for two or more hours a day, while a TV set doesn't mind at all. Remember this about television viewing: While the child is watching TV he's not doing other things. There must be a balance between the good he's deriving from viewing and the deficit he's accruing from not having other experiences. More than an hour and a half of viewing a day is probably too much. Actually, however, most 18- to 36-month-old children won't sit still for more than a few minutes at a time—usually just for a few commercials.

MUSIC

MUSIC, like every other product of organized human thinking, has a pattern, a definite set of rules. It doesn't simply take off and course around the scale a few times before making a crash landing. It follows rules and patterns.

The 18-month-old child should already be familiar with some of these rules and patterns. He should have experienced many lullabies. Hopefully he'll experience many more. In addition, he should hear other kinds of beats and arrangements. If possible he should have his own records, which he can listen to during a certain part of the day. He should also learn to express himself with music. That's where you come in. Dance with him. Set him on your lap and keep time by jostling him up and down to "Hi Diddle Dee." Let him do rolls or somersaults to "Oh! Susannah." Let him march to the *1812 Overture*. Let him feel music; give him a chance to learn music's real justification at a young age.

HOW THINGS WORK

THE 18-MONTH-OLD doesn't question the world because it is all he knows. For him everything is natural—the trees, the air, the fact that things fall, the washing machine and so forth. But not everything in the world is "natural," and one of the most helpful distinctions the child can learn to make is between things that take their orders from man and things that don't. Point out the "man-made" things in his world and briefly explain how they work. Don't go into detail. Just let him know that they have a *function*. For instance, when he's watching water pour from a faucet, point out that you can control the stream of water simply by turning the handle. "Here's how we get that water ... just turn the handle."

Here are some other gadgets the child should come to know something about before he reaches 3. (Note: Most of these are lethal. Make strict rules about touching them, climbing on them, etc., and enforce these rules.)

Vacuum cleaner: Show what it does. Demonstrate the vacuum principle by sipping (not too vigorously) from a glass.

Kitchen range: Show how the dials control the gas or electricity and thus control the temperature of the burners. Explain why we cook food.

Washer and dryer: Show how these work to wash and dry clothes.

Typewriter: This is one of the safer gadgets. Let the child hit the keys. Show him where the ink comes from and how it gets on the paper.

Piano: Show him how depressing the keys makes the sound.

Also, light bulbs, beaters, toasters, coffee-makers, knife sharpeners, can openers.

TASK SCHEDULE UP TO 3 YEARS

AGE (IN MONTHS) FOR WORKING ON TASKS

TASK	PAGE REFERENCE	Age span (months) for working on task
Locating Parts of the Body	103	Pre-18 – 23
Naming Parts of the Body	103-104	Pre-18 – 35
Locating Regularly Contacted Objects	104	Pre-18 – 25
Naming Regularly Contacted Objects	104	20 – 35
Learning Names of Animals from a Book	105-107	24 – 35
Learning Names of Letters:	107-116	
Capital	111-112	30 – 35
Lowercase	113-116	33 – 35
Color	117	25 – 35
Light-Dark	118	25 – 35
Hot-Cold	118	25 – 35
Action Words	118-119	19 – 35
Action Words of the Senses	119-121	29 – 35
Geometric Shapes	121-123	28 – 35
Position Relations	123-127	30 – 35
Comparative Words	127-129	31 – 35
Counting—Number Recitation	129-130	24 – 35
Right-Left	130-131	24 – 35

Age scale (months): Pre-18, 18, 19, 20, 21, 22, 23, 24, 25, 26, 27, 28, 29, 30, 31, 32, 33, 34, 35

CHAPTER VII

Three Years
to Four Years

DURING THIS PERIOD the child in the active environment learns to read, learns the fundamentals of arithmetic, and learns many new patterns of logical thought. In most cases he learns much more slowly than an older child would on the same tasks. For instance, it will take the child in the active environment a year to learn as much about reading as the average first grader learns in four months. Traditionally, this slowness has been interpreted as proof that the younger child's nervous system is not mature.

Actually, however, the slowness is merely proof that the task of learning to read is not the same for the younger child as it is for the older one. Reading is the sum of many prerequisite skills. Some of these involve interpreting space. Some involve motor abilities. Some involve "memory." While these skills are poorly developed in the younger child, they are developed to a much higher degree in the older child. In other words, a race between these two children is a little unfair because one child is much closer to the finish line when the reading lessons start.

In many ways, the 3- to 4-year-old child will seem slow, sometimes frustratingly slow, but try to remember that the tasks he is tackling are not the same as they are for you. On the following pages, we outline some of the assumptions underlying the tasks he will encounter. Try to appreciate their sheer difficulty. And when the year is over and you look back on what the child has learned, you'll discover that he has achieved rather astonishing gains.

READING

THE CHILD SHOULD spend about half an hour a day on formal material. His reading lesson should last 10 to 15 minutes. Other lessons, which should be handled more casually than reading, consume another 15 minutes. What is learned during these formal periods should be related to the child's other daily activities. Always try to make the point that what is learned is *useful*.

Which method of teaching reading should you use, the look-say or the phonic? The controversy rages, with educators on the side of the look-say or sight method saying, it's bad to start by teaching letters because the child then becomes bored and develops the habit of looking at words atomically. The phonetic advocates counter with the argument that the English language is an orderly set of phonetic rules—a neat code. Teach the rules and the rest will take care of itself.

Both positions are weak, but each has something to recommend it.

THE LOOK-SAY METHOD

The look-say theorists notice that experienced readers read words not as sums of the atomic elements, but as wholes, gobbling up five or more of them in a single glance. From this observation, they draw two conclusions: (1) adults see total forms (else how could they read so fast?) ;

(2) children should learn to read the way experienced readers read; they should learn to see whole words, total configurations. Both of these conclusions are false. Let's take them one at a time.

Adults do not see words as total forms or objects. They see a progression of elements from left to right, no matter how fast they read. You can demonstrate this point to yourself by covering up the lower one half of the words on any line of this page. Now read. You will read at a speed of about ninety per cent of your normal rate, and you will not be in doubt about any word. You have changed the total shape of each word and made each word look like a different object; all of the letters are identifiable, however, so you can read without appreciable loss of speed. Now cover up the top half of the letters. Reading is more difficult and you have to infer some words, especially those that contain n, h, r, l, i, f—such as *fill, nill, hill.* Notice, you can no longer "read" the words although *you have not changed the total shapes any more in this demonstration than when you covered up the bottom half of the letters.* The ability to recognize the words has little to do with the total shape of the word. It stems from the ability to recognize each letter in the word. When you cut the word in half one way, you can read. When you cut it in half the other way, you can't. And if you want to make the relationship between the total shape of the word and the letters ridiculously obvious, cover up the front half of each word and try to read. Now you have completely destroyed some of the letters. As a result, you're left with nothing but pure conjecture about most words.

Another way to demonstrate the weakness in the look-say approach is to analyze the assumption that words are objects. If they are, we should be able to make the same general statements about words as we can make about any other object. If we cannot make the same statements, the concepts are not the same and should not be taught in the same manner.

So we make up a list of statements, such as these:

1. We learn about words through experience.
   We learn about objects through experience.
2. We can perceive words visually.
   We can perceive objects visually.

So far, so good. But somewhere down the list will be this pair of statements:

A word may lose its identity if it is reversed in a mirror or turned upside down.

An object does not lose its identity if it is reversed in a mirror or turned upside down.

In a mirror *dud* becomes *bub*. Upside down *pond* becomes *puod*, *sop* becomes *dos*, and *sun* becomes *uns*, although *suns* remains *suns*. Therefore, there is a fundamental difference between words and objects.

Reading is not a mere extension of object identification. Reading is a code. The elements in the code are letters, and the ground rules state that you must know how these letters function. They are not thrown together any old way. A certain formation produces a certain word. Reading cannot be reduced to anything simpler.

Even if reading were mere object identification, the look-say method would be on pretty wobbly supports, because you don't learn to identify complicated objects by referring to their general "configuration." Remember the difficulty the person who had been blind from birth encountered when trying to identify a triangle and square? He noted the details, not the general shape. So it is with words. The reader must learn to see the details—the specific details—that make one word different from another.

The look-say conclusion that the child should learn to read whole words because the experienced reader apparently reads whole words is like saying that beginning typists should learn to talk and engage in other activities while they type because experienced typists talk and engage in other activities while typing. The tasks simply aren't the same for the beginner and the experienced performer, because the experienced performer has been "modified." The look-say method was formulated long before we knew much about the mechanics of perception or learning. It is a legacy that's based on archaic knowledge. Fortunately, we don't have to inherit it.

The history of the look-say method is interesting, if a little distasteful. The method had been in existence for some time by the turn of the century. It had been tried out by schoolmasters in New England, who wrote eloquent pieces on why it is an inferior method. When John Dewey was promoting the notion of learning by doing, he needed examples of instant learning by doing (other than those provided in the cooking or sewing classes). Somebody pointed out that there was a method of teaching reading that involved simply reading, not the preparation of learning letters and learning the skill of blending the individual sounds together. The method, although it had never been demonstrated to be a viable method, was immediately adopted by the educational establishment. It radiated from the large metropolitan centers (Chicago, New York, and the major California cities). And it became a vogue.

The method is poor because it doesn't provide clear demonstrations of how the code works. The child may believe from the teacher's demonstrations that the idea is to look at a picture and then say things that are true of the picture. The child may simply memorize the pages in the reader and recite the "words" that are supposed to go on the page. Later, the child may learn somewhat painfully that reading is not verbal recitation or page memorization.

THE PHONIC METHOD

The phonic method is based on the idea that the printed word is not the smallest unit open to analysis by the beginning reader. Letters make up the word and the letters play a role in directing the reader to pronounce the word. Ideally, each letter makes a sound and the sum of the sounds is the word. Teaching through phonics involves teaching the letters first, then teaching some rules or procedures for analyzing the arrangement of letters in a specific word.

The major problem with the phonic method is that the letters must be given some sort of arbitrary sound value. Unfortunately, our language is fraught with irregularities. The letter *a* doesn't always make the same sound in different words. Here are some of the possible variations: *what, are, all, eat, at, bear*, etc. Which is the "true" sound for *a*?

The method presented on the following pages is a fairly manageable phonics method. Note that it is neither the most elegant method nor the easiest way to teach some of the skills. Since writing this book, we have developed commercial programs that are more effective in teaching beginning reading, but are quite expensive. We are, however, working on a program for parents to be published in an inexpensive book form. Until then, the method outlined on the following pages will work reasonably well. Most of the teaching is achieved with work on a blackboard (or possibly index cards). Once the child has mastered the basic words, we suggest introducing beginning books. The problem at this stage of the program is that most books that are available at the bookstore or library are very poor for initial teaching because they present a highly irregular vocabulary. The initial teaching should involve very few irregulars, so the child becomes facile with the basic decoding operation.

TEACHING THE LETTER SOUNDS

Every letter not only has a name but makes a sound, just as every dog has a name (Fido, perhaps) and makes a sound (arf, arf). The letter b makes the sound b̲ill; the letter s makes the sound s̲ill—all quite logical so far as it goes.

The big trick in teaching the various letter sounds is to

reduce chaos to some kind of order and present the sounds in a way that will show the child how they are derived from the letter names he's spent so long learning.

The letter names provide a point of departure for learning the letter sounds, and the child who has learned the names already has a good start toward learning the sounds. You can help him use what he already knows by dividing the letters into four basic groups.

Group One consists of f, l, m, n, r, s and x. The name of each of these letters starts out with a vowel sound and ends with a consonant sound. If you want to know the sound the letter makes, take the vowel sound off the letter name and you've got it. Consider f. You pronounce it "efff." If you want to know what sound it makes, drop the ĕ sound and you've got it: fff. The same for el (–l), em (–m), en (–n), es (–s), ex (–x), and ar (–r)–drop the initial vowel and what remains is the sound the letter usually makes.

Group Two consists of the letters b, d, p, t, v, z, j and k. This is a more difficult group, because it contains b, d and p–three troublemakers. The names for the letters in this group start out with a consonant and end with a long vowel sound. "Be." To derive the letter sound from the name, say the name of the letter, knock off the final vowel sound, and you've got it: "bbb." The same for dee (dd), pee (pp), tee (tt), vee (vv), zee (zz), jay (jj), and kay (kk).

Group Three consists of exceptions, c, g, h, q, w, y–*and unless they are treated as exceptions, they'll conceal the logic behind the letters in Groups One and Two.* The letters c and g seem to be Group Two letters; they both begin with a consonant sound and end with an "ee" sound. Therefore c should make the sound "sss," and g should make the sound "jjj." But they don't always make these sounds. Usually they make the sounds kkkk and ggg. The letter h looks as if it might be a member of Group One, but it's not. It doesn't make the sound "ch." It makes the sound "hhh."

Group Four consists of the vowels. The vowels in English

make an appalling variety of sounds, but we will consider only the most common sounds, the short sounds and the long sounds. The short sounds are: and, end, in, on, up. They are difficult for the child to say, and more difficult for him to hear. Their relation to the names of the letters is not obvious. Reading would be much easier to teach if we didn't have to bother with them. But we do.

The Group One Letter Sounds: f, l, m, n, s, x, r. Before you start teaching these, make sure that you can produce each sound properly. Pay special attention to whether or not a letter is voiced or whispered. Only some letters should be pronounced with a voice, and if you make the others into voice letters, you'll simply teach the wrong pronunciation. The *f* sound, for instance, is a whispered sound. Place your fingers on your throat and say the word *fan.* Your voice mechanism is turned on for the an but not for the f. If you try to put a voice behind the *f,* you simply change it into a *v* sound.

Here is how the Group One letters are properly pronounced.

    f—Usually makes the sound *f*ill. (No Voice.)

       Occasionally of. (Voice.)

    l—Makes the sound lill. (Voice.)

   m—Makes the sound mill. (Voice.)

   n—Makes the sound nill. (Voice.)

   r—Makes the sound rill. (Voice.)

   s—Usually makes the sound *s*ill. (No voice.)

      Sometimes wise. (Voice.)

   x—Usually makes the sound ax. (No voice.)

      Sometimes exact. Occasionally xylophone. (Voice.)

Present only the first sound for each letter, but be aware of the others.

Begin by writing all the Group One letters (lowercase) on a chalkboard. Arrange them so that you can proceed from left to right, just as you would on the printed page.

      f l m n r s x

Have the child identify the letter name. "What's the name of this letter?" "Small f." Then point out that the letter makes a sound. "It has a name and it makes a sound. Listen: fff." Show him how the sound derives from the name. (Note: you may have a tendency to tack an ŭŭ sound on the end of various letter sounds—fffŭŭ, lllŭŭ, mmmŭŭ, and so forth. The tendency is strongest for letter sounds that are whispered. Putting a voice behind them seems to complete them and make them louder. But try to keep them clean.)

"The *name* of this letter is small f and it makes the sound fff. Did you know that? The sound is right in the name. Listen: ĕ-fff. Listen again. Hear it in the name? Ĕ-fff. Ĕff. Can you say it?"

"Foo."

And so on through the rest of the letters that remain, l, m, n, r, s, and x.

After the introductory session, print all Group One letters on the chalkboard. Mix up the order.

1. Ask the child the letter name.
2. Repeat the name after him in an exaggerated manner that makes the letter sound more obvious.
3. Ask him what sound the letter makes.
4. If he has difficulty, pronounce the letter name so that the letter sound becomes increasingly obvious.

What's the name of this letter? . . . Yes, this is small m. Small e-mmmm. What sound does e-mmm make? . . . Listen, the sound is in the name. e-MMM. Did you hear it? . . . Yes. Em makes the sound mmm."

The child should master the Group One letters in two weeks or less, but don't rush him.

Some 3-year-olds have pronunciation trouble. The most common difficulties are the lisp (pronouncing the s sound as "th") and the habit of pronouncing the r sound as a w (stweet for street). Since both of these difficulties involve Group One letter sounds, the easiest time to start correcting them is now, when the child is working on sounds.

To teach the s̲ sound to a child who lisps, have him clench his jaw. This may not be easy for him at first. Give him something to bite on and let him use a mirror. After he's mastered clenching, teach him to smile with clenched jaw. Finally, have him make the "sss" sound while smiling through a clenched jaw. He'll make the correct sound because he won't be able to get his tongue between his teeth to say "th." *Saying* the proper sound will also help him *hear* the difference between the "ssss" and "thh," something he was probably unable to do before. Continue to teach the s̲ sound in this exaggerated fashion until the child gains some control over it. Then relax the procedure.

Correcting the *stweet* tendency is somewhat more difficult. Probably the best way is to play lion with the child. Roar. Exaggerate the throaty guttural quality of the rrr—make it rattle. "Now you try it. Rrreally rrroar." After some practice, he'll be able to produce the sound. Keep it exaggerated until he gains control over it; then begin to refine it. This can take several months, although he may master it in a couple of weeks.

The Short Vowel Sounds: The child can attack words when he knows nothing more than the Group One consonant sounds and the short vowel sounds. He is laden with less information and can therefore concentrate more on the mechanics of moving from left to right and of blending the various sounds.

But you can't make words out of Group One consonant sounds alone, so the short vowel sounds come next.

They are: ănd, ĕnd, ĭn, ŏn, ŭp. Learn them. Here are some words that will help you remember the correct sounds:

a—And, apple, ant.
e—End, egg, elephant.
i—In, it, is.
o—On, ox, odd.
u—Up, under, until.

Memorize this list, or keep a copy of it handy during your

lessons. It's easy—too easy—to forget the correct short sound and make this kind of mistake. "Say the short a sound, as in the word *all*."

All short vowel sounds are quite similar; all are formed with the mouth open; all are voiced. The easiest way to help the child produce them is to take them out of isolation and put them together in a set—a rote pattern: a e i o u (and end in on up). The pattern functions something like the melody of a song. Try to produce the fourth note in the song "Stardust," and you'll see what we mean. Producing the note is easy if you start at the beginning of the song and produce the notes that precede it. But without these, the task is pretty difficult. The vowel sounds are as fragile as the individual notes in "Stardust." They are much easier to produce when they have a "melody," a set, to hold them together.

Print the vowels on the board: a e i o u. (Note: Not ɑ but rather, a.)

1. Ask the child to name the letter.
2. Tell him that the letter makes more than one sound.
3. Present the short sound.
4. Give examples of words that *start* with the sound.
5. Have him repeat the sound and identify it as the short letter sound (the short e sound or the short u sound).

"What's the name of this letter? . . . Good. Small e. e makes a lot of sounds. It makes long sounds and short sounds and funny sounds. *Short e* makes this sound. ĕĕĕ. Your turn . . . ĕĕĕ. Good. Do you want to hear the short-e sounds in some words? Listen . . . ĕĕĕ-gg, ĕĕĕ-nd, ĕĕĕvery. Your turn. Say ĕĕĕ-gg . . ."

The short e sound is a potential source of trouble. Six of the seven Group One consonants have the short e sound in the letter name: ef, el, em, en, es and ex. After the child masters the vowel sounds, he'll be trying to blend the short e sound with the sounds of Group One consonants. Anticipate the trouble he'll have.

"The short e sound is in some of the other letters. Listen.

ĕĕĕ-ff. Hear the ĕĕĕ? But the letter f makes the sound fff, doesn't it? The letter e makes the sound ĕĕĕ."

After you've acquainted the child with the individual short vowel sounds, introduce the short vowel pattern, ă-ĕ-ĭ-ŏ-ŭ. Print it on your board from left to right.

"Okay, here are the letters small a, small e, small i, small o and small u. Here are the sounds they make [pointing] ăă . . . ĕĕ . . . ĭĭ . . . ŏŏ . . . ŭŭ. Your turn . . . ăăă think of the word ănd . . . ăă-nd; ĕĕĕ . . . think of the word ĕgg . . . ĕĕĕ-gg; ĭĭĭ . . . think of ĭn, ĭĭĭ-nn; ŏŏŏ . . . think of the word ŏŏ-nn; ŭŭŭ . . . think of the word ŭŭ-nder."

When the child has learned to repeat the sound pattern after you say it, switch emphasis to locating the letters. Present the pattern in the usual order: a e i o u. Run through it several times. Then say, "I'm going to make the sound of one of these letters. See if you can find the letter. Listen hard. ăăă. Which letter makes the sound ăăă? . . . Good. The letter a. Let's say it. The letter a makes the sound ăăă . . ." Continue through the other letters *in the a e i o u order.*

During the following lessons speed up the locating process, making the questions shorter, the answers more concise. "What makes the sound ăă? a makes the sound ăă. What makes the sound ĕĕĕ? e makes the sound ĕĕĕ." Proceed in the a e i o u order. "Okay, I'll make the sounds and you point to the letters that make them. Think hard. ăăă . . . ĕĕĕ . . . ĭĭĭ . . . ŏŏŏ . . . ŭŭŭ. Good. Let's say them together . . . ăăă . . . ĕĕĕ . . ."

Present the series on the board in the usual order. Recite the sounds and have the child follow. Then point to any letter in the group, i for instance. "What sound does i usually make? Let's figure it out." Do this by going back to the a and reciting the sound pattern until you reach i. ăăă . . . ĕĕĕ . . . ĭĭĭ. i makes the sound ĭĭĭ." Point to another letter, perhaps u. "What sound does u usually make? Let's figure it out. ăăă . . . ĕĕĕ . . . ĭĭĭ . . . ŏŏŏ . . . ŭŭŭ. u makes the sound ŭŭŭ." Repeat for the other vowel sounds.

147

This exercise provides good practice in working from left to right. If the child has trouble following the left-right order, have him point to each letter as he says the sound it makes.

Reading Words Formed with Group One Consonants and Short Vowel Sounds: Words follow different patterns. The easiest for the child to learn is the consonant–short vowel–consonant pattern (as in the words *big, his, let*). This is the pattern to present first. Print the vowels and three rows of words on your chalkboard in this manner.

```
    a   e   i   o   u
   → fan        fan         fan
   → run        run         run
   → mad        mad         mad
```

1. Begin the lesson by referring to the vowels at the top of the board and running through the short vowel sounds.

2. Next, refer to the arrows that are to the left of each row. "These tell you the way you should read. Make your finger look like the arrow . . . pointing the way the arrow points . . . like this and read. We always read the top first, so we start here and go this way."

3. Model the sounding-out process. Touch under each letter and say the sound of that letter. Try not to stop or create a pause between the sounds. Don't say, "ff--a--n." Say the word slowly: "fffaaannn," making sure that you are clearly touching under the letters that you say. The demonstration must show that you are saying the sound for each letter as you touch under that letter.

Repeat the model several times. Then tell the child, "Your turn." Hold your finger where the arrow is; quickly move under each letter as the child says the sounds.

If the child has trouble saying the sounds without stopping, model the pronunciation. To do this, move away from the board and say, "Listen to me. ffffaaaannnn. Say that with me . . ." Repeat the model and continue responding with the child until the child seems to be performing well.

Then say, "Your turn," and let the child say the sounds. Finally, return to the board word and say, "That's what you say when I touch under these letters." Perform the sounding-out with the child as you point to the word.

4. Demonstrate how to say the word fast. "I'm going to sound out the word, then say it fast." Sound out the word. Then touch the arrow and say, "Say it fast: fan." As you say the word, move your finger quickly under it. Tell the child, "Your turn to sound it out and then say it fast." Present the task to the child. If the child has trouble saying the word fast, present the task as a purely verbal task. Move from the chalkboard. "Listen: fffaaannn. Say it fast." If necessary, demonstrate the task several times. Then present it to the child.

5. Handle the second and third words in each line in an abbreviated manner. Note: The same word is repeated in each row. For the subsequent words in the line, demonstrate sounding out and saying it fast. "My turn. I'm going to sound out this next word and then say it fast." Start with the arrow, touch under each sound, sound out the word without pausing between sounds. Then return to the arrow and say, "Say it fast." Slash under the word and say it. After modelling the procedure, give the child a turn. Make sure that the child doesn't "jump the gun." Warn the child. "You have to watch my finger. Don't say sounds before I touch under them."

6. Repeat the procedure for the second row of words. Don't be surprised if the child tries to say "fan" for the first word in the second row. This mistake is the price you pay for making the subsequent words in each row easier. To correct the mistake, simply require the child to "say it fast" when you present the word verbally. In fact, you may present "fffaaannn" and "rrruuunnn" in a kind of game. "See if you can say the right word fast. The word will be fan or run. Listen . . ."

7. After you've gone through all three lines of words, review by giving the child a *location task*. "Look. Here's the

word fan. How many other words <u>fan</u> can you find? Remember, they have to be the same as this one."

8. Present a new three-word group (using f, l, m, n, s, r and the short vowels) every day for two weeks. Then mix up the order of the words in the block to wean the child from set cues.

man	fin	man
run	man	run
fin	run	fin

Don't let the child charge into errors, which is precisely what he'll do unless you alert him to the new task. After he finishes the first word in each line, warn him, "Both of these are not <u>man</u>. Only one is. Can you find the one that says <u>man</u>? Remember it has to look just like this word."

After he finds the other <u>man</u>, go back to the middle word, <u>fin</u>. Treat it in the usual manner. Then have the child read all of the words in the line. Help him if he gets stuck. Proceed to the next line.

Spend a total of about five weeks on exercises involving Group One consonants and short vowels. Don't expect the child to learn any words accurately during this period. Remember, he's not dealing with simple "objects." He's dealing with a code, a very difficult one.

The Group Two consonants:

<u>b</u> makes the sound big. (Voice.)
<u>d</u> makes the sound dill. (Voice.)
<u>j</u> makes the sound Jill. (Voice.)
<u>k</u> makes the sound kill. (No voice.)
<u>p</u> makes the sound pill. (No voice.)
<u>t</u> makes the sound till. (No voice.)
<u>v</u> makes the sound very. (Voice.)
<u>z</u> makes the sound zoo. (Voice.)

The Group Two letter sounds are difficult to pronounce in isolation. It's very easy to get in the habit of saying bbŭŭ, dŭŭ, and so forth. In fact, you can't help but make a slight vowel sound of some kind after even the cleanest *b* or *d*.

Teach these sounds as you taught the Group One sounds:

1. Write the Group Two letters on your board from left to right:

> b   d   j   k   p   t   v   z.

2. Have the child identify the first letter, b.

3. Indicate that the name of the letter contains the sound it makes: "b makes a sound. Listen and you can hear it in the name—b-$\overline{ee}$; b makes the sound b."

4. Have the child repeat the sound and say, "b makes the sound b."

5. Continue through the other letters in this fashion.

After a week, the child should have a pretty good grasp of the Group Two letter sounds.

Reading Words Formed with Group Two Consonants and Short Vowel Sounds: The procedure is almost identical to the one you used with the Group One consonants. Select three words from the simple words that you can make up using the Group Two consonants and short vowels: bat, bet, bit, but, dad, dell, did, dip, dot, jet, job, pat, pet, pit, pod, pot, tap, top, tub, vat, zip. Present the words in this fashion:

tub	jet	tub
jet	zip	jet
zip	tub	zip

When you sound out these words, point with a finger from each hand. Start with the pointing finger from the right hand under the vowel and the left hand finger in front of the word. Tap the right-hand finger under the vowel and say the vowel sound (*uuu* for the word *tub*). Then demonstrate the sounding out. Quickly move the left-hand finger under the letters *t* and *u* as you say, "Tuuu . . ."

Don't try to hold the *t* sound. It can't be done. Simply blend it with the *u*. Practice the procedure before you use it. When the child is attempting to sound out the words, say, "Take a good look at the letter over my finger. Then get ready to say the letters I point to."

After the child reads the individual words in a line, let

the child read all the words in a line. If the child has trouble with words containing *b* or *d*, delay the introduction of *b* but continue to present words that contain *d*.

If the child has trouble with the words that begin with stop sounds (*j, d, p*) erase the first letter from each of these words and have the child sound out and identify the two-letter words. Then add the initial stop sound consonant and say the word. (Start with *et*, then add *j* to form *jet*.)

Play a game in which you may add different sounds to the beginning of the word (some sounds from group one and some from group two). Start with an ending such as *at*. Add *s, m, p,* or *t* to the beginning. Note that this is a hard game. Model the correct responses and respond with great admiration when the child performs correctly.

Point out that you can spot a d at the beginning of a word bcause the d faces away from the word. "This word is *dip*—you know, like a dip of ice cream. Dip. Say it. Listen. Ddd-ip. It begins with a dd sound. What letter makes that sound? Yes, d. And how do we know this is a d? Look at the way it's facing. It's facing away from the word, isn't it? We're reading this way →. But the d is facing this way ←."

Spend about three weeks on Group Two words. Don't be afraid to repeat words. Try to set your pattern up so that the words are not too similar in appearance or sound.

The Group Three Consonants: This group consists of six letters: c, g, h, q, w, y. They belong together because they are all exceptions. All of them except w look as if they belong to one of the other groups. A child who says that the letter y makes the sound "wwww" or that h makes the sound "chh" or that c makes the sound "sss" is not a slow child. Actually, he is bright. He's extending workable rules that he made up about letter-sound patterns. The letter sounds, not the child are at fault. The child deserves credit for a smart conclusion. Here are the exceptions:

c   usually makes the sound <u>c</u>at; sometimes *c*ity. (No voice.) Would always make the sound *c*ity if it were a regular Group Two letter, like b.

g usually makes the sound gun; sometimes gin. (Voice). Would always make the sound gin if it were a regular Group Two letter, like b.

h usually makes the sound hat. (No voice.) Would always make the sound chick if it were a regular Group One letter, like f.

q makes the sound queen. (No voice on the kkk sound; voice on the www sound. Would make the sound cat if it were a regular Group Two letter.

w makes the sound win. (Voice.) Perhaps no voice on some words, depending on where you live.

y usually makes the sound yyes; sometimes my, happy, day. (Voice.) Would make the sound win if it were a regular Group Two letter.

Teach the Group Three letter sounds as exceptions. "We're going to study some funny letter sounds now. These are all mixed up."

Put the Group Three letters on the board left to right.

c g h q w y

1. Ask the child the name of the letter.

2. Repeat the name, and ask him what sound he thinks it should make. (See list above.)

3. Point out that the letter sound doesn't behave that way. "Yes, you'd think that g would make the sound jjj. And sometimes it does. But most of the time it makes the sound *ggg*. Can you say that?"

Note: the child may have trouble producing some of these sounds—especially ggg, hhh, qqqw, wwww. If he does, give him a word to hang onto: gun, hat, queen, window.

"It's hard to say: qqqw. Try it once more. Almost. Listen, and you can hear it in this word: *queen*. Hear it? qqqw-een. Can you say that?"

After about a week, make the task more difficult by switching emphasis from location to identification.

1. Name the letter.

2. Have the child give the appropriate sound. If he gets stuck, tell him the sound.

Spend as much time as the child requires to learn Group Three sounds thoroughly. Time spent now represents time and ego saved later.

Reading Words Formed with Group Three Consonants and Short Vowel Sounds: Form simple words that *begin* with Group Three letters and have a short vowel sound. Don't worry if the ending letters are not from Group Three: One irregular in a word is enough. Cat, cup, get, gas, gun, hat, hit, will, yes, yet.

Put three groups of words on the board, and go over them in the usual manner.

hat	will	hat
will	gas	will
gas	hat	gas

Present a new Group Three word block every day for about a week.

The Long Vowel Sounds: The long sound for each vowel is the same as the name of that vowel. The letter a makes the long sound ā (as in ate) ; the letter e makes the sound ē (as in eat) ; i makes ī (as in iron) ; o makes ō (as in open), and u makes ū (as in use). All quite logical, and there actually isn't much for the child to learn. The main ideas he has to get are (1) that the vowels are capable of making more than one sound, and (2) that when you want the long sound of a vowel, you say the letter name.

After you've gone through the long sounds of the a e i o u pattern several times, present long vowel words: he, we, I, go, so.

"This word is so. Say it. Yes. We start with the sss sound and then we have a long o: sss-ō. Your turn. Good. And this word is he. Say it: hhhh-ee. The hhh sound here and then the long e . . ."

Don't try to make the long sound seem reasonable, because it isn't. For every so and go, he'll have to grapple with a to. So just point out the words.

READING FROM BOOKS

There are many books on the market for beginning readers. Most of them are extremely difficult for a beginning reader to handle. They are typically loaded with irregular words (such as *said, were, where,* and *mother*). The words are not presented frequently enough to assure that the child masters them. And the syntax of the stories is often designed so that the child "knows" the next word before reading—a situation that may encourage undue guessing.

The best source for beginning books may be your school library. Ask the librarian if it is possible for you to check out beginning readers from a linguistics or phonics program. Note that you don't want the beginning books from a sight-reading program.

Before reading the books with the child, go through them and identify words that are irregular. These are words that are not spelled the way they sound. The word *what* is irregular because it is not spelled *wut*. The word *said* is irregular because it is not spelled *sed*.

Preteach these words. Teach them as strange words. Follow this general procedure:

1. Identify each word and make sure the child can pronounce it. "This word is *said*. What word?"

2. Show how the word is spelled by referring to the sounds. "Here's how the word sounds: sssaaaiiid. But that's not how we say the word. We say *sed*."

3. Direct the child in sounding out the word. Then ask, "But how do we say the word?" For the first few words, the child may need quite a bit of prompting to remember the word.

Work on the irregulars that appear in the story until the child is firm on them. Then follow these steps:

1. Make sure that you can identify the irregular words in the story. Remember, the child doesn't know that the letters *ck* make only one *k* sound, that two *ll*'s make only a single *l* sound, or that an *e* at the end of some words makes no

155

sound at all. Expect the child to make mistakes. Don't get impatient. Be consistent and point out how the letter combinations work. If the child has particular trouble, play a game with the words involved in the problem.

Remember what the child knows. Don't assume he knows more, because he doesn't. He knows the sounds of the consonants, and he knows two sounds for each vowel. He doesn't know exactly when to produce a given vowel sound, and he can't always produce the given sound on command. He has a vague idea that words follow the form of consonant–short vowel–consonant (and sometimes consonant–long vowel–consonant). He has an idea that the elements in a word make the sounds, and he knows something about reading from left to right. He may think he knows a word or two and maybe he does. But the simplest kind of reading assumes a far greater knowledge than he possesses.

2. Map out the material you plan to read during the lesson. *Aim for twenty words.*

3. Begin the lesson with the short vowel sounds.

4. If the book is new, explain what it is and what it's about. "This is a book we're going to read. It tells about a boy and his duck." In fact you may want to read the book to the child before he tries it.

5. Look at the pictures before you start reading. If you don't let the child at least partially satisfy his curiosity about the pictures before you start reading, he'll probably look at them when you want him to look at the words. Explain what's happening in each picture. Identify the characters and point out the details that are clues to the setting and action. "How do I know it's cold out? Look at the heavy coats they're wearing."

6. Have the child simply *locate* all of the words in the assigned material going from left to right and from line to line in the prescribed manner. Have him touch every word. Remind him of the rules he's learned about reading (starting left and going right, interpreting the spaces as gaps be-

tween words, and starting each new line at the left). Take his hand and demonstrate first. "Remember, when we read we always start as far over here as we can and as far up here as we can. Here we go. *Let's see if we can touch every word.* Here's one . . . here's the next one. Oh, oh, we're at the end of the line. Where do we go now? All the way back and then down to the very next line. Now we start all over and touch every word."

Note: The child may not have the motor ability necessary to touch the words he wants to touch. Don't hurry him.

7. Point with a pencil, so you can touch the individual letters in the words.

8. Pronounce each word, and have the child repeat it.

9. Sound out all words that are *not underlined;* point to the letters as you pronounce them. Have the child follow. This is big. B—see, it faces in—iii-g. B-iii-g. Your turn."

10. Sound out all irregular words *as if they were regular,* with a regular short vowel sound. Then prompt the idea that they are funny words. "Let's sound it out [pointing with pencil] . . . www . . . hh-aa-tt. Www . . . hat. But we don't say 'www . . . hat.' We say, 'what.' "

The purpose in treating words this way is to help the child relate the words in his book to what he knows about words in general. It shows him how irregular words are regular, namely that they still go from left to right, that the individual letters make their usual sounds, but that the word doesn't add up in the usual way.

So treat every deviation from what the child knows as an exception, even if the deviation is a common letter combination.

11. After you've gone through all twenty words, review them. Use the same procedure you used during the initial presentation, but go faster, and ask the child if he can identify some of the easier words. "Do you remember what this word is? Think hard." If he doesn't know, tell him. Then show him how the letter sounds make up the word.

"This word is <u>some</u>. It looks like it should be ss-ŏŏ-mm-ĕĕ, but we say 'some.' "

Remember, you want the child to respond as much as possible. Let him point to the words. Ask him where the next word is. Ask him which way you go when you read. Ask him what you do when you come to the end of the line. Ask him what it means when a word is underlined. Ask him to repeat the words after you. Ask him to repeat the sounds after you. Keep him involved throughout the lesson.

Use this basic method of teaching reading until the child is 4, but as the child begins to catch on to words, change the ground rules to take advantage of his new knowledge.

1. Increase the number of words until you're covering about thirty-five a session.

2. Ask him if he knows familiar words. If he doesn't, provide him with clues. "Remember, we had this word before, when Jack brought the duck home." Sometimes the statement, "We had this word before," or "I'll bet you remember this word," is enough to let the child look at the word as a familiar pattern. But don't be surprised by erratic performances. The clues that make a word "familiar" are so fragile that the child can recognize a word two times in three lines of print and fail to recognize it the third time. For some reason—perhaps because of the word's position on the line or perhaps because of the words surrounding it—the word is no longer familiar, and all the clueing in the world won't change it. When this happens—and it will, many, many times—tell him the word and don't make an issue of it.

3. Encourage the child to guess, but not wildly. Recognize that the child will make two different types of wrong guesses. He'll generalize about a word from some detail, usually the beginning letters. When he calls *wonderful* "won't," he's making this kind of mistake. The other type is

an inference pattern or context guess. He'll think he knows what word should come next, so he'll say it. When he calls the word *elephant* "him" he is making this kind of mistake.

Don't treat guessing as a cardinal sin. It is a step in learning how to read. The good reader has worked out a set of rules about the context of what he's reading. He knows that only a limited number of words or phrases occur in a given context. This is sentence an example of one in which expected cues are not present. For a child all sentences read this way.

Don't treat context mistakes as cardinal sins, but don't go too far the other way and encourage wild guessing. If the child goes on a guessing spree, bring him back to the printed page with a statement something like this: "Well, take a good look at this word." Don't tell him he's wrong. Just bring him back for another look. Then show him how the elements work.

4. *Teach phonic rules through examples of familiar words.* You can pound the table and tell the child over and over that the letter group ou makes the sound "ow," and the child will fail to see the ou in the word shout. Only the very sophisticated reader can take a word apart and concentrate on the ou sound. And the sophisticated reader, even a sophisticated reader who has received careful drilling in phonetic rules, doesn't actually isolate words according to diphthongs and digraphs. He may think that he does. Actually, however, he's operating much more by analogy. He sees the word out in shout, and so he automatically knows the ou sound.

Teach the phonetic rules, yes. But not in isolation. Tie them to a familiar word. During the lessons you should call attention to the common beginnings: th, ch and sh; the common combinations: ai, au, ea, oa, ee, oo, ou, ow and ck; and the common endings: s, ed, ing. Also point out how the final *e* makes a preceding vowel long. If the child doesn't know a word that contains the combinations, use the present word as the example. "This is a funny word, isn't it? It looks like ss-hip. But we say ship. This is a funny word all right. But take a good look at it, because you know something? We're going to have more words that begin the same way, with sh. The word short, the word shave, the word shoe—they're all sh words just like this one."

Remember, when you present sounds like ed, that there is more than one example of them. "Yes, this word is asked—aa-ss-kk-tt. Hear the ed on the end, just as in the word looked."

There are also two th's—this and thing.

Endings come slowly, and internal sounds come even more slowly. Just keep reminding the child of a model word and he'll show progress—in time.

5. Give the child more responsibility in sounding out words. Stick to regular words, and don't make too many sounding-out demands on him. It is far faster and more efficient to tell the child a word, thus placing the emphasis not so much on the methods of attacking words but on *words*.

6. Don't rush the child. His rules are delicate. He has to handle them just so or he'll be left holding a bunch of broken pieces. Sometimes he can't find in his repertoire the word he sees. Other times he finds it, but he can't make his vocal cords say it. The worst thing you can do is rush him. He needs time to find and pronounce even the most familiar words. The next worst thing you can do is to allow him to stew over a word too long. Give him a clue about the word, remind him of which book it was in. Wait about four or five seconds. Then help him out. "It's *duck*. I'll bet you remember it now, don't you? What is this word? Good."

7. Use the child's reading knowledge outside of the daily lesson. Let him read signs and words in the newspaper. Note: Signs are usually in uppercase letters. The child will probably not recognize a familiar word if it appears in up-

percase. Also, the child learns to read signs because of the outside cues he receives. A child can learn to read a stop sign from a distance of three blocks during a snowstorm and be unable to recognize *stop* in a book. He hasn't learned the word as much as capital letters in a given setting, on a sign of a certain shape and color.

By the time the child is 4, he should have a sight vocabulary (words he can recognize without help) of about one hundred words and he should read very hesitantly. These gains are anything but spectacular when you compare them with those achieved by the average first-grader. But this is not a fair comparison. The first-grader has already worked out motor skills, rules about space, and rules about word occurrences before he started reading. The preschool child hasn't. But by the time the preschooler reaches the first or second grade, he'll read on a level far superior to that of a first-grader (and probably superior to all but the smartest third-graders).

ARITHMETIC

EDUCATORS HAVE ALMOST COMPLETELY MISSED the point on arithmetic and how to teach it. They have turned to the Greeks and their geometric approach; they have turned to the Arabs and their abacus; they have turned to "experts" who are almost universally wrong on everything they say. They have turned to gimmicks, shortcuts and calculating tricks.

But mathematics is almost pure logic. It is not the tables and the facts, the rules and counter rules you learned when you were in school. It is not the abortive games and tricks and Mickey Mouse that your child may now be learning. Mathematics is a series of basic rules and universal opera-

161

tions. Mathematics is almost pure deduction. This means that if you are given a very few fundamental facts and relations, you can deduce a great many conclusions. Surprisingly, a great many of the necessary facts and relations are contained in the apparently simple and unimposing task of counting. The child who knows how to count with understanding already has laid the groundwork for addition, subtraction, algebra problems and the concept of "equal." An understanding of counting is extremely important, but not nearly as easy to achieve as it might seem. Counting is not a simple task.

COUNTING OBJECTS

The child already knows how to recite the number series from one through ten. But for him, counting is just a series of sounds. There is absolutely nothing in the names of the numbers that explains the complicated operation of counting objects. The rules the child has to master before he can count four blocks with any degree of understanding are:

Rule 1: To touch every block—but *only once*.

Rule 2: To coordinate the counting with the touching, so that he says "one" when he touches the first block, "two" when he touches the second, and so forth.

Rule 3: To give a block only a certain number, the one that is next in the series.

Rule 4: To number each block according to its position, not according to its characteristics. The position is the only thing that tells him which block is "three" and which is "four." If he shuffles the blocks around, the "three" block may become the "one" block.

Rule 5: To understand that the last number he says tells something about all of the blocks he's counted. If the block is "four," he must understand that it is the "fourth" block and that if he were to put aside all of the blocks he's counted so far, he would have four of them.

Plan to work with the child at least twice a week in sessions that last no longer than five minutes. Put three blocks in a row on the floor. Then explain the purpose of counting. *"How many blocks are here?* Let's count them and find out." Next, explain the rules of the game. "When we count we must touch all the blocks and count them, but we must touch them only once and count them only once. Watch me. I touch the first block and say 'one.' Now I touch the next block and say 'two,' and now I touch the last block and say 'three.' " Always count from left to right. After you have finished counting, draw a conclusion about what counting has told you. "I counted all of the blocks. There are three blocks here. One . . . two . . . three— three blocks."

Now rearrange the blocks and count them again.

1. State that you are going to count, and that counting will tell you *how many* blocks are here.

2. Count from left to right, slowly, touching each block as you count.

3. Conclude: "I counted them and there are three blocks here."

The purpose of rearranging the blocks after counting them is to isolate the relationship you're trying to present. You don't want the child to think that the "two" or the "three" belongs to a particular block.

Next, let the child count. Take his hand and touch the first block. Say "one." Guide his hand to the second block. "Two." And the third. "Three." Then conclude: "We counted all of the blocks and there are three of them."

After three or four introductory sessions (during which you demonstrate counting with different objects), begin to increase the child's responsibility in counting.

1. First let him try counting as you guide his hand. Also begin to ask him questions about why you count and what

the counting has told you. "Why do we count?" Answer: To find out how many blocks are here. "You counted up to four. What does that tell you about the blocks?" Answer: There are four blocks here. (If the child doesn't know the answer, help him out.)

2. Next, let the child count and point at the same time. He'll find the task easier if you arrange the blocks so that the spaces between them are large (six inches to a foot). When he counts well-spaced blocks, he stands a better chance of remembering where he has been and where he is going.

3. After the child has been counting for a month, begin increasing the number of blocks, until you reach ten.

Learn the five rules that govern counting (page 162). When the child makes a mistake, he's breaking one of these rules. Analyze his mistake and then correct it by strengthening the rule that is weak. If the child tries counting a block twice, spread the blocks out further, on the chance that he forgot where he had been and where he was going. "After you count this one, you have to count the next one. That's the rule. Here, watch me, and then you do it again . . ."

PICKING UP BLOCKS AS THEY ARE COUNTED

After the child has been counting objects for about three months (don't worry about overlearning), introduce a new task that acts as a transition betwen counting all of the objects and counting only a certain number of objects. The new task involves picking up each block as you count it and putting it in a pile.

Start with three or four blocks and work up to ten. Demonstrate the new task several times before letting the child try it. "How are we going to find out how many blocks are here? Yes, by counting them. Here we go. Watch me. When I count a block, I put it over here. One . . . two . . . three.

There, I counted three blocks. Did I count all of them? I must have because *there aren't any left.*"

When the child tries this kind of counting, he'll probably become so absorbed in manipulating the blocks that he'll lose his place. Help him out at first by playing a game in which *he* moves the blocks and *you* count them. Then, change off, with you moving the blocks and the child counting. Finally, after the child is fairly handy at both tasks, put them together and let him both move the blocks and count them.

COUNTING OUT A SPECIFIED NUMBER OF OBJECTS

By the time the child is 3½, he should be ready to learn how to count three blocks or five blocks from a pile of ten blocks. By now, he knows something about the relationship between the last number he says and all of the objects he has counted. He knows that when you count to four you can say, "There are four blocks here." Now we're going to ask him to apply his knowledge to a different situation. We're going to change counting from a question of "how many" to a directive: "this many." He counts not until all the blocks are gone but until he reaches a certain number.

He's going to have to learn a rule. If you want four objects, you stop as soon as you say "four." If you want two hundred and three, you stop as soon as you say "two hundred and three."

Counting until you reach a certain number is more difficult than counting all of the objects, because you've got to keep more things straight in your mind. You have to remember, in addition to everything else, the number that tells you when to stop.

1. First get the child used to stopping after he says a certain number. Explain the task. "I want you to count to three." Explain the rule. "The rule is this. Stop counting as

soon as you say 'three.'" Demonstrate. "Listen to me. I'll count to three. I'll stop as soon as I say 'three.' One . . . two . . . three. Your turn. Count to three. Stop after you say three." Repeat with other numbers through ten. Expect the child to have trouble with the larger numbers, simply because he'll probably forget the number at which he is supposed to stop.

2. After the child is reasonably proficient at stopping (two or three weeks), coordinate the new rule with block counting. Set out a row of ten blocks. Let the child count all of them. Then tell him that you want to count out four of them. Remind him of the rule. "That means we stop counting as soon as we say 'four.' I'll put them over here. You count. Remember, you count every time I pick one up. Here we go. One . . . two . . . three . . . four. Oh oh, I said 'four.' That means I have to stop counting." Point out that you can check your accuracy by referring to the pile of blocks you have counted. "We wanted four blocks. If we counted four blocks, we must have four blocks here. Let's see if we do. Count them. Good."

Stay with this procedure for three or four sessions, then let the child move the blocks while you count. This should be fun for him.

3. The final step is a solo in which the child counts, piles the counted blocks, and stops at a specified number.

Start out with the smaller numbers (below five). Remind him of the rule. "Stop counting as soon as you say _____." Encourage him to work fast. The longer it takes him to finish counting, the greater the chance he'll forget the number he's shooting for or his place in the number series or both.

4. Show the child how counting plays a part in every day activity. Let him count common household things like three forks, four stamps, two cupfuls of flour, and so on.

By the time the child is 3¾, he should be fairly proficient at all the types of counting you've presented. Expect him to

THREE YEARS TO FOUR YEARS

fail occasionally on counting out seven or more objects. The time lapse is against him on larger numbers. The remedy is practice—lots of it.

COUNTING TO THIRTY

Present the series in the same manner you used to teach the numbers from one through ten. Make it a part of the bedtime ritual beginning when the child is about 3 years old. Teach five new numbers at a time, starting with eleven through fifteen. Make it clear how these numbers fit into the familiar series. "We're going to learn to count from one to fifteen. First we count from one to ten. Do you want to do that for me? Good. Now we go on to fifteen. Listen to me. Eleven—say it—twelve—say it—thirteen—say it . . ." Have him repeat each number after you for about a week. By then he should be ready to try the whole series at once. Say it for him first, starting with one. Then let him try starting from one. If he gets stuck, help him out.

Finally let him recite the series without first hearing you say it. "Okay, I'm going to put the light out on fifteen. Your turn to count."

Present the remaining groups of five numbers in the same manner.

COUNTING BACKWARD FROM TEN TO ZERO

After the child has learned to count to thirty, present the task of counting backward. "We're going to learn to count down, just as they do when they blast rockets off into outer space. And when we say 'zero, blast off,' I'm going to turn the light off. Counting backward, here we go. Ten, nine, eight, seven, six, five, four, three, two, one, zero, blast off." When counting backward is presented in this manner, the child learns it very fast. The "blast-off" technique can be used also in connection with different games. "Okay, shoot the dart at the target when I give the signal. Count down: Ten . . . nine . . ."

THE NUMBER SYMBOLS THROUGH 10

Identifying the number symbols is not related to any of the other forms of counting and can be presented at any time during the year. We suggest presenting it when the child is about 3¾ years old.

Procedure: Write the symbols from 0 through 10 in crayon from left to right on a large sheet of paper (larger than standard notebook paper). Form them as they appear in books:

0   1   2   3   4   5   6   7   8   9   10.

Be careful in writing the 1 and 9. Mount the chart in the kitchen or the child's room at the child's eye level. Go over it at least a couple of times a week, using the same approach you used to teach the letters.

1. Give each number its name. "The name of this number is *one*," or "This is how we write *one*."

2. Point out the distinguishing characteristics of each written number symbol:

    0—Looks like an o.

    1—Looks like a small l.

    2—Curved top with flat bottom.

    3—Hump on top and hump on bottom.

    4—Leg with L-shaped arm coming out of it.

    5—Bar at top, big curve at bottom.

    6—Big curve with egg at bottom.

    7—Big bar at top of leg.

    8—Egg at top; egg at bottom.

9—Big curve with egg at top.

10—A one and a zero side by side.

3. Trace the letters with the child, guiding his finger. "See? Big bar on top. Then here comes a slanting leg . . ."

4. After the child becomes fairly familiar with the symbols (a month after they are introduced), ask him to *locate* the numbers as you say them. "Can you find 7?" If he has trouble, remind him of the symbol's distinguishing characteristics. "Remember, 7 has a big bar across the top and it stands on a slanting leg. See if you can find a number that looks like that."

5. Watch out for the most common mistakes—confusing 2, 3 and 5, and confusing 6 and 9. Stress the guides for recognizing each of these symbols.

6. After the child has learned to *locate* the number symbols consistently, have him identify them. "What's this one? Think hard, now." Again, remind him of the rule if he has trouble. "Look at it carefully. What's this across the top? That's right, a bar. And what is this? Okay, what number has a big bar across the top and stands on a slanting leg? Sure, 7."

7. The final step involves taking the symbols out of the familiar context. Use your chalkboard for this phase of number learning. "I'm going to write a number on the board. See if you can tell me what it is."

The child should know the symbols from 0 through 10 flawlessly by the time he is 4 years old.

WHAT NUMBER COMES NEXT?

It is easier to add $268 + 1$ than to add $268 + 37$. The reason is that you can follow a simple rule when adding 1 whereas there is no simple rule for adding 37. The rule for adding 1 is, "Go to the next number in the counting sequence." It is a simple rule with great implications. It demonstrates that adding is an extension of counting. Adding is not an extension of sheep and apples, of murky relationships that are logically independent of either adding or counting. Adding is an extension of the familiar, abstract series, one, two, three, four . . .

The rule seems simple enough, but the act of finding the next number is not too easy. It involves isolating a number and stripping it from the familiar context cues.

As a transition betwen counting and finding the next number, present four different kinds of counting games that help the child become handier at isolating a given number and seeing it in relation to the other numbers in the series. These games or patterns should be presented when the child is about two months away from his fourth birthday.

Pattern One, Counting Every Other Number: Tell the child that you're going to play a game in which you say one number, he says the next, and so forth. "I'll start out. One. You say, 'two.' Three. You say, 'four' . . ." The child will have some trouble at first. He's not used to handling the numbers in this manner. He'll forget his place and want to say more than one number when his turn comes. Work on Pattern One for about three weeks.

Pattern Two, What Comes after One? This pattern extends what the child learned in the first pattern. In this pattern, the child must answer the question, "What comes after one (or two or three or four, etc.)." Always start with "What comes after one?" Then continue through the familiar number series. "What comes after two? . . . and what comes after three? . . . and what comes after four? . . ."

When the child gets stuck, show him how to find the next number. "Let's figure out what comes after six. We go back to the beginning and count to six. Then we see *what comes next.*"

Spend about three weeks on this pattern.

Pattern Three, The Skipping Pattern: This pattern treats the number series in a more abbreviated manner than Pattern Two. It is a very easy pattern for the child to learn. "What comes after one? . . . [two.] And what comes after three? . . . [four]. And what comes after five? . . ." When this pattern goes smoothly, the numbers occur in the very familiar sequence: one, two, three, four, five, etc.

Spend two weeks on this pattern. Then review all the patterns.

Pattern Four, The Backward Pattern: This is far more difficult than any preceding pattern and should be presented only after the child has a pretty good foothold on the others. Actually, the child probably won't see this pattern as a clear-cut pattern. For him it will be more an exercise in which you've obliterated most of the familiar context cues. Start with nine and work backward. "What comes after nine? . . . and what comes after eight? . . . and what comes after seven? . . ." Take it slowly, and give the child plenty of time to think.

By the time he's 4, the youngster should have an idea of how "the next number" is related to the familiar number series. He should have a feel for the various patterns and know how to figure out what number comes next. He should have all of the skills and understanding necessary to take the next step up the ladder of mathematical abstractions, addition.

STATEMENTS ABOUT
THE WORLD

AT 3 YEARS, the child is ready to take a big step. Until now, the basic unit of communication for him has been words—*grass, fast, big, hurt, dog.* But now things change. The unit becomes the *statement*. *The statement is a formula.* It means more than a couple of words added to the stipulation, "Hot, Mommy," because, by adding a couple of words, the child has come upon a code for handling many, many relations. "The stove *is* hot."

This statement contains inferences that are not readily found in the individual concepts. For instance, it contains the notion that the stove is not cold. This fact cannot be inferred from the individual concepts *hot* and *stove*. Therefore, statements are extremely important in the learning hierarchy. They enable the child to do such things as make deductions about whether or not the stove is cold without burning himself.

Teach statements as basic, irreducible concepts that generate questions and answers. Here's the general procedure.

1. Start with a "model sentence." "Dogs have four legs," "Daddy works hard," "Big boys run fast."

2. Show that the original statement generates questions. Do this by asking and answering questions based on the original statement. For instance:

The stove is hot.

Is the stove hot?

Yes, the stove is hot.

Is the stove cold?

No, the stove is *not* cold.

This pattern of reasoning expresses the basic assumptions of our language and of the relationship between statements and the physical world. The child has only one way to learn the basic formula—through specific examples, about butterflies, Daddies and trucks. So when you present a statement, get in the habit of following it up with a question and the answer to the question.

That tree is big. Is that tree little? No, that tree is not little. That tree is *big*."

"Planes fly high. Do they fly low? No, they fly *high*."

"This is a book. Is it a crayon? No, it is a *book*."

3. When the child is about 3½, let *him* try answering the questions that are implied by simple fact-statements. "There are seven days in the week. Are there seven days in a week? Are there twenty days in a week?"

4. Whenever possible, relate the fact-statement to something the child knows. "Planes fly high, Billy. Do you know how high? Well, if Daddy took a stone and threw it just as high as he could, it would go so high you would hardly see it. But do you know what? It wouldn't even come close to that plane up there." When the facts are not relatable, don't try to find a "meaningful" explanation. Just give it to him straight. "Evergreens keep their needles all year round."

5. Do not make the classic mistake of waiting for the child to ask questions. His questions are limited by what he knows. If you wait, therefore, you may find yourself answering the questions of a middle-aged man. The idea that children—even "precocious children"—run around trying to satisfy their thirst for knowledge by asking questions is a myth. Question-asking 3-year-old children are usually children who have learned a device to control adults.

6. Do not devote a special time to fact-learning. Instead, take the facts as they come. When the child is watching you cook, tell him what's happening. When you're gardening and he's tagging along, explain something about what you're doing. In your presentation, however, try to boil the key fact down to a simple statement. "The oven bakes bread because the oven is hot."

WHAT FACTS TO TEACH THE 3- TO 4-YEAR-OLD

Every name the child has in his vocabulary is the subject for a dozen facts, ranging from simple observations, "This is a grasshopper, Mom," to rather sophisticated relationships, "Your Daddy is my Grandpa." If we tried to outline all of them, or even most of them, we would have to record nearly every exchange between mother and child throughout the day. However, the following statement areas are particularly important because they lay the groundwork for logical thought.

Facts about the Child's Formal Relations with Others: Teach the child his name and address by conducting imitation interviews. These can be fun, especially over toy telephones.

"Hello, little boy. What's your name?"

"John."

"John what? There are lots of Johns."

"John . . . I don't know."

"I'll bet you're John Baker."

"John Baker."

"And where do you live, John Baker?"

"I don't know."

"I'll bet you live at 1634 Tulip Drive. Can you say that? 1634 Tulip Drive."

"16 . . . 34 Tulip Drive."

"In what city?"

"Tulip Drive?"

"Norman, Oklahoma."

"Norman, Oklahoma."

Later introduce his telephone number.

By the time the child is 3½, he should give correct answers fairly consistently, but he'll still make mistakes from time to time when he's 4.

He should also learn practical definitions for *brother, sister, mother, father, husband, wife, aunt, uncle, grandmother, grandfather, son, daughter, grandson, granddaughter, cousin.* Seems like a pretty drab list, and it is—or it can be. It can also be fairly interesting if you relate your definition to something the child is interested in. The secret is to gossip.

Subject: Husband and wife. "I'm Daddy's wife. Did you know that? Who do you think Mr. Wilson's wife is? [Neighbors.] Why, Mrs. Wilson. And who do you think Mr. Snider's wife is?" [More neighbors.]

Use the who's-who-in-the-neighborhood approach for defining the other familial relationships.

A good time to deal with the grandmother-grandfather relationship is when you're planning a trip to their place or when you're en route.

"Do I have a mother? Sure I do. And do you know who she is? Do I have a father? Does Grandfather Jones have a daughter?"

By the time the child is 4, he should have a pretty good grasp of all these relations if you remind him of them from time to time.

Time Concepts: You probably get a little weary of reading over and over again about the difficulty of the concepts a youngster encounters, but they are difficult. And it's a mistake, a drastic mistake, not to recognize their difficulty. The notion of time is among the more difficult. To be oriented in time you must know how to classify events of the past, not in terms of their logical relation to other events nor in terms of their importance or vividness, but in terms of something as trivial as which one happened first. A child goes for an airplane ride with his grandparents; a month later he has a tooth filled at the dentist's. Now you come along and try to tell him that these two events are related. The child looks puzzled. He simply wants to remember the plane ride and forget about the drilling.

Even by the time he's 4, he won't have a perfect grasp of that invisible quality we attach to events, that dimension called time. But he'll be on his way. He will know about the days in the week and the months in the year. He'll also know what *tomorrow, today* and *yesterday* mean.

Days of the Week: Make a wall chart, which you can hang in his room. Title it, "The 7 Days of the Week." Then list the days vertically.

> Sunday
> Monday
> Tuesday
> Wednesday
> Thursday
> Friday
> Saturday

Teach the sequence in the same manner you taught the number series.

1. Make sure that the child can pronounce each name properly.

2. Have him repeat each name after you as you run through the series.

3. Have him try repeating the whole series after you say it.

4. Have him recite the whole series without hearing you say it first.

Ask questions about the heading of the chart. "How many days are there in a week? Yes, seven. Are there seven days in a *year?* No. A year is a long, long time. Are there seven days in a *month?* No, a month is a pretty long time, too. There are seven days in a *week.* Say it. Seven days in a week."

Try to give each day a personality. "Sunday is a family day. Daddy doesn't work on Sunday. He doesn't work on Saturday, either. He works on Monday [pointing to the chart] . . . Tuesday . . . Wednesday . . . Thursday and Friday. What day do we go shopping on? Yes, Friday. Does the garbage man come on Fridays? Yes, he does. Does he come on Saturdays? No."

Today, Tomorrow, and Yesterday: After the child has learned to recite the series with reasonable accuracy, introduce the concepts of *today, tomorrow*, and *yesterday.* The rule you want to demonstrate is this: Today is this day. It can be any day in the series. Tomorrow is always the following day. And yesterday is always the day before.

The rule implies the manner of presentation.

1. Tell the child what day it is. "Today is Thursday."

2. Have him find Thursday on the chart. "Find Thursday, and put your finger on it. Today is not any other day, is it? It's not Sunday."

3. Give him the rule for figuring out *tomorrow.* "Tomorrow is always the next day. So if today is Thursday, tomorrow must be the next day. Move down to the next day. Tomorrow must be . . . yes, Friday. Good thinking."

4. Go back to "today," and present the rule for figuring out *yesterday.* "Yesterday is always the day *before* today. The one above. So if today is Thursday, yesterday was the day before. Yesterday was . . ."

These rules are completely skeletal. They are accurate and fit virtually any situation. But until the child actually fits them to a variety of situations, they won't have a very deep meaning. They won't be "intuitive."

The Months of the Year: After the child has mastered the days of the week (which he should do by the time he's $3\frac{3}{4}$), introduce the months of the year. Use the same basic approach. He'll require more time to learn the months because there are more elements to learn and because they aren't as easy to demonstrate as the days of the week.

Make a wall chart. Title it "The 12 Months of the Year," and list the months in a vertical column.

> January
> February
> March

April
May
June
July
August
September
October
November
December

Stress the meaning of the heading. "The twelve months of the year. Not the seven months of the year. Not the twelve months of the week. The twelve months of the year." Later ask questions about the heading.

Teach the months in *groups of four at a time*, starting with January, February, March, April.

1. Recite the entire sequence, all twelve months.

2. Present four months, carefully pronouncing the name of each. Have the child repeat each name after you. "Feb-ru-ary. Say it. March. Say it . . ."

3. As the child becomes more familiar with the four names, have him repeat all four after you say all four. Then have him recite all four with no prompting.

4. After he has mastered four, move on to the next four. Always start from the beginning—from January—and have the child recite the entire series up to the present material.

Explain that a year is a long time. "It goes all the way from last Christmas to next Christmas. From your birthday when you were three years old until your next birthday when you'll be four years old."

Talk about the months. When a new month begins, tell the child about it. When he sees a winter story on TV, explain that snow usually comes during the months of December, January and February. When you talk about the family vacation or swimming, explain to him that the warm weather months are June, July, August and September.

QUALITIES, ACTIONS, GEOMETRIC PATTERNS, AND RELATIONS

HERE ARE SOME of the raw concepts the child should learn during the year, along with hints about presenting them effectively.

Before and After: Present in connection with learning *today, tomorrow* and *yesterday. After* is the next day down the list; *before* is the preceding day up the list. Actually, this is a poor explanation, but it should be sufficient, providing you demonstrate how to use the concepts in different contexts.

First and Second: Teach in connection with counting. The *one* block is the first block; the *two* block is the second block. No further explanation is necessary.

New-Old (Young-Old): Teach in connection with animals. "Baby animals are young. Big animals are old." Demonstrate with both small and large animals so the child doesn't get the idea that all elephants are old.

The Same and Different: This is another of the difficult concepts. When you say that two things are the same, you are merely stating that you can make an identical statement about both of them. You're not specifying what this statement is. It may be, "This thing is hot," or it may be, "This thing is called a 'chair.' "

Define *same* by showing its relation to statements. For instance, refer to two red blocks. "This one is red . . . this one is red . . . so they must be the same. They must be the same *color*—red." Build two block trains the same length. "There are four blocks in this train. There are four blocks

179

in this train. These trains must be the same. They are the same in number."

The notion of *different* should be introduced after the child has a reasonable grasp of *same*. "This one's blue. This one's *not* blue. Are they the same? No. *So they must be different.*" Use this question-answer pattern in different situations to make the point that *not-same* and *different* are the same concept.

Because: Rule: *Because* always answers the question "why?" "Why do we have cars? Because we want to go places fast." "Why do you have to stay in the yard? Because the mother is boss and she says to stay in the yard."

The child soon learns that when a statement contains a *because*, it is a powerful argument. So he tries to use it to fortify his own arguments, and he's not fussy about strict usage. He may walk up to you and state, "Because I want a cookie," which statement seems so logically commanding that no mother could possibly refuse. While the proper usage of *because* grows out of the desire to answer "why?" the child's usage grows out of the desire to use the word *because*.

The best way to present *because* is to relate it to the appropriate question. Do it in a way that allows the child to see the relation. "So you want a cookie, eh? Why? Is it because you're wearing your red shirt or because you're hungry? I see. Because you're hungry. Well, can you say the whole thing? I want a cookie because I'm hungry . . ."

Patterns: Acquaint the child with stripes, checks, polka dots and plaids. Refer to these patterns when you're dressing him. "This shirt has stripes on it. See these lines going in the same way? Those are called stripes."

Visual Inferences: A cartoonist puts down a few simple lines and swirls and you understand not only that they represent a person, but that they represent a person with a certain expression. Now the cartoonist goes further. He draws four pictures in a row. The setting for the illustrations may be the same, and to the untrained eye (namely the child's eye) the pictures may look alike. Not to you, however. They tell a story. You notice the subtle differences between the pictures: you read the inferences.

When you read inferences from a cartoon, you're using a kind of basic deductive reasoning. You use the same kind of reasoning every time you consider certain facts and deduce what must have happened. You start with the rule. For example, "If a man gets hit with a pie, he'll have pie splattered all over his face." Then you flip it over so that it says, "If he has pie splattered all over his face, he got hit with a pie." The rest is easy.

Cartoons are a good medium for presenting "what happened" deductions. So go through the comics with the child about once a week, especially the funny ones. Point out the details which function as rules. If Louis is happy, point to the detail that shows he's happy. If he is going to slip on a roller skate, point out the impending danger. State the rule: "If you slip on the skate, you could fall and hurt yourself, couldn't you?"

Also point out background details. "Look at these things coming out of his mouth. Do you know what they are? They're musical notes. See the way his cheeks are puffed up. He's whistling. Usually when people whistle they are happy, so I'll bet he's happy. Do you know where he is in this picture? Well, look back here. Here's a house, and here's a mailbox . . ."

Don't expect the child to catch on to cartoon interpretation overnight. It will take him a long time. But by the time he's 4, he should be able to make some of the simpler inferences. "Louis likes the dog . . ."

Right-Left: When the child was 2, you started teaching right-left. You called attention to his right and left members when you dressed him. In addition, you helped establish a basis for distinguishing between left and right by always squeezing the right member, never the left.

Continue the procedure throughout his third year. When the child is about 3½, he should be able to follow simple *right-left orders*. But his knowledge will be quite fragile. He may respond correctly two or three times and then fall into a bumble of confusion.

Right and Left Turns: Teach this task in steps.

Step One: Ask the child to raise his left hand. "Think hard now: your *left* hand. Good."

Step Two: "Put your left hand straight out to the side. Way out. Good."

Step Three: "Now look at your left hand. Keep looking at it."

Step Four: "Now turn toward your left hand. Go after it. Watch out now. Don't let your left hand go after you."

Step Five: Let the child spin around and around after his hand.

Don't try more than a couple of repetitions at a standing. Give the child ample thinking time, and don't be surprised if he makes mistakes from time to time. The most difficult part is learning to turn toward the hand. Once he masters this task, the rest comes fairly easy. To help him out, have him touch a wall with his extended hand. Mark the spot and have him face it. "Okay, now just face the spot. That's it. You're turning toward your left hand. That means you're turning left." By the time the child is 4, he should be able to turn left and right with a little prompting and reminders of the steps.

IDENTIFYING THE PLANETS

SEVERAL MAPMAKERS put out charts that show the various planets and give information about their size, distance from the sun, and so forth. Buy one of these charts or make one of your own.

Go over the chart at least once a week, beginning when the child is about 3¾. Tell him what these balls on the chart are. "These are the planets in the solar system." Then explain what that means. "We live on the earth. It looks flat. But if we could fly far up in the sky we'd see that the earth is not flat. It curves. And if we could fly far enough, the earth would start to look like a ball in the sky, the same way the moon sometimes looks, and the sun looks. The earth is one of the planets that revolve around the sun. But there are others. Some are much bigger than the earth, and some are much smaller. Sometimes at sunset we can see one of them, Venus. It looks like a bright, bright star. Now we're going to learn the names of all the planets in the solar system. Can you say that: the planets in the solar system."

After the explanation:

1. Name all of the planets, starting from the sun and working outward.

2. Have the child repeat each name after you say it.

3. Go over the first three planets (Mercury, Venus, Earth) about four times and have the child repeat each name after you.

4. Direct him to think about the planets in terms of how close they are to the sun. Do this by asking him questions. "Look at the chart now. Which planet is closer to the sun, Venus or Earth? Sure, Mercury is the closest. Venus is next closest, and then comes Earth."

5. Repeat this procedure during subsequent sessions until the child can name the first three planets without prompting. Then move on and concentrate on the next three.

6. Relate his new knowledge to the stunning display that goes on overhead on a clear summer night. You may have to let him stay up past his bedtime to see the show, but it's well worth the price. Explain what he's looking at. "Years ago, men used to think that those were white holes in a dark cloth. But do you know what they really are? Stars. *Suns.*

Like our sun. But some are so big that our sun would be just a tiny *speck* next to them. Look at all the stars."

IDENTIFYING DINOSAURS

THE IDEA BEHIND TEACHING the child the names of the planets is to help establish a limit or boundary for understanding space and size. It's like setting a stake out in the middle of a barren field before you start plowing. The post tells you how far to go. The child has already picked up a few bits of information about the relative size of blocks, people and things. During the next few years, he will work back and forth between this knowledge and that of planets until he's filled in a reasonably consistent and productive knowledge of size and space.

The reason for teaching the child to identify dinosaurs is to establish the limits for understanding *time*. Again the procedure involves erecting a rather dramatic landmark way out in the field, then using it as a reference point for finding your way.

At this writing, there are at least three good children's books on dinosaurs, all of which sell for less than a dollar. If the current trend in children's books continues, none of these books might be on the market when you read this passage. But a dozen new books will be. And they will probably be as good. We therefore simply suggest that you select the book that shows the major dinosaurs: sauropods (*Brontosaurus, Brachiosaurus*), theropods (*Tyrannosaurus rex*), ankylosaurs, ceratopsians (*Triceratops*), ornithopods (*Trachodon*), and stegosaurs. Select a book that has good illustrations and captions that use the dinosaurs' *real* names. Not all books do. In some educational circles, people think that the name *ankylosaurus* is somehow more difficult than *hippopotamus* or *automobile*. It isn't, and we don't recommend those books that refer to Brontosaurus exclusively as the Thunder Lizard and Tyrannosaurus rex as the tyrant king.

Go through the dinosaur book about once a week, beginning when the child is almost four years old.

1. Define the task as "learning about the dinosaurs." "Dinosaurs were huge animals that lived on earth *millions of years ago.* Were there any dinosaurs around when Daddy was a boy? No. Were there any when Grandpa was a boy? No. There weren't always human beings on the earth. And we have to go way back before human beings were alive to find the dinosaurs . . ."

2. Tell something about how we know that dinosaurs existed. "No men were there to see the dinosaurs. Nobody could take pictures of them. So how do we know about them? We have found their bones and their bones tell a story . . ."

3. Explain something about what the earth was like when the dinosaurs lived. "Were there houses and buildings? No. Were there horses? Cows? Dogs? Sheep? Cats? No. Were there pretty trees like those out there? No. Were there flowering bushes like those in front of the Doners' house? No. The plants and the animals were different then. Very different. The plants were like they are in this picture. See the funny trees?"

4. Give the names for three or four dinosaurs, taking them in the order they appear in the book. Have the child repeat each name. Tell something about each dinosaur's size and appearance. Point out the identifying characteristics. "See the long neck and the long tail. See the big thick legs. That's Brontosaurus. If his head was in the kitchen do you know where his tail would be? In the Ellises' backyard! Brontosaurus. Say it."

5. Close each session with a quick review of the dinosaur names.

HOW THINGS WORK

CONTINUE HELPING THE CHILD see the difference between the man-made part of his world and the part that is natural. The man-made part works. Show him how it works. Explain the way appliances work. Gear your presentation to his increased level of understanding. Give him more details, more facts. And don't be afraid to say that you don't know how something works. Show him that you like to learn things, too. For instance, if he asks about a doodad on the water heater, admit, "I really don't know what that does. Let's ask Daddy when he comes home. He can probably tell us."

OBJECTS

DESPITE ALL OF THE NEW DIMENSIONS the child will add to his intellectual diet during this year, the main course will still be object names. Things. Your presentation can now be quite casual. The child has worked out a very efficient set of rules for learning object names. So you don't need to make a production out of presenting them. But don't overlook them. Make sure he uses the proper names and make sure your explanations are expressed (at least for the most part) in words he understands.

TASK SCHEDULE FROM 3 YEARS TO 4 YEARS

AGE (IN MONTHS) FOR WORKING ON TASKS

Task	Page Reference	36	37	38	39	40	41	42	43	44	45	46	47
Group One Letter Sounds	143-145	♦	≈	≈	≈	≈	≈	≈	≈	≈	≈	≈	≈
Short Vowel Sounds	145-148		♦	≈	≈	≈	≈	≈	≈	≈	≈	≈	≈
Words Formed with Group One Consonants and Short Vowel Sounds	148-150			≈	≈	≈	≈	≈	≈	≈	≈	≈	≈
Group Two Letter Sounds and Their Words	150-152					≈	≈	≈	≈	≈	≈	≈	≈
Group Three Letter Sounds and Their Words	152-154						♦	≈	≈	≈	≈	≈	≈
Long Vowel Sounds	154						♦	≈	≈	≈	≈	≈	≈
Reading from Books	155						♦	♦	♦	♦	♦	♦	♦
Counting Objects	162-164				♦	♦	♦	♦	♦	♦	♦	♦	♦
Picking Up Objects as They Are Counted	164-165				♦								
Counting Out a Specified Number of Objects	165-167									♦	♦		
Counting to Thirty	167						♦	♦	♦	♦	♦	♦	♦
Counting Backward	167-168										♦	♦	
Number Symbols	168-169										♦		
What Number Comes Next?	169-171											♦	
Statements about the World	171-172					♦	♦	♦	♦	♦	♦	♦	♦
Answering Questions	173-174					♦	♦	♦	♦	♦	♦	♦	♦
Name, Address, Relatives	174-175					♦	♦	♦	♦	♦	♦	♦	♦
Time Concepts:	175												
Days of the Week	176												
Months of the Year	177												
Learning Right and Left Turns	182							♦	♦	♦	♦	♦	♦
Learning Planets	182-184							♦	♦	♦	♦	♦	♦
Learning Dinosaurs	184-185							♦	♦	♦	♦	♦	♦

PRIMARY TASK ♦♦♦
REVIEW ≈≈≈

CHAPTER VIII

Four Years
to Five Years

IT IS DURING THE CHILD'S FIFTH YEAR that the active environment differs most radically from the "standard" environment. This is the year of the greatest gains in capacity and performance—the year of the big jump. It is both an easy and a difficult year for the teacher. It's easy because the child is extremely receptive. He can distill the meaning from a very casual, hazy presentation. The pace of the learning is fast, however, and the material abstract. The teacher must work harder to stay a jump ahead of the child. And she must devote more of her time to formal sessions.

READING

THE CHILD WANTS TO READ FAST, the way you read. Unfortunately, he learns (in a series of painful stages during the year) that reading fast is not as simple as it seems. The mistakes he makes give a pretty good clue about the kind of shortcuts he experiments with.

At first, he tries identifying a word by considering only the first couple of letters. Thus, he calls any word beginning with *ha* "have," whether the word is *have, hat, hand* or *hamamelidaceous.* The approach works fine as long as he's confronted with only one word that begins with a given letter combination. The child reluctantly discovers that the approach isn't very handy when dealing with more than one word that starts out a given way. So he searches for something else and finds the word endings. These are very important, he learns. So he concentrates on them with such intensity that he forgets about the first part of the word. Now he may call *save* or *gave* "have," simply because they end in *ve*.

Then he goes through a period of slower, careful reading. This is a period of consolidation. The child is gun-shy. He is tired of making mistakes.

The urge to read fast persists, however, and the child once more starts through the cycle. But this time he's more sophisticated. His mistakes are not as flagrant. He may call *one* "on," *off* "of," *started* "starting," all of which are generalizations from the beginning of the word. Similarly, he may call *truck* "duck," *this* "is" and *or* "for." Again, these are more refined mistakes.

He continues through this cycle throughout the year, each time getting a little closer. Then, just before he starts to show real signs of reading progress, he'll make a mistake that shows he has learned to evaluate both the beginnings and the endings of words. He'll reverse a beginning part and an end part. For instance, he'll call the word *time* "mite," or the word *tag* "gas." Educators are usually appalled by this kind of mistake, but it is quite natural and quite necessary. A child who makes it is showing that he considers both the beginning and ending parts of a word, and he does it very quickly, so quickly that they get turned around.

By the end of the year, the child will be reading on a fair beginning second-grade level. There is a possibility that he'll read better than this, but don't count on it.

The materials: Continue to read out of such books as the

Easy Reader series. During the year, the child will read and re-read at least six of these books.

The schedule: Conduct daily lessons that are about fifteen minutes long.

The method: Present the reading task as you did during the latter part of the preceding year.

1. Go over the material beforehand and underline all irregular words.

2. Plan to read about sixty words a session at the beginning of the year, gradually increasing to about a hundred and fifty words by the time the child is 5.

3. Look at the pictures before you start reading; explain something about the story.

4. Point to the words. As the year progresses, let the child take over the pointing responsibilities. Usually, he should not be required to point to more than several lines of print before you take over.

5. Ask the child if he knows regular and irregular words that he has had before. If he doesn't know them, identify them, and then sound them out. Always sound out irregular words as if they were regular. As the year progresses, the child can do more sounding of *regular words only*.

6. Re-read the passage with emphasis on recognizing familiar words. ("I'll bet you remember this funny word.")

7. Point out endings and beginning of words. Always refer to familiar words. "See the *ain* part of this word, *gain*. That's the same as the end part in the word *train*."

The needs of the child are somewhat different from what they were during the preceding year when he was working out the bare rudiments of the reading code. The approach should be modified to accommodate these needs. Here are some suggestions:

1. Recognize that reading requires an attitude that the child hasn't quite mastered. One day he'll have a better hold on it than the next. One day he'll read more slowly and make an almost uninterrupted stream of mistakes. The next day

he may read better than he'll read again for three months. Don't make him feel that he's failed if he has a bad day. More important, don't try to evaluate his performance on the basis of a single day's performance. Always consider three or four days at a time.

2. Don't stress speed. The child is already motivated—perhaps too strongly—to read fast. He is engaged in a running battle between going faster and being more accurate. Don't jump in on the side of speed and overpower his attempts at accuracy. Speed will come with time. The ability to read well is dependent on a certain amount of practice.

3. On the other hand, don't let the child become too atomic in his approach. Remember, he's supposed to be *reading words*, not piecing together a sound puzzle. After he's had about four seconds to examine a word, help him out.

4. Use your pencil to give the child clues about how to attack each word. On words that he should know, move your pencil further below the line of print and more toward the middle of the word. This pulls him past the beginning sounds and helps him see the word as a whole. If the word is unfamiliar, or if he balks, move up under the first part of the word and move along the word as you pronounce it.

5. Use an every-other-word game to help speed up his reading. The results of this game are rather dramatic. What it does is to pull the child out of a rut by forcing him to look several words ahead. It works like this: After the child reads his assignment, tell him that you're going to re-read it, playing a game in which you read the first word, he reads the second, and so on. Then go to it. Use this game as often as you wish. It's good, potent medicine.

Progress: The words the youngster encountered as a beginning reader are the words that often will give him the most trouble now. It's not at all uncommon for a 5-year-old who reads well to have trouble with *and* or *he,* words he has seen several thousand times. The reason for his difficulty is relatively simple: the first words are loaded with *false as-*

sociations, false starts. When the child was exposed to them, he was trying to learn a difficult code, a very confusing code. He made many persistent mistakes. As he progressed, he perfected the code, made fewer mistakes. He is able to learn the word *calendar* now in only about four trials, whereas last year he required eight hundred to learn the word *them.*

Because of this process, the child, starting shortly after he's $4\frac{1}{2}$, exhibits a strange reading ability. He reads a familiar *Easy Reader* at a moderate to slow rate. Yet he is capable of reading *more difficult* material at about the same rate. At 6, he is *still* working the lumps out of the beginning words. Yet, at this age he can read about dinosaurs and geology as fast and fluently as he can handle *The Cat in the Hat.* Most of the words in the dinosaur book are clean, while those in *The Cat in the Hat* are garbled with interference.

Don't underestimate his ability to handle more difficult material. Don't wait for him to read easily in the *Easy Reader* books before moving on to something more difficult. Shortly after he's $4\frac{3}{4}$, introduce him to books that are slightly more difficult. Among the better ones are *Pickle for a Nickel, The Whale Hunt, George the Gentle Giant, Jonathan and the Dragon, The King Who Learned to Smile.* In some of these books the type face is different from the familiar kind: g for g, a for a.

Interest: During the first half year, the child probably won't display much interest in reading outside of his lesson, because reading isn't much fun for him (unless his motivation to read is exceptionally strong). Reading is plain old hard work. And the work overshadows the reward. About the time he reaches the half-year mark, however, the balance tips. He'll read words on cereal boxes, on TV slides, on buildings. And he'll start reading on his own.

Reading and spelling: About the time the child shows interest in reading outside the lesson, he's ready to look at reading a little more academically and start thinking about words in terms of the way they are spelled. He's probably forgotten much about his alphabet. If you test, you'll probably discover that he doesn't know the names of quite a few letters. You can refresh his memory with a two-day review of the letter names, or you can simply start spelling words and letting these demonstrations serve as the review. We prefer the second method. Use spelling to distinguish between potentially confusing words in the reading lesson. "This is *want*, w-a-n-t. *Went* is spelled with an *e*."

As the child approaches his fifth birthday, have him print words on the chalkboard. Select a few letters such as: a f t s. Write these at the top of the board. Then ask the child to form words that utilize these letters. "Make the word *fat*." Don't assume that he will write well because he reads well. He will print like a rank amateur regardless of how well he reads. He may make an *f* that looks like this: ʔ ; an s that looks like this: ℥. In learning discriminations for reading, he has not had to formulate rules about the direction of most letters. Now, however, direction becomes very important.

It is a good idea to teach the child how to print because his teacher in school may find it difficult to believe that a "gifted" child who can read well cannot write well also. She may conclude that child is not actually trying very hard.

MATHEMATICS

READING IS NOT CONSISTENT; mathematics is. This means that in mathematics the number of rules is small compared to the number of applications. Not so with reading. The number of rules is much greater, the scope of application much smaller. There are so many rules and so many skills that it is not expedient to make all of them explicit. It's more practical to present the reading task in a semi-sloppy fashion, allowing the child to work out the various rules on his own. No method of reading ever will achieve astounding results with all children because of the nature of the task. The situation is quite different with mathematics. Since mathematics is deductive, a teacher can take advantage of the consistency to teach operations in one year that children normally don't learn in eight. Astounding results are possible because mathematics is a neat and clean subject.

You will find that our method is different. But it is not arbitrarily different. It is different because it is based on two fundamental assumptions:

1. The child does not have to understand each rote fact of addition or multiplication before he moves on; what he needs to understand are the *operations* of addition and multiplication.

2. Many of the advanced concepts in mathematics are explainable only in terms of prior concepts. In other words, you shouldn't try to define division in terms of sheep any more than you should try to define colors in terms of blocks or balls.

Diagrams: Begin weaning the child from the concrete by demonstrating the notion of a diagram. The simplest kind of diagram assumes that you can let a mark stand for a thing in the physical world. What is true of the mark will be true of the physical thing.

Draw 4 circles on your chalkboard, leaving a good space between them. Explain that this is a diagram.

O   O   O   O

Beneath each circle, place 1 wood block on the base of the chalkboard. Show which circle stands for which block by drawing a line from the block to the appropriate circle.

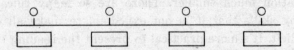

Have the child count the blocks and then the circles. "Yes, there are 4 circles and 4 blocks." Then tell him that you're going to let the circles stand for the blocks. "I can do this because *I can say the same thing about the circles and the blocks when I count*." Refer to the first circle-block: "This circle stands for this block . . ." To keep the child from getting the idea that there's a special connection between a particular circle and a particular block, show him that the order of the blocks does not matter. "Look, I can mix the blocks up. It doesn't matter, because there is still a circle for every block." Have him follow the lines to see which circle goes with which block.

Take 1 of the blocks away. "Count the blocks and see how many are left. Yes, 3. Now watch what happens when I take 1 circle away." Erase the corresponding circle. "Count them. Yes, 3 circles. When I start out with 4 blocks and take 1 away, I have 3 blocks. When I start out with 4 circles and take 1 away, I have 3 circles. *Anything I can say about counting blocks, I can say about counting circles*."

Add 2 blocks to the row. "Look. I'm putting 2 blocks down here: 1 . . . 2. Now let's count all of them and see how many I've got . . . 5 blocks. Now let's see what happens when I add 2 circles. Yes, 5 circles." Draw the lines showing the connection between the new blocks and the new circles. "See? Anything I can say about counting blocks, I can say about counting circles."

Repeat with various demonstrations, taking 1 away, taking 2 away, taking all 3 or 4 away, and so forth. Always tie the demonstration to the rule: What you can say about counting blocks, you can say about counting circles. Repeat the exercise.

Now you've established the fact that you can let circles stand for anything. "When I want to talk about counting sheep, I can make circles on the board and say, 'Each circle stands for a sheep.'" Draw 4 circles on the board. "How many sheep are there on the board? And what if I want to let the circles stand for houses? How many houses have I made on the board? Sure, 4. Because each circle stands for a house . . ." Ask questions such as, "What if I wanted to talk about 5 horses? How many circles would I put on the board?"

From now on, practically all of your work will be done on the board. What is true of your representations will be true of things.

Showing the Relationship between Counting and Adding:
1. Draw 2 small circles on the board.

> O   O

2. Count them, pointing as you count: "1 . . . 2 . . ."
3. Let the child count them. "Your turn."
4. Define adding so that it ties in with what the child knows about counting. If I add 1 more, I'll have . . ." Draw another circle, and count them.

> O   O   O

"Three circles." Repeat. "I have 3 circles. If I add 1 more, I'll have . . .

> O   O   O   O

". . . 1 . . . 2 . . . 3 . . . 4. I'll have 4 circles. If I add 1 more, I'll have . . ."

> O   O   O   O   O

And so on. Add circles until you reach 20. Repeat the procedure several times.

As soon as the child catches on to the idea that when you say, "Add 1," you're going to the next number in the counting series, start speeding up the operation. "I have 7 circles and if I add 1 more, I'll have . . . yes, 8. I have 8 circles. If I add 1 more, I'll have . . . Good."

5. Present the rule for adding 1: Draw 5 circles on the board. "Here's a rule for adding 1. You first see how many you start out with. How many are here? Sure, 5. And you say, 'I have 5. If I add 1 more I'll have . . . If you don't know, you ask yourself what comes after 5? What's the next number? Sure, 6. So if I have 5 and add 1 more, I'll have 6."

Give examples in which the circles stand for horses or dogs. Rule: "What is true about circles is true about anything: dogs, blocks, people, anything." This is an important rule. Repeat it often.

Reading Addition Problems:
1. Present $3 + 2 = 5$.
2. Identify the $+$ as plus, the $=$ as the equal sign.
3. Then read. "We read just the way we do in the book. We start over here [left] and say, 3 . . . plus . . . 2 . . . equals . . . 5–3 plus 2 equals 5. Your turn . . ."
4. Point out that you can add any two numbers together. Demonstrate with various examples. Let the child give the numbers and you write them down. "Pick any numbers you want."
5. After he can read addition problems and properly identify the terms (which may take at least an entire session), show him how to *interpret* addition problems. Begin by pointing out that in addition you start out with one number and end up with another. Put the problem $3 + 2 = 5$ on the board. "The problem tells us that we start out with 3 and end up with 5." Give the child practice on several other problems. Then present the problem

$$4 + 5 =$$

"What about this one? We start out with the 4, and we end up with—*you don't know*. That's what we have to figure out. I know that when you start out with 4 and add 5 you end up with 9, so I can write . . ."

$$4 + 5 = 9$$

"I solved the problem. Read it . . ."
Repeat with examples until the child catches on to the idea of starting out and ending up. This is an extremely important notion. Make sure he learns it.

Translate symbols into the operation of adding.

$$3 + 1 =$$

"Look at what the problem tells you. It tells you to start

197

out with 3. Then the plus sign tells you to add. It says, <u>Get more numbers</u>. How many more? [Point to the 1.] Look. It says get <u>1 more</u>. Start out with 3 and get 1 more. And when you do that, you'll end up with *4*.

$3 + 1 = 4$

Read it."

Keep the presentation straight and simple: start out with the number on the left (at least in the present problems); the plus sign tells you to get more, the number after the plus sign tells you how much more; and the number after the $=$ sign tells you what you end up with.

6. Diagram the problem.

$$\bigcirc \ \bigcirc \ \bigcirc \ + \ \bigcirc \ =$$
$$\bigcirc \ \bigcirc \ \bigcirc \qquad \bigcirc$$

The top row shows you what you start out with and what you add. The bottom row shows what you end up with. The bottom row is equal to the top row because you can draw a line from every circle in the top row to a corresponding circle in the bottom row.

$$\begin{matrix} \bigcirc & \bigcirc & \bigcirc & + & \bigcirc & = \\ \bigcirc & \bigcirc & \bigcirc & & \bigcirc \end{matrix}$$

To find out how many you end up with, simply count the circles in the bottom row. You can see where each one came from. *You can see the relations between the three terms.*

Stress the idea that the term you start out with and the term you add are reflected in the answer. Point to the bottom row, "See, here's the 3. And here's the 1. 3 plus 1 is 4."

Rule: For every circle in the top row there must be a circle in the bottom row.

7. After the child understands how to read an addition problem and how to interpret it (which will probably take three sessions and 40–50 examples), introduce the rule for adding 1 to other numbers.

$3 + 1 =$

"What do we start out with? . . . Yes, 3. And what do we do (pointing to the + sign)? . . . Yes, get more. And how many do we add? . . . Yes, 1. . . . And what do we end up with? . . . We don't know. But I know a way to figure it out. Is there a 1 in this problem? . . . See if you can find it. . . . Yes. So I draw a circle around the 1.

$$3 + \textcircled{1} =$$

"We're adding 1 to which number? . . . To 3. [Pointing to the 3.] When you add 1 to a number, you end up with the next number. We're adding 1 to 3 so we're going to *end up with the number that comes after 3*. What comes after 3? . . . Sure, 4. So we're going to end up with 4. Let's write it down."

$$3 + \textcircled{1} = 4$$

Summarize the problem as an addition fact. "3 plus 1 is 4. Say it."

8. Follow with a series of problems. Include some in which the 1 is first $(1 + 3 =)$ and last $(7 + 1 =)$. Have the child read the problem. "7 plus 1 is . . . we don't know." Then ask, "Are we adding 1?" Have him locate it. Circle it. "What's the rule when you add 1?" Help him state the rule. "When you add 1 to a number, you always end up with the next number." Have him find the number to which 1 is being added. He should have no trouble, because it's the only uncircled number in the problem. "What comes after 7? Good. So we'll end up with 8." Write the answer.

$$7 + \textcircled{1} = 8$$

Diagram the problem with circles.

9. Don't introduce $1 + 1$ or $1 + 0$ until after the child has worked on $+ 1$ problems for a week or so. Solve them the same way you would any other $+ 1$ problem. In $1 + 1 =$, circle only a single 1 and ask what comes after the other 1.

In $1 + 0 =$, explain how to handle the zero (which the child already knows vaguely from counting backward). "We call this *zero*. And zero means that you have nothing. When I say I have zero shoes, it means I don't have any shoes." Give other examples. Then tell the child that 1 comes after 0. Tie this in with what he knows about counting backward.

10. Demonstrate that the rule about the next number applies only when you're adding 1. The child probably will get the idea after the first few sessions that addition is simpler than it actually is. Find the 1; look at the other number; then say the number that comes next. Pretty easy. To keep him honest, present a series like this.

$$1 + 4 =$$
$$5 + 4 =$$
$$5 + 1 =$$
$$6 + 11 =$$
$$1 + 9 =$$

"Now remember, we can't use the rule for adding 1 unless we find a 1 in the problem. Do we find a 1 in the first problem? Good. Then we can use the rule. Let's do it. Do we find a 1 in the second problem? No. So we can't use the rule. The problem 5 plus 4 is 9 is one you just sort of have to remember. Say it . . ."

11. Present continuity exercises. For the next month, spend about five minutes at the beginning of each session on the $+1$ problems. Here are several series of problems you can present. They show the relation between $+1$ and counting.

$0 + 1 =$	$9 + 1 =$
$1 + 1 =$	$8 + 1 =$
$2 + 1 =$	$7 + 1 =$
$3 + 1 =$	$6 + 1 =$
$4 + 1 =$	$5 + 1 =$
$5 + 1 =$	$4 + 1 =$
$6 + 1 =$	$3 + 1 =$

$$7 + 1 = \qquad 2 + 1 =$$
$$8 + 1 = \qquad 1 + 1 =$$
$$9 + 1 = \qquad 0 + 1 =$$

Stress the addition facts: "2 plus 1 is . . . well, what comes after 2? . . . 3. So, 2 plus 1 is 3. Say it . . . 3 plus 1 is . . . What comes after 3? . . . 4. So, 3 plus 1 is 4. Say it . . ." These series are quite similar to the What comes next? games the child played during the preceding year.

Word Problems Involving Adding 1: Introduce word problems after the child has been exposed to +1 problems for at least two weeks. The idea to get across is that the rule for adding works with dogs, sheep, cows or anything else the child can name. The idea is not that these prove the rule. You wouldn't try to convince the child that a red ball proves the concept red. It is merely an example of red, just as adding pies is an example of adding.

Present problems like these: "I have 8 dollars. Then I get 1 more. How many do I have?" "A farmer buys 4 sheep. Then he buys 1 more. How many does he have?"

1. Tell the child specifically how to translate the words into mathematical symbols. The parallel between the everyday language we use and the language of mathematics is not obvious—not even logical. Conventions: The first number you mention is the one you *start out with*. If the first number mentioned is 7, you start out with 7. The words *more*, *adds*, *gets*, *buys* tell you that you're adding. You indicate these on the chalkboard with a plus sign. Then you add as many as the farmer *gets* or *adds* or *buys*. If he steals 1, you write $7 + 1$. Next, you put an equal sign, and ask the question the problem poses.

$$7 + 1 =$$

How many does he end up with? We don't know. That's what we have to figure out.

2. Diagram the problem on the board, using circles for

each number in the problem. If the farmer has 8 bulls and buys 1 more, diagram the problem this way:

$$8 + 1 = \underset{\text{(8 circles)}}{\text{OOOOOOOO}} + \text{O} =$$

Explain that each circle stands for a bull. "For every bull we have in the top row we must have 1 in the bottom, so we draw them in the bottom row and count them—that's how many bulls the farmer has."

Introduce one or two word problems during each session for at least two weeks. Don't be afraid of repeating problems framed in the same situation (such as bull-buying). The only way the child will learn the key words is to hear them over and over.

Number pairs: After the child has been on +1 problems for about two weeks, introduce number pairs: $1 + 1 = 2$, $2 + 2 = 4$, $3 + 3 = 6$, $4 + 4 = 8$, $5 + 5 = 10$. These play an important role in the child's understanding of mathematics. They become stepping-stones, and they make good stepping-stones because they are easier to remember than standard addition facts. They contain fewer elements. The child doesn't have to remember three different numbers when he deals with number pairs because two of the numbers in the problem are the same.

1. Present the first five number pairs on the board:

$$1 + 1 =$$
$$2 + 2 =$$
$$3 + 3 =$$
$$4 + 4 =$$
$$5 + 5 =$$

2. Point out that you're adding 1 in the first problem only.

3. Diagram each problem:

$$2 + 2 \quad =$$
$$\text{OO} + \text{OO} =$$
$$\text{OO} \quad\ \text{OO}$$

"Count the circles in the bottom row. That's how many you end up with."

4. Summarize the problem as an addition fact. "Yes, 2 plus 2 is 4. Let's say it together . . ."

5. Repeat the same basic exercise for about two weeks. Omit the diagramming after the first session and begin to emphasize the number pairs as rote facts. Do this by erasing the answers to the series and asking the child to give the answers. "Okay, take a good look at them because I'm going to erase the answers . . ."

6. After the child has learned the number pairs through 5 + 5 (which should take two weeks), introduce the number pairs 6 + 6 =, 7 + 7 =, 8 + 8 =, 9 + 9 =, and 10 + 10 =. Use the circle demonstration only during your first session. Go over these pairs every day until the child knows them as facts. Use the same procedure suggested for the first number pairs.

ALGEBRA PROBLEMS

No, algebra is not necessarily a high-flown, abstract subject. In fact, the child already knows algebra. He simply doesn't know that he does.

1. Write this problem on the board:

$$3 + 1 = B$$

It is an algebra problem with one unknown—the B.

2. Explain that we *read* the problem as, "3 plus 1 is B." Then give him a rule for *interpreting* an unknown. "Whenever you have a letter in a problem, it asks you '*How many?*' This problem asks, '3 plus 1 is how many?' It asks, 'How many do you end up with?' "

3. Work it as you would any other +1 problem. "We're adding 1, so we say, 'What comes after 3?' Good: 3 plus 1 is 4."

4. Explain that you know what B equals when you answer the question, "How many?" "When you add 3 plus 1 you end up with how many? You end up with 4. So we can say B equals 4." Write:

$$3 + 1 = B$$
$$B = 4$$

Give the child six to eight algebra problems of this form during each session for about a week. Use familiar +1 and number-pair problems. Use a variety of uppercase letters for unknowns, but avoid I, O, Q, S and X. Here's a typical exercise:

Problems	Solutions
$3 + 3 = K$	$K = 6$
$8 + 1 = R$	$R = 9$
$1 + 13 = D$	$D = 14$
$6 + 6 = M$	$M = 12$
$4 + 4 = U$	$U = 8$
$4 + 1 = E$	$E = 5$

Algebra Problems Involving +1: The unknown in an algebra problem asks the question "How many?" regardless of where it is in the problem. The equation $3 + 1 = F$ tells you that if you start out with 3 and add 1 more, you'll end up with—how many? You'll end up with 4. So, $F = 4$.

The problem $3 + F = 4$ tells you that you start out with 3 and add *how many* to get to 4. So, 3 plus *how many* is 4? If you answer the question "how many?" you solve the problem: 3 plus 1 is 4. $F = 1$.

1. Present the problem

$$6 + C = 7$$

2. Explain, "This is a new kind of algebra problem. See? The *C* is here in the middle. But it still asks 'How many?' This problem says, '6 plus how many is 7?' You say it. Good."

3. Show the child how to use a variation of the rule for adding 1 to solve the problem. "Look. We're adding something to 6. How many? We're adding something to 6 and

we're ending up with 7; *7 is the next number after 6. We're adding something and we're ending up with the next number.* We must be adding *1*. Because what's our rule? When you add 1 to a number, *you end up with the next number.*"

The pattern of logic involved in this kind of deduction is basic, so basic in fact that we, who are used to it, have trouble reducing it to words. The child is not used to it. He has to learn it. And he'll learn it more rapidly and more thoroughly if you show him the steps you're taking. Study the sample explanation we just gave. Practice it.

4. Summarize the problem so that the child can see the relationship between the familiar +1 fact and the present problem: "6 plus *how many* is 7? 6 plus 1 is 7. Say it. Good."

5. Write the answer.

$$6 + C = 7$$
$$C = 1$$

Give the child six to eight problems of this kind during each session for the next week. Put the unknown first in some problems and second in others. Here would be a typical exercise.

$$A + 2 = 3$$
$$9 + C = 10$$
$$4 + R = 5$$
$$V + 6 = 7$$
$$F + 6 = 7$$
$$1 + G = 2$$

The explanation is the same whether the unknown comes first or second. For instance, to explain $A + 2 = 3$, you point out that you're adding something to 2 and *ending up with 3.* How much are you adding? Well, you're ending up with the number that comes after 2, so you must be adding 1. How many plus 2 is 3? 1 plus 2 is 3. $A = 1$.

The child will soon spot a shortcut for solving these problems. He'll learn that all he has to say is, "C equals 1," or, "A equals 1," without really knowing why. The best way to handle this is to say, "That's right. And how do we know that A equals 1? We know it because we're adding something to 3 and ending up with the number that comes after 3. Right? Let's hear you say it. How do we know we're adding 1?" Help him through the explanation.

Algebra Problems Involving Number Pairs: Introduce these problems only after the child is used to relating algebra problems to addition facts. "3 plus how many equals 4? 3 plus 1 equals 4."

1. Present the problem, $4 + H = 8$.

2. Show that the rule for adding 1 does not apply. "Look. We're adding something to 4 and we're ending up with 8. Are we ending up with the next number after 4? No. So we're not adding 1."

3. See if the child can answer the question "How many?" "Think hard: 4 plus *how many* is 8? . . . 4 plus . . ."

4. If he doesn't know, show him how you can figure it out. Represent the problem this way:

$$O\ O\ O\ O\ +\ \underline{\hspace{2cm}}\ =$$
$$O\ O\ O\ O\quad\ O\ O\ O\ O$$

Explain, "We start out with 4 and we add. We don't know how many we add, but we must end up with 8. The problem tells us that we started out with 4 of those 8. Let's draw lines to show which ones we started out with."

"Those are the four we know about. The ones that are left are the ones we must have added. How many are left? Let's count and see . . . 4." Fill in the diagram so that it looks like this:

"The circles that are underlined are the circles we must have added. 4 plus how many equals 8? 4 plus 4 equals 8."

5. Refer to the original problem.

$$4 + H = 8$$
$$H = 4$$

The sample problem above shows the relationship between the answer term and the unknown in a way the child can appreciate. Use it liberally during the first three or four number-pair sessions. Then discontinue it, and encourage the child to solve the problem by remembering the addition fact. "Come on. You can remember that if you think hard: 3 plus how many is 6? 3 plus . . ." If he doesn't remember, tell him.

Include a few +1 problems in with the number pairs. Also, introduce number-pair problems in which the unknown comes first, $C + 6 = 12$. The child should catch on to these algebra problems rapidly. He should be able to work all +1 and all number pairs involving an unknown a month after you introduce the first algebra problem.

IF-THEN PROPOSITIONS

Mathematics is a deductive science. That means that you can go from a simpler form to a more complicated form if you play according to the rules of the game. To make the correct move, however, you have to make the right kind of statement. Almost always, this statement can be expressed as an if-then proposition. "If 8 plus 1 is 9, 80 plus 10 must be 90." "If 8 plus 8 is 16, 8 plus 7 must be 15." "If 8 times 5 is 40, 8 times 6 must be 48." "If 8 equals the fractions $8 \times \frac{1}{1}$, $8 \times \frac{2}{2}$, $8 \times \frac{6}{6}$, it also equals the fraction $8 \times Dg/Dg$."

Present if-thens this way:

1. Make a green mark on a piece of paper with a crayon. Next to it, make another green mark. Explain, "We're going

to figure things out a new way. We're going to *if-then*." Point to the first mark. "If this is green . . . [point to the second mark] this is green. We can say that because they are the *same*. Let's do it once more. If this is green, this must be green." Repeat with two blue marks and two red marks.

2. Introduce something a little more complicated. Take two books. Don't tell the child what they are called. Just show that the first book has pages with printing on them. Show that the book has a cover. Now show that the second book also has pages, printing, and a cover. Conclude: "They're the same, just as the colors were the same. So I can say, 'If this is a book, this other one must be a book.' Your turn . . ."

3. Put a green mark on your paper. Next to it make a red mark. "Here's a new kind of if-then. If this one is green, this one *can't be green*. It can't be green because it's not the same. We can't figure out what it is, but we know that it can't be green." Repeat with different color combinations. Then use the book again. Place it next to a block, and make the line of if-then reasoning more specific. "If this is a book, this can't be a book."

"When we if-then, we always start out with what we know. We know that a book has pages, has printing, has a cover. Does a block have pages, printing, and a cover? No. It can't be the same."

4. Repeat with various examples, comparing spoons with dishes, lamps with rugs, and so on.

5. Demonstrate some basic if-thens with number-type concepts. Put a row of 4 circles on your chalkboard. Beneath it put another row of 3 circles.

○ ○ ○ ○
○ ○ ○

Have the child count the circles in the top row. Then say, "If there are 4 up here, there can't be 4 down here *because these rows aren't the same.*" Show why they're not the same by drawing a line from every circle in the top row.

"If these lines were the same, there would be a circle below for every one above. But there's no circle for the last circle."

Give similar examples in which the line below is either the same or different from the line above.

6. Introduce if-then with addition. Start with the familiar problem, $3 + 1 = 4$. Represent it with circles.

Next to the original problem present $3 + 2 =$. Modify the $3 + 1$ diagram.

The difference between $3 + 1$ and $3 + 2$ is now evident. A circle has been added to the right of the heavy vertical line, changing the 1 into a 2. The top row is no longer equal to the bottom row. To make it equal we have to add 1 circle.

We can translate the diagram into an if-then proposition by covering up the portion of the problem to the right of the vertical line and saying, "If 3 plus 1 is 4 . . ."

Now uncover the top row to the right of the vertical line, ". . . 3 plus 2 can't be 4. It has to be 1 more than 4." Uncover the bottom row to the right of the vertical line. "It has to be *5*." Repeat, "If 3 plus 1 is 4, 3 plus 2 is 5."

$$\begin{array}{cccccc} \bigcirc & \bigcirc & \bigcirc & + & \bigcirc & | & \bigcirc & = \\ \bigcirc & \bigcirc & \bigcirc & & \bigcirc & | & \bigcirc \end{array}$$

By using the diagram properly, you can show the child just exactly why 3 plus 2 can't be 4, and why it has to be 1 more than 4 (because the circles in the top row must correspond to circles in the bottom row).

Present six to eight if-then problems during each of the next fifteen sessions. Base these on familiar +1 and number-pair facts: $6 + 1 =$, $3 + 3 =$, $1 + 4 =$, $5 + 5 =$, $5 + 1 =$, $2 + 2 =$. Always change the *second* number, never the first. If $6 + 1 = 7$, $6 + 2 = ?$ Take the child through the steps in reasoning. Don't expect him to pick up the pattern overnight. He won't.

7. Use diagrams during the first four or five sessions. Then drop them and work from the problems, using a modified approach.

$$2 + 2 = 4$$
$$2 + 3 =$$

"Look. We start out with 2 plus 2. In the second problem we don't have 2 plus 2; we have 2 plus 3. We know that 3 is bigger than 2—1 bigger." Draw a line from the 2 down to the 3, and put a +1 in the middle of it. "We added 1 . . .

$$2 + 2 = 4$$
$$+ 1$$
$$2 + 3 =$$

"Here's a rule. If we add 1 on this side of the equal sign, we have to add 1 on the other side of the equal sign.

$$2 + 2 = 4$$
$$+ 1 \quad + 1$$
$$2 + 3 =$$

"What's 4 plus 1? Sure, 5." Write it, completing the bottom equation. "Let's go though the whole thing. We start with 2 plus 2. If 2 plus 2 is 4, 2 plus 3 *can't be* 4. It must be five." It helps to phrase the if-then the way we suggest here. The child finds the line of reasoning easier to follow if he knows that 2 plus 3 *can't be* 4. He can see then that it has to be 1 more than 4. It has to be 5.

Keep the child responding. As he becomes handier with if-then reasoning, let him do more and more of the talking. "What are we starting out with? How are we changing it? What's the rule? If we add 1 here, we must . . . Good. So give me the whole if-then. Fine."

8. After the first two weeks, introduce if-thens in which the first term changes.

$$3 + 3 = 6$$
$$4 + 3 =$$

Show that they diagram the same way as the original problems and that they follow the same rules.

$$O \mid \begin{matrix} O \ O \ O + O \ O \ O = \\ O \ O \ O \quad \ O \ O \ O \end{matrix}$$

They should present no real stumbling blocks.

By the time the child has been working if-thens for two weeks, he should be able to phrase an if-then conclusion and he should have reached the point where the words are starting to mean something. But it will be a while before the full meaning comes through.

Rule for +2: By now the child doesn't have to figure out $7 + 1 =$ (most of the time). He knows it as a fact, which means he's ready to take another step up the ladder of abstraction. He's now ready to use his knowledge as a base for adding 2 to a number. The rule is a combination of what the child knows about +1 and if-then.

"When you add 2 to a number, it's just like adding two 1s. To figure out the answer, you first find out what comes after the number, just as you did when figuring out a +1 problem. Then you do it again, to find out what a +2 is."

$$6 + 2 =$$

"We know that 6 plus 1 is 7. What comes after 7? 8. So 6 plus 2 must be 8."

Put a series of mixed problems on the board.

$$3 + 3 =$$
$$5 + 2 =$$
$$2 + 7 =$$
$$5 + 5 =$$
$$8 + 1 =$$
$$6 + 2 =$$

Point to the first one. "Are we adding 2? No. Then we can't use our rule." The second. "Are we adding 2? Sure. To which number? To 5. Do we know what that equals? No, but we can figure it out. Point to the 5 and say, 'I know what 5 plus 1 is. Five plus 1 is *6*. So 5 plus 2 must be 1 more than 6; 5 plus 2 must be *7*.' "

$$5 + 2 = 7$$

2. Diagram one or two problems, using the vertical line to show what +1 would be and why +2 has to be 1 more.

"We have 1 more in the top row so we have to have 1 more in the bottom row."

3. Present six to eight problems involving +2 each day for the next week. Mix them up with other problems. Work toward a shorter and shorter explanation. After about the third day, you should start approaching the problems this way.

$$3 + 2 =$$

"I don't know what 3 plus 2 is, but I know what 3 plus 1 is: 3 plus 1 is 4. So 3 plus 2 can't be 4. It must be 5."

Keep the child responding and using the rule.

Continuity Game: After the child has been adding for a couple of months, introduce the continuity game, a game designed to dramatize the continuity of numbers and relate adding to counting. The game is fun, and while it won't do much to teach specific addition facts, it will help the child get a broader view of the number system.

To play Continuity, simply draw a series of figures on the board—stick-men, cars, balls, cups or hats—and show the different ways there are to add them. For example, draw six stick-men on the board. Have the child count them, and then put the number below the men.

Now draw a heavy vertical line to the left of all of the men.

$0 + 6 = 6$

Ask the child how many men are to the left of the line. None. How many are to the right? 6. So you write $0 + 6 = 6$. Show where you got the numbers. Point to the left of the line. "None here. So we say 'zero.'" Now to the right. "And 6 here. When we add 0 and 6, how many do we end up with? 6."

Don't expect the child to see what's happening immediately. He will in time.

Next, move the vertical line one place to the right.

$1 + 5 = 6$

Explain. "There are still 6 men here. So we're going to end up with 6. But look at this." Again, ask the child how many men are to the left of the line. 1. "And how many to the right? Count them . . . 5." Write $1 + 5 = 6$. "Zero plus 6 is 6, and 1 plus 5 is 6. Let's say it: 1 plus 5 is 6." Keep moving the line and adding until you've added $6 + 0 = 6$.

The exercise will show the child that there are different combinations that add up to the 6, and that as one term you are adding gets smaller, the other gets larger.

Make the continuity game a part of every lesson for about a month. Use the larger numbers (6 through 10).

Subtraction: Usually, subtraction is presented only after the child knows a great many addition facts. This is a hollow convention. The facts aren't nearly as important as an understanding of the operation. Subtraction is quite similar to addition. The problem consists of three numbers, the two you start out with and the one you end up with. There are two signs, just as there are in addition. And you approach the problem in the same manner, from left to right. Even the pattern of the problems has a vaguely familiar ring.

1. Define the operation. Addition is a way of talking about counting forward. Subtraction is like counting backward. The plus sign tells you to get more; the minus sign tells you to take some away. The number that follows the sign tells you how many to take away. Show how subtraction works, with a circle demonstration.

○ ○ ○ ○ ○ ○ ○ ○ ○ ○

"Okay, I have 10 circles. How many will I have if I take 1 away?" Cross 1 out:

○ ○ ○ ○ ○ ○ ○ ○ ○ ∅

"Count them. Sure, I have 9. How many will I have if I take 1 more away?" Continue through the series until you have crossed out all circles.

Repeat the exercise with a slight twist. Introduce the terminology used to describe subtraction: "10 minus 1 is 9 . . . 9 minus 1 is 8 . . ."

2. Diagram a subtraction problem this way.

$$5 - 2 = 3$$

(a) ○○○○○   (b) ○○○∅∅
Start out with 5.   Take away 2.

(c) ○○○∅∅
End up with 3.

3. Explain: The problem tells you to start out with 5. Do you add any? No. You subtract. You take some away. How many? 2. So you cross out 2 circles. Now, you've done what the problem says, so you should end up with a circle for every circle that's not crossed out. 3 circles. 5 minus 2 is 3.

Repeat with several other examples.

4. Give the child a rule for subtracting 1. This rule takes the same form as the rule for adding 1; the child should have no trouble with it. "Remember, when you add 1 to a number, you end up with the next number. Well, when you subtract 1 from a number, you end up with the number that *comes before.* Just like counting backward."

Give the child a series of problems.

$$2 - 1 =$$
$$9 - 1 =$$
$$5 - 1 =$$
$$6 - 1 =$$
$$10 - 1 =$$

"Are we subtracting in the first problem? Are we subtracting 1? Good. Then we can use our rule. What number are we subtracting 1 from?" If the child has trouble, circle the 1. Then he shouldn't have much trouble finding the number from which he's subtracting 1. "Okay, we point to the 2 and say, 'What comes *before* 2?' That's our answer: 1. 2 minus 1 is *1.* Say it . . ."

As the child becomes more familiar with the operation, speed up the explanation. "6 minus 1 is—what comes *before* 6? 5. 6 minus 1 is 5." Present —1 problems for about a week.

5. Use algebra problems to compare addition and subtraction. Take two numbers, such as 4 and 5. Write them on the board this way:

$$4 \qquad = 5$$
$$5 \qquad = 4$$

Refer to the problem in the top row. "Which of these numbers is bigger, the 4 or the 5?" If the child has trouble, remind him of the relation between bigger numbers and counting. "Well, let's count and see, 1, 2, 3, 4, 5. Which one came last, 4 or 5? So 5 is the bigger number. *We're ending up with a bigger number*. That means we have to *get more;* we have to add. So put in the plus sign.

$$4 + \qquad = 5$$

"How many do we have to add? We don't know, so we can put the letter *K* to stand for *how many*."

$$4 + K = 5$$

Now read the problem and solve it: "4 plus *how many* is 5? . . . 4 plus 1 is 5. So K must equal 1. Wherever there's a K you can put a 1."

$$4 + 1 = 5$$

The bottom problem (5 $\quad$ = 4) tells you that you start out with the 5 and end up with the 4. "Which number is bigger? The 5. So you're starting out with a bigger number and ending up with a smaller one. That means you have to take some numbers away. Put down a minus sign.

$$5 - \qquad = 4$$

"How many do you take away? You don't know. So you can let the letter D stand for *how many*." The problem now reads:

$$5 - D = 4$$

Solve the problem. "You start out with 5, and how many do

you have to take away to end up with 4? Five minus 1 is 4. D is 1, so we can put a 1 wherever there's a D."

Now compare the two equations:

$$4 + 1 = 5$$
$$5 - 1 = 4$$

Conclude: "The three numbers always go together. When you have two of them, you always have the third one. And they always work together. When you add, you always *end up* with the bigger number. When you subtract, you always *start out* with the bigger number."

These points are important. Go over them until the child can repeat them. Remember to use them in future problems.

Work on the relationship between addition and subtraction for about a week. Present six to eight problems during each session. Use all of the addition facts the child knows as a basis for these problems—all the +1 and the number-pair problems. Define subtraction as akin to addition.

$$4 \quad\ \ = 8$$
$$8 \quad\ \ = 4$$

Do this by showing that the 8 and the 4 in the bottom problem correspond to the 8 and the 4 in the top problem. Draw lines to connect the same numbers.

"Remember, the three numbers in a problem go together. If we find the missing number for the top problem, it will also work for the bottom problem. In the top one, we're ending up with a bigger number—so we're adding. 4 plus how many is 8? 4 plus 4.

"What are we doing in the bottom problem, adding or subtracting? Subtracting, because we're ending up with a

217

smaller number than we started with. And the missing number is the same as it was in the top problem: 4. 8 minus how many is 4? 8 minus 4 is 4."

After the first few sessions, mix the problems up so that occasionally the subtraction problem comes first. Here is a typical set of problems:

$$6 \qquad = 3$$
$$3 \qquad = 6$$

$$5 \qquad = 6$$
$$6 \qquad = 5$$

$$9 \qquad = 8$$
$$8 \qquad = 9$$

$$7 \qquad = 6$$
$$6 \qquad = 7$$

$$8 \qquad = 4$$
$$4 \qquad = 8$$

$$4 \qquad = 3$$
$$3 \qquad = 4$$

Always set your problems up so that you end with an easy one. You want the child to walk away from the lesson with the impression of success, not failure.

If the child has trouble with those problems in which the subtraction fact comes first, refer him to the addition problem below it. After a week, present all of the problem pairs with the subtraction problem first.

6. Give the child a precise rule for relating addition and subtraction problems. Illustrate with this pair of equations:

$$5 + 1 = 6$$
$$6 - 1 = 5$$

Rule: When you add, you always end up with the *big num-*

ber. The other two numbers are the parts. When you subtract, you always *start out with the big number.* The other two numbers are the parts.

Draw a box around the big number in each equation.

$$5 + 1 = \boxed{6}$$
$$\boxed{6} - 1 = 5$$

The parts always add up to the big number. "Look at the bottom problem. The parts are 5 and 1. 5 plus 1 is 6. 6 is the big number." Illustrate with other problems. Get the two important points across: When you subtract you always start out with the big number. And the two other numbers always add up to the big number.

7. Present subtraction problems involving number pairs and other familiar addition facts. The child now has a precise rule for solving subtraction problems. Use it.

$$8 - 4 =$$

"The problem tells us to start out with 8 and take 4 away. How many will be left? Well, what do we know? We know that when we subtract we always start out— Yes, with the big number. Let's put a box around it."

$$\boxed{8} - 4 =$$

If 8 is a big number, 4 must be a— Yes. A part. What do we know about big numbers and parts? The parts always add up to the big number. So 4 plus [pointing to space after equal sign] how many is 8? Yes. So the other part must be a 4. That's our answer then: 8 minus 4 is 4. Say it."

Note: The presentation we suggest seems more laborious than teaching subtraction as facts. Later, however, the child will use his knowledge of the "big number" and the "parts" to solve problems that can't be solved as facts.

Give the child six to eight subtraction problems during each of the next fifteen sessions.

8. Play a continuity game. When the child understands

the rule for subtraction introduce a version of the continuity game you used to demonstrate addition. Draw a series of similar figures on the board, stick men, cars, cups. Put the number below the figures.

Now draw a heavy vertical line to the right of all of the men.

$6 - 0 = 6$

Explain: "These are the men we start out with. Now we're going to subtract. The men on this side [right] of the line are how many we subtract. How many are there? None. So we say, 'Six minus 0 is—.' Count them and see how many. Six minus 0 is 6."

Now move the line one place to the left.

$6 - 1 = 5$

"We still start out with 6 but now we take 1 away. We start out with all of them and take this one [right of vertical line] away. How many are left? Count all of those we haven't taken away. Six minus 1 is 5."

Repeat until the vertical line is to the left of all of the men $(6 - 6 = 0)$.

Play Continuity every day for about a month. Concentrate on the larger numbers, 6 through 10.

9. Introduce if-then for -2 problems: These should be introduced only after the child has a pretty firm hold on -1 problems and knows at least a few -1 facts. Base your -2 problems on the -1 facts he knows. If he knows $5 - 1 = 4$,

give him $5 - 2 =$. If he knows $9 - 1 = 8$, give him $9 - 2 =$. And so forth.

Approach the problem by acknowledging that you don't know the answer as a fact: "5 minus 2. We don't know what that is, do we? But we do know what 5 minus 1 is . . . Yes, 5 minus 1 is 4." Write the familiar fact above the problem.

$$5 - 1 = 4$$
$$5 - 2 =$$

"If 5 minus 1 is 4, 5 minus 2 must be less than 4 because the more we take away, the less we end up with. If we take 1 away, we'll end up with 4. If we take 2 away, we'll end up with *1 less* than 4. We'll end up with 3. Now here's how we say the whole thing: 'If 5 minus 1 is 4, 5 minus 2 is 3.' Your turn . . ."

Actually, this is a tricky if-then. If you take away more you end up not with more but with less. You'll probably find that the harder you try to explain why, the more confused the child will become. So keep the explanations short. Tell him that it's tricky, and then teach it more or less by rote method. "If 9 minus 1 is 8, 9 minus 2 can't be 8, it must be 1 *less* than 8—7." Expect him to have some trouble.

REVIEW

You have presented all of the fundamental rules the child needs to understand the logic of adding and subtracting. However, he needs practice in using these rules. So, during the fifth month, devote the first five or ten minutes of every lesson to a review of what he's learned—about adding 1, if-then, algebra, relating adding and subtracting. Use the continuity games to show him the various ways of arriving at the "big number." Point out the general rules of adding and subtracting: the big number and the two parts always go together; when you add, you always end up with the big number; when you subtract you always start out with the big number.

The abstract concepts that are coming up hinge on these rules.

MULTIPLICATION

Introduce multiplication with a large number chart at least 14 inches by 14 inches on which the numbers are arranged like this:

1	2	3	4	5	6	7	8	9	10
11	12	13	14	15	16	17	18	19	20
21	22	23	24	25	26	27	28	29	30
31	32	33	34	35	36	37	38	39	40
41	42	43	44	45	46	47	48	49	50
51	52	53	54	55	56	57	58	59	60
61	62	63	64	65	66	67	68	69	70
71	72	73	74	75	76	77	78	79	80
81	82	83	84	85	86	87	88	89	90
91	92	93	94	95	96	97	98	99	100

Place the chart near your chalkboard. Open every session for about a week by having the child read to 30. To help reduce the confusion about reading numbers like 21 and 12, teach the rule that the first number you read tells you whether you're talking about a teen or a twenty. If the first number is a 2, you're talking about 20. If the first number is a 1, you're talking about the teens. The number 12 belongs with the teens.

Refer to the task as counting by ones. "That means counting one at a time."

Next, introduce multiplication as an extension of counting. Explain: "When you count by ones you *start with 1* and you count every number. But you don't have to count by ones. You can count by *any number*. You always start with the number you want to count by. If you want to count by twos, you start with 2. If you want to count by eights you start with 8. And if you count by twos you count *2* numbers at a time. If you count by eights, you count *8* numbers at a time."

Illustrate counting by twos, using the number chart. Circle the numbers you count. "When we count by twos, we start with 2 and count two at a time."

1   ② 3   ④ 5   ⑥ 7   ⑧ 9   ⑩

11   ⑫ 13   ⑭ 15   ⑯ 17   ⑱ 19   ⑳

"Let's count every number that's circled: 2, 4, 6 . . . Your turn." Tie the counting in with adding 2. "When you count by ones, it's just like adding 1. You always go to the next number. When you count by twos, it's just like adding 2. You don't go to the next number but to the one after that."

Present the following series of +2 problems every day for about a week:

$$0 + 2 =$$
$$2 + 2 =$$
$$4 + 2 =$$
$$6 + 2 =$$
$$8 + 2 =$$
$$10 + 2 =$$
$$12 + 2 =$$
$$14 + 2 =$$
$$16 + 2 =$$
$$18 + 2 =$$

After the child supplies the answers, read down the answer column with him, "2, 4, 6, 8, 10 . . ." Explain, "This is counting by twos. When you count by twos, it's just like adding 2 to the answer each time." Demonstrate that the series comes out the same regardless of how the problems are set up—0 + 2 or 2 + 0.

Repeat the demonstration with eights and tens. Use a

triangle to mark each of the eights on the chart (8, 16, 24
. . . 80) and a square for the tens. Get across the ideas that
you can count by any number, and that counting by that
number is just like adding with that number. Let the child
practice counting by twos, eights and tens.

Next introduce a *multiplication chart*. Make it at least as
big as the number chart, preferably bigger. Print the numbers of each *vertical* row in a different color, so that it is
easy to read down any row.

1	2	3	4	5	6	7	8	9	10
2	4	6	8	10	12	14	16	18	20
3	6	9	12	15	18	21	24	27	30
4	8	12	16	20	24	28	32	36	40
5	10	15	20	25	30	35	40	45	50
6	12	18	24	30	36	42	48	54	60
7	14	21	28	35	42	49	56	63	70
8	16	24	32	40	48	56	64	72	80
9	18	27	36	45	54	63	72	81	90
10	20	30	40	50	60	70	80	90	100

The number chart showed how you go about figuring out
how to count by twos or eights. The multiplication chart
shows what the various counting series look like when you
put them side by side. The ones move out vertically and
horizontally from the upper left corner of the chart. The
twos move out horizontally and vertically crossing at the
4. The threes cross at the 9, the fours at the 16, and so

forth. If you want to count by a number, such as 7, follow the ones across the top of the chart until you reach 7. Then go down. If you want to count by sevens 4 times, go down the 7 row until you're on a line with the 4 in the far left vertical row. If you want to count by sevens 10 times, go down the 7 row to the bottom of the chart (which puts you on a line with the 10 in the far left vertical row).

Using the chart, teach the child to count by the various numbers starting with the easiest series and progressing to the more difficult: 1, 10, 2, 5, 9, 8, 4, 6, 7, 3. Devote approximately two to five minutes to counting at the beginning of each session. After the child has mastered a series, let him recite it without referring to the chart. Try to arrange it so that you're working on more than one series at a time, reviewing one and learning another. The child should be able to learn all of the series by the time he's 4½, but he'll learn them at different speeds. He'll master the tens, twos, fives and nines fairly quickly, but he'll probably find the remaining series difficult. And he'll have good reason. The remaining series interfere with one another. They cross paths and lure the child from one path to another. He will make mistakes. Many can be anticipated and prevented, however, by teaching the child checkpoints to help distinguish one series from another.

Ones: 1, 2, 3, 4, 5, 6, 7, 8, 9, 10. No checkpoints are necessary because the child is already familiar with the series. Point out that when you count by ones, you always start with 1.

Tens: 10, 20, 30, 40, 50, 60, 70, 80, 90, 100. Remind the child of the similarity between counting by tens and counting in the teens. Because of the similarity, the child will have a tendency to make this kind of mistake when counting by tens: ". . . 60, 70, 80, 90, 20." You can reduce this tendency by providing a checkpoint. "When you count by tens you always end up with 100."

Another checkpoint is helpful. The first two numbers of

the ten series are 10 and 20—not 10 and 11. Incorporate these checkpoints into a nonrigid rule that the child recites before he counts. "When you count by tens, you always start out with 10; you hit 20; and you end up with 100."

Twos: 2, 4, 6, 8, 10, 12, 14, 16, 18, 20. The checkpoints for the two series are: (a) you start with 2; (b) you end up with 20.

Fives: 5, 10, 15, 20, 25, 30, 35, 40, 45, 50. The pattern for fives is easy if the child gets the rhythm. You can help him by singsonging the series. Point out that the last digit in the series goes 5–0, 5–0, 5–0. The pattern is easier after it reaches 20, because then the rhythm becomes more obvious: 25–30, 35–40, 45–50. Point out that every number that ends in 0 is also a number in the ten series. Checkpoints: (a) start out with 5; (b) end up with 50. There are no real trouble spots in this series.

Nines: 9, 18, 27, 36, 45, 54, 63, 72, 81, 90. Counting by nines plays on a variation of a familiar theme, counting backwards. 9, 18, 27, 36, 45, 54, 63, 72, 81, 90. And as the second digit is shrinking, the first (starting with 18) is proceeding forward by ones. When you present the nine series to the child remind him of two important checkpoints: When you count by nines (a) you end up with 90; (b) you always hit 63. The pattern for eights and the pattern for nines are like two lines that come closer and closer, finally crossing at 72, and then gradually diverging. That's why the greatest area of confusion occurs around 72. The child who knows how to count by both eights and nines finds himself forgetting which line he's supposed to be traveling when he approaches 72. He may anticipate 72 by jumping from one line to the other, saying 64 instead of 63. Again he may say 80 after he says 72. The seven series also crosses paths with the nines. So the child may think that he is counting by sevens and jump from 63 to 70. That's why the checkpoints are important. "You hit 63 and you end up with 90." The child who finds himself saying 70 after 63 knows that he made a mistake because he should end up with 90, not 70.

Eights: 8, 16, 24, 32, 40, 48, 56, 64, 72, 80. The series is somewhat similar to the one for nines. The last digit gets smaller each time you count, until it reaches zero. Then it pops back up to 8 and starts all over. 8, 16, 24, 32, 40, 48, 56, 64, 72, 80. In this series, however, the last digit gets *2* smaller each time you count. "It's just like counting backward by twos: 8, 6, 4, 2, 0." The series for eights is full of trouble spots. Since 8 is twice 4, every number in the eight series is a number in the four series. The eight series also crosses paths with the six series, the seven series, and the nine series. Its most serious encounters are with the nine. Probably the best way to help the child keep the eight series straight is to stress the following checkpoints: (*a*) you always hit 40; (*b*) you always hit 64; (*c*) you always end up with 80. The purpose of the first checkpoint is to show the child that the pattern repeats itself. You can help him acquire the feel of the pattern by reciting it in two stanzas. "8, 16, 24, 32, 40 [pause] 48, 56, 64, 72, 80."

Fours: 4, 8, 12, 16, 20, 24, 28, 32, 36, 40. The four series crosses paths with a lot of other numbers, but there is no real area of entanglement as there is with eights and nines. The greatest difficulty occurs after 20. Stress these points: (*a*) you always hit 20; (*b*) you always hit 28; (*c*) you always hit 32; (*d*) you always end up with 40. Recite the series in two stanzas, pausing at 20 to indicate that the pattern is repeating itself.

Sixes: 6, 12, 18, 24, 30, 36, 42, 48, 54, 60. Many of the encounters with other series are serious. Unless the child is well versed in the checkpoints of the other series, he'll have troubles with sixes. Probably the most important checkpoints are these: (*a*) you hit 30; (*b*) you hit 48; (*c*) you end up with 60. Recite the series in two stanzas, pausing at 30. Expect the child to confuse the series with the nines, eights,

sevens and fours. You can reduce the confusion by having
him overlearn the sixes.

Sevens: 7, 14, 21, 28, 35, 42, 49, 56, 63, 70. This series is
difficult in a different way. It has no repeating pattern. The
twos, fours, fives, sixes and eights repeated their pattern at
least twice. Not so with the seven series. It just rambles on,
crossing paths with other numbers here and there. It causes
its greatest confusion in the neighborhood of 35, 42 and 63,
where it crosses with fives, sixes and nines. But at least part
of this confusion stems from the fact that the series seems
long. Stress these checkpoints: When you count by sevens
(*a*) you always hit 35; (*b*) you always hit 49; (*c*) you always end up with 70.

Threes: 3, 6, 9, 12, 15, 18, 21, 24, 27, 30. This series, like
the sevens, is long-winded: its pattern does not repeat itself. On the other hand, the series has no really serious
encounters with other numbers. The last part is the most difficult: 21, 24, 27, 30. Stress these checkpoints: When you
count by threes (*a*) you always hit 21; (*b*) you always hit
24; (*c*) you always end up with 30.

Multiplication Problems: Introduce multiplication problems after the child has been counting with the multiplication chart for about three weeks (at which time he should
be working on tens, twos and fives). Follow these steps:

1. Explain how to read the problem. There's a difference
between what the problem says and the operation it specifies. Start with what it says.

$$5 \times 3 =$$

Explain, "We read the problem this way: 5 times 3 equals
how much? It looks something like an addition problem, but
we read this mark [times sign] as 'times.'" Give the child
practice in reading problems. Review the reading operation
for the next three or four lessons.

2. Explain how to translate the problem into an operation.

$$5 \times 3 =$$

"The times sign tells us that we're going to count by a number. Which number? The 5. *Count by fives*, that's what the 5 × tells us. But how many times should we count? That's what the other number tells us. Count by fives *three times*."

3. Demonstrate how the counting operation works on the chart. Divide the demonstration into two parts. First show the child how to count three times on the chart. Then show him how to tell what his answer is. Refer to the 5 column of the multiplication chart.

1	5
2	10
3	15
4	20
5	25
6	30
7	35
8	40
9	45
10	50

Explain, "Every time I count, I move one place down the 5 row. When I count one time I'll be here at 5; when I count two times. I'll go down one place to 10, when I count three times, I'll move down again and end up at this number—15. That's my answer."

Note: In this kind of counting you have to ignore the face value of each number and treat it as if it were worth 1. The 5 is worth 1, the 10 is worth 1, and so forth. Then, after you're through treating each number as an object, you turn around and read off the face value of the final number. There's nothing easy about this kind of counting. So take it slow, and make it quite clear when you jump from treating numbers as objects with a value of 1 to treating them according to their face value.

4. Give the child practice in working problems that in-

volve counting by twos, fives and tens, 1, 2, or 3 times. Here is a typical set of problems:

$$5 \times 3 =$$
$$10 \times 1 =$$
$$2 \times 3 =$$
$$5 \times 2 =$$
$$2 \times 1 =$$

Present such series for about a week.

5. Next, introduce problems that require the child to count by twos, fives and tens 4, 5, and 6 times. Show the child how he can use the far left column of the multiplication chart to find his place. For instance, the problem $2 \times 6 =$ tells you to count by twos 6 times. The child would probably lose his place if he tried working the problem in his head. Fortunately, he doesn't have to. He can find the sixth number down in the far left column, move to the right and read the answer in the 2 column.

1	2	3	4
2	4	6	8
3	6	9	12
4	8	12	16
5	10	15	20
6	12	18	24

"Find the number of times you're supposed to count, and go across to the row you're counting in."

Work on problems like these for about a week.

6. Introduce zero as the second number in the problem.

$$2 \times 0 =$$

"We read it, 'Two times zero equals how much?' We translate it, 'Count by 2 no times at all.'" Demonstrate how it works with pieces of chalk. Hand 2 pieces to the child. "There. I gave you 2 pieces of chalk. How many times? *One time.* If I gave you 2 pieces of chalk two times, I'd give them to you once, and then I'd give them to you again. Like this [give child 4 pieces of chalk]. Now I'm going to give you 2 pieces of chalk *zero times*. Here goes. [Make no move to give the child any chalk.] There. How many pieces do you have now? [Child will be puzzled.] You don't have any, do you? When I count by twos zero times, I don't count at all. That's kind of tricky, isn't it?" (The child should have fun counting by familiar numbers zero times.)

7. For the next month, devote part of every lesson to multiplication. Have the child count by a number and then work three or four problems involving other familiar numbers. Let him count without referring to the chart if he's familiar with the number, but always let him use the chart when he's trying to figure out a problem. About a year and a half from now, as he approaches his sixth birthday, he'll begin to work multiplication problems without referring to the chart, but don't try to wean him from the chart too soon. No good will come of it. As he becomes more familiar with the chart, however, he should be able to find his place visually, without pointing to the numbers or requiring you to point.

Multiplication Involving Algebra: Introduce this task after the child has been working regular multiplication problems for two or three weeks. Here's how:

1. Formulate problems that involve counting by fives, twos or tens no more than three times. *Always set them up so that the unknown is the second term.* Always $5 \times D = 15$. Never $D \times 5 = 15$.

Read the problem by identifying each symbol, starting from the left and proceeding right. "Five times D equals 15."

2. Interpret the problem in much the same way you interpreted addition and subtraction problems that involved an unknown. Interpret the D (or any other unknown) as *"how many times?"* The problem $5 \times D = 15$, therefore, tells you to "count by fives *how many times* to get to 15?"

3. Figure out the answer by referring to the multiplication chart. The problem indicates that you should count by

fives until you reach 15. Then figure out how many times you counted. This can be done on the chart by counting down the 5 column to 15 and then referring to the far left row to see how many times you counted.

$$
\begin{array}{ccccc}
1 & 2 & 3 & 4 & 5 \\
2 & & & & 10 \\
3 & \longleftarrow & & & 15 \\
\end{array}
$$

The number of times you counted is the value of D. You counted three times, so D = 3.

$$5 \times D = 15$$
$$D = 3$$

4. Make sure the child understands what question the problem is asking. It is asking him "How many times?" Have him answer this question, using the word *times*. "Count by fives how many times to get to 15? Count by fives three *times*."

5. Show him that the answer to the problem can be substituted for the unknown. Erase the D and put a 3 in its place. "D equals 3. That means wherever there's a D, I can put a 3 and the statement will always be true."

$$5 \times D = 15$$
$$5 \times 3 = 15$$

6. After the child finishes with a problem, state the entire problem as a multiplication fact and have him repeat it after you: "5 times 3 is 15."

7. During the next week, present a mixture of both regular and algebraic multiplication problems. The child may have trouble remembering the question that each type asks. Remind him that the regular problem, $2 \times 5 =$, tells you what number to count by and tells how many times to count. It doesn't tell you what you'll end up with. You may find it helpful to present the problem like this: $2 \times 5 = C$. "If you count by twos five times, you'll end up with how many?" The algebra problem, on the other hand, asks how many

times you have to count: $2 \times C = 12$. "Count by twos how many times to get to 12?" This problem asks *how many times?* If the child gets confused, ask him these questions: "Do we know what number to count by? Do we know how many times? Do we know what to end up with?" The answer to one of these questions will be "no."

AREA OF RECTANGLES

If somebody hands you a sheet of graph paper and says, "How many squares are there on this sheet?" he is actually asking you to find the area of the graph paper and give your answer in squares. So what do you do? Perhaps you count each square individually. This method will certainly give you the correct answer but it's a little slow. Another way, a faster way, is to count the squares in bunches. Instead of counting each square, count each *row* of squares. If there are 10 squares in a row, count by tens until you've counted all the rows.

1. Draw a horizontal rectangle on the chalkboard and label it in this manner:

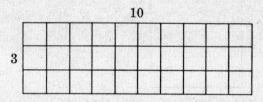

Explain: "This is a rectangle, and we want to find out how many squares are in it. Let's count them." After the child has counted them, write the total on the board: 30 squares.

"I'll bet there's a faster way to count them. What if we counted a whole row all at once?" Draw a line through the entire top row. "We would be counting by *ten*, wouldn't we? And how many *times* would we count?" Draw a line through each row: "1 row, 2 rows, 3 rows. So we count by tens 3 times."

$$10 \times 3 =$$

"There it is. Count by tens 3 times. Do it . . . We end up with 30 squares. That's the same answer we got when we counted by ones."

2. Present one or two area problems a day, similar to the one described above. Draw in the squares. Make the point that you can solve the problem by counting complete rows, and that you count as many times as there are rows. If the problem involves a rectangle that is 9 squares across and 4 squares down, you can solve it by counting by nines 4 times.

After you've explained the procedure several times, let the child tell you how to write the multiplication problem. "Okay, we want to count by twos 7 times. How do I write that? Yes, $2 \times 7 = C$. We want to find out how many squares we end up with."

3. Introduce rectangles without interior squares after the fourth or fifth session.

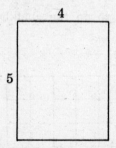

"I didn't draw in the squares in this rectangle, but look at these numbers. They tell us how many rows of squares there are. There are 4 across this way and 5 down this way. Every time we count a row, we count 4 squares, and how many times do we count? Five times. Count by fours 5 times to find out how many squares there are in the whole thing." If the child has trouble following the explanation, draw in the squares lightly and go through the explanation again. Present one or two problems of this kind during each session.

4. Introduce story problems. Children like area problems, especially those connected with something they would like to do.

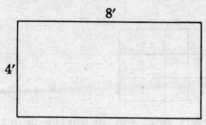

"Here's a wall, and you want to paint it. But you don't know if you have enough paint. You have a can of paint, but it will only cover 40 square feet and you don't know if this wall is more than 40 square feet. So you have to figure it out. See this mark after the 8? [Point to 8']. That says *feet*. Count by eights 4 times . . ."

Repeat with problems that involve building and making things. A farmer wants to know how many square miles are in a tract; a carpenter wants to know how many square inches are in a board, and so forth. Don't be afraid to use symbols for feet and inches. Children have no trouble with these.

5. Demonstrate that the problems can be worked from different sides of the rectangle. This demonstration should come after the child has been working area problems for two weeks or more. Begin by presenting a rectangle with two sides labeled.

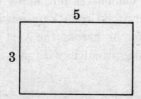

Now see if the child can figure out the length of the un-labeled sides. "If this line on the top is 5 units long, how long is this line on the bottom?" If the child has trouble, draw in the squares and show him that the bottom line has to be as long as the top line.

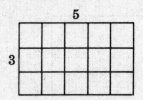

"There are 5 in every row: 5 in the top row, 5 in the middle row, and 5 in the bottom row. So the bottom line is 5 units long, just like the top."

Next, show that the side across from the one labeled "3" also has to be 3 units long. Present several other rectangles with two sides labeled and have the child specify the un-labeled sides.

6. Present problems in which the bottom and righthand sides are labeled.

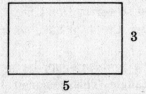

Make the point: "It doesn't matter where you count from, as long as you count all of the squares."

For the final part of the demonstration, show him that he will get the same answer if he counts up or down the horizontal rows ($5 \times 3 = 15$) or across the vertical rows ($5 \times 3 = 15$). Give the child practice with a variety of similar problems.

Area Problems Involving an Unknown:

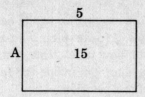

Explain: "This one's a little different. We know how many squares there are in the whole thing. This 15 tells us that. And we know how long the top side is. But do we know how long this side is? No. But we can figure it out. This problem tells us to count by fives *how many times* to get to 15. How would I write that?"

$$5 \times A = 15$$

Have the child use the chart, count by fives to 15, and refer to the left column to figure out how many times he counted.

"Yes, A equals 3. We count by fives *3 times* to get to 15."

Present one or two of these problems during each session for several weeks. At first, set them up so the unknown is on the left vertical side of the rectangle. Then begin shuffling the unknown around. Make sure that the child sets the problem up so that the unknown is always the second term in the problem—always $5 \times E = 20$; never $E \times 5 = 20$. Make up story problems about painters, farmers, children and so forth.

TELLING TIME

The code for telling time is extremely difficult. To master it, the child has to learn when to call a 3 "three" and when to call it "fifteen." He has to learn when he should say so many minutes *after* an hour and when he should say so many minutes *before* the next hour. The code, difficult as it is, can be broken down into small digestible chunks. But don't expect the child to learn to tell time in a few days. Teach the component tasks in the order indicated below, and make sure he's mastered each task before moving on to the next.

1. The hours on a clockface. After explaining to the child that you're going to teach him how to tell time, draw a large circle on the board. Put *four* numbers inside the face—12, 3, 6 and 9. Have the child note their position.

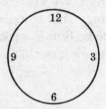

"Now remember, the 12 is always at the top . . . the 3 is always here . . . the 6 at the bottom . . . and the 9 over here." Erase the numbers and ask the child if he remembers where to put the 12, 3, 6 and 9. Then indicate the other numbers.

"There are twelve hours on a clockface and the 12 is always at the top."

2. The big hand is the minute hand; the small hand is the hour hand. To dramatize this rule, draw the minute hand extending past the edge of the clockface.

"See? The hour hand points to numbers on the clock, but the minute hand doesn't. The hour hand is pointing to the 4. So we say it's 4 o'clock." Draw the hour hand in different positions. Repeat the rule. "The short hand is the hour hand. The hour hand points to the numbers on the clock. It points to 5, so we say the hour is 5 o'clock."

3. A clock always moves this way. ⟩ Acquaint the child with the motion of a clock by having him draw circles in the air. Start at 1. "Remember, a clock always moves to the bigger numbers, so it has to move this way." Demonstrate with a clock that has only an hour hand. Draw the hand in different positions and ask what hour it is.

Then ask, "What's the next hour going to be? And the hour after that? And after that? Show me which way the hand will move." Let the child watch a real clock that has a second hand so he can see how the hand rotates.

4. The long hand is the minute hand. "The hour hand points to the numbers in the clock. The minute hand doesn't. It points outside the clock, *and we have to figure out the minutes*. We cannot read them." Indicate the minutes outside the face.

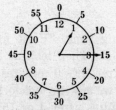

"See, the minute hand points to these numbers. Zero is at the top and then comes 5 . . . and then 10 . . . It's just like counting by fives. What's the hand pointing to now? . . . 15 minutes *after*." Explain the procedure for figuring out the value of the minute hand. "We always start at zero and count by fives until we come to the minute hand. We say, '0, 5, 10, 15'—15 minutes *after*. Your turn." Present problems on a clockface that has only a minute hand.

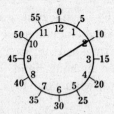

Introduce only examples in which the hand points directly to the numbers outside of the face. No 6-minute or 13-minute-after problems. Don't read off the answer. Start at 0 and count by fives until you reach the minute hand. Then express the answer in terms of minutes *after*. "It's 10 minutes after an hour."

5. O'clock problems. Present problems that show the minute hand at zero.

Introduce a procedure for telling time. "First figure out how many minutes after the hour. Then look at the hour hand to see what hour you're after. It's 0 minutes after 4. And when it's 0 minutes after 4, we say it's 4 o'clock. Do we say it's 4 o'clock when it's 5 minutes after 4 or 15 minutes after 4? No. Just when it's 0 minutes after 4." Give the child plenty of practice in working o'clock problems.

240

6. Minutes-after problems. Now give problems in which the minute hand is at 5, 30, 55 or another number (not 0).

Use the same procedure introduced above. "First figure out how many minutes after the hour. Start at 0 and count by fives until you come to the minute hand . . . 20. So you say 20 minutes after . . . Now we figure out after *what* hour. Look at the hour hand. What's it pointing to? 3. So it's 20 minutes after 3. Say it." Always draw the hour hand so it is obviously pointing to the number the child will read.

7. Make the minute hand so that it sticks out of the clock, but omit the numbers outside the clockface. Draw the hand so that it goes through one of the numbers on the clockface.

"Look, there are no minutes on this clock, but we can figure it out, can't we? Remember the rule. Start at the top, at 0, and count by fives until we reach the minute hand. 0 . . . 5 . . . 10 . . . 15 . . . 20 . . . 20 minutes after. Look at the hour hand. After *1*." Give the child plenty of practice with problems like this one. Start out with problems that don't indicate more than 25 minutes after an hour. But as he becomes more familiar with the procedure, introduce problems up to 55 minutes after. Always make the hour hand point to a number.

241

8. Introduce after-before. This exercise involves only the hour hand. Draw it between any two numbers on the clock-face.

"Okay, now this is the hour hand. It is after one hour and before another. Which hour is it after? Well, which way does the clock move? It moves this way [indicate a ⟳ circle with hand] *so it must be after the hour it just passed.* Which one did it just pass? It just passed the 2. So it's after 2." Introduce various other *after* examples. Don't introduce *before* until the child has a pretty good idea of *after.* He may have trouble figuring out where the hand has just been. Help him out by circling the clockface very slowly, stopping at the hand. "Okay, what number did I pass last?" The *before* hour is the next one the hour hand will touch. "The hour hand just passed 2, so it's after 2. What's the next number it will reach? 3. So it's before 3." Give the child practice in associating before and after. Do this with a series of if-then problems that don't involve the clock. "If the hour hand is after 7, it is before . . ." This pattern of reasoning is difficult because it is different from the *after* concept used in determining the next number.

9. Introduce before-the-next-hour. The final step in teaching how to tell time involves providing the rules for figuring out how to express the time in terms of *before* an hour. Introduce an operation that holds true under all circumstances.

(*a*) Look at the hour hand. It is after the hour it has just passed and before the hour it will reach next. In this example the hour it will reach next is 10, so it is before 10.

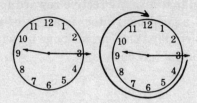

(*b*) How much *before* 10? The hour hand is after 9 and be-fore 10. How much before 10? To find out, touch the minute hand and say "Zero." Then begin counting by fives in a clockwise direction until you reach the *12* on the clock. The number you will say when you reach 12 is the number of the minutes before 10. "Five [pointing to the 4] . . . 10 . . . 15 . . . [keep going until you reach the top of the clock]. So the time is 45 minutes before 10." This procedure works with *any example*.

10. Reduce the size of the minute hand. After the child has worked time-telling problems (one or two during each math session) for about a month or more, reduce the size of the minute hand—but try to keep the difference in size between the two hands obvious. After the child has worked time problems for three or four months, you may want to intro-duce the notion that it's possible for the time to be 23 or 16 minutes after an hour. Do this by introducing dots be-tween the numbers on the clockface.

Have the child count in a clockwise direction to the number immediately preceding the hand. Then add on the dots, as-signing each a value of 1. "Yes, we're up to 15 minutes after, but look, we haven't reached the hand yet. So we have to count these dots. We're at 15, so this one is 16 . . . this one is 17 . . . this one is 18. It's 18 minutes after."

11. We have found that a very effective reward for learning to tell time—and a good motivator—is a gift of a watch for Christmas or a birthday. You can pick one up with large legible numbers for only a few dollars.

FRACTIONS

Present the following tasks. The child should master each task thoroughly before proceeding to the next.

1. Demonstrate how to *form* fractions. Do this by drawing a circle on the board.

"How many pieces are in this pie I just made? One piece. One whole." Write a 1 on the board. Now shade in the entire circle.

"How many pieces did I just shade in? One piece, the whole thing." Write a 1 above the original 1, forming the fraction $\frac{1}{1}$. "This is a *fraction*. It tells about the pie. *The bottom number tells that I made a pie with 1 piece.* The top number tells that I *colored* 1 piece." Draw a few other circles and show how the approach works.

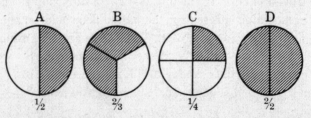

244

A. How many pieces did I make? . . . 2. So the bottom number is 2. How many pieces did I color? . . . 1. So the top number is 1. ½.

B. How many pieces did I make? . . . 3. The bottom number is 3. How many did I color? Count them . . . 2. So the top number is 2. ⅔.

C. How many pieces did I make? . . . 4. The bottom number is 4. How many did I color? . . . 1. So the top number is 1. ¼.

D. How many pieces did I make? . . . 2. So the bottom number is 2. How many did I color? . . . 2. So the top number is 2. 2/2.

2. Teach the child how to read fractions. The usual procedure for reading a fraction is to say the top number, then say the bottom number and stick a nice moist *thhh* on the end of it. One ninth. Four sevenths. Five twenty-eighths, and so forth. Unfortunately, not all fractions follow this rule. We don't normally say one twoth, one threeth or one fiveth. Teach the general rule first, with such fractions as ¼, ⅚, ⅜, ⅞. Then present the exceptions. Thirds and fifths aren't so bad. "We don't call it threeths when there's a three on the bottom: we call it thirds. Think of *thirteen* or *thirty*. When there's a five on the bottom, we call it fifths. Think of *fifty* or *fifteen*." However, there is no handy reminder for halves. "We call this 'halves.' You just have to remember it." The child should learn to read fractions with very little trouble.

3. Show the child how to go from fraction to diagram. This exercise is simply the reverse of the original demonstration. It involves the same rules. Put a fraction on the board and draw a circle above it.

½

"What does this fraction tell us to do? The bottom number tells us how many parts to make. The top number tells us how many parts to color. Make 2, and color 1."

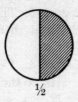

½

Repeat with various examples. The child should have a good grip on the operation after only a few examples.

4. Present the fundamental rule for adding fractions. This rule is particularly important because it applies to adding anything, not merely fractions. The rule is this: When you add, the terms must be talking about the same thing. If one term is talking about hats, the other must be talking about hats. If one is talking about dogs, fourths, or *A*, the other term must talk about dogs, fourths, or *A*. This simple rule is one of the most important the child will learn.

To teach it, first show the child how you know what a term is "talking about." The formula is simple. Read the number and then say, "What?" For instance, if the term is 3 hats, read the *3* and then say, 'What? 3 whats?' 3 hats. So you're talking about hats."

Put a series like this on the board:

A	B	C	D
2 dogs	1A	3 hats	9 boys

A. "I cover up everything but the number. I read the number. 2. Now I say, '2 *what?*' I uncover this part and look. It says *dogs*. 2 *what?* 2 *dogs*. I'm talking about dogs."

B. "I cover up everything but the number. I read the number: 1. But 1 *what?* Look: 1 *A*. I'm talking about *what?* I'm talking about *A*s."

C. "I cover up everything but the number. 3. I say, '3 *whats?*' I uncover and see that I'm talking about *hats*."

D. "I cover up everything but the number. 9 *whats?* Look : 9 boys. I'm talking about boys."

5. Next, clarify the role of the number. "The number tells you *how many.*" That's all there is to it. Give the child practice in answering the questions, "What is it talking about?" and, "How many?" with more hat and dog terms :

2 boys   7 dogs   5 hats   3 rats

"Look at the first one. Now think hard. What is the term talking about? Yes, boys. And how many boys? 2.

"Look at the next term. How many is it talking about? 7. What is it talking about? Dogs . . ."

This approach works out fine for dogs and hats, but what about fractions? Fractions involve two numbers, so if you cover up everything but the number, you won't cover up anything. And how do you know which number tells "How many?" Explain, "The top number tells you how many and the bottom number tells you what you're talking about." The bottom number is actually the one that answers the question, *"What?"* You can make this point very nicely by writing a series of fractions on the board :

$\frac{2}{4}$ $\frac{3}{8}$ $\frac{2}{9}$ $\frac{8}{10}$ $\frac{1}{3}$

Then cover up the bottom of each fraction and read the top. "The first one says '2.' 2 *what?* I uncover the bottom number and it tells us what : 2 *fourths.* The top number tells us how many, and the bottom number tells us *what.* We're talking about fourths and we have 2 of them."

Go through the remaining fractions this way.

6. Next, show that it's impossible to add unless both terms are talking about the same thing, and that if you can add, your answer must talk about the same thing as the other terms.

3 boys + 3 hats =

"The first thing you have to do is figure out what we're talking about. The first term is talking about *what?* About boys. The second term is talking about *what?* About hats. How can we add boys and hats? We can't, *because we're not talking about the same thing.* So we're going to end up with 3 boys and 3 hats." Change the problem to read "3 boys + 3 boys." "What is the first term talking about? Boys. What is the second term talking about now? Boys. Both terms are talking about the same thing. So we can add. *And we're going to end up with boys.* 3 boys plus 3 boys is 6 *what? Boys.* How many boys? 3 plus 3."

Use the same aproach to work fractions.

$$\tfrac{3}{7} + \tfrac{1}{4}$$

"Can we add these? Figure it out. The first term is talking about 3 *whats? Sevenths.* Is the other one talking about sevenths? No; so we can't add." Change the problem to read "$\tfrac{3}{4} + \tfrac{1}{4}$." "What's the first term talking about now? Fourths. Is the other term talking about fourths? Sure. So we *can* add. And our answer will be in *what?* Fourths."

$$\tfrac{3}{4} + \tfrac{1}{4} = \tfrac{}{4}$$

7. The final rule for adding fractions: You don't do anything to the bottom numbers; *you simply add across the top.* When you're adding 4 hats and 3 hats, you don't change the word *hats;* you simply add up the 4 and the 3. So it is with fractions. When you add $\tfrac{4}{5} + \tfrac{3}{5}$ you don't do anything to the bottom number. It merely tells you *what you're talking about,* and, like hats, it must remain unchanged.

The best way to make this point is to have the child work addition problems in steps. "First figure out what you're talking about. *Then* figure out how many."

$$\tfrac{3}{6} + \tfrac{2}{6} =$$

"Are both terms talking about the same thing? Yes. What are they talking about? Sixths. So what are we going to end up with? Sixths."

$$\tfrac{3}{6} + \tfrac{2}{6} = \tfrac{}{6}$$

"Now all we have to do is figure out how many sixths. The top number tells us that: 3 plus 2, that's how many sixths. Since 3 plus 2 is 5, we'll end up with 5 sixths."

$$\tfrac{3}{6} + \tfrac{2}{6} = \tfrac{5}{6}$$

8. Give the child practice in adding fractions that involve $+1$, $+2$, and number pairs. Present three or four problems during every session for at least a week. Throw in an occasional unaddable problem such as $\tfrac{3}{6} + \tfrac{3}{5}$ to keep the child alert.

After the child has a reasonable grasp of the conventions involved in adding two of anything, shorten the procedure for attacking the problem.

Subtracting Fractions: The rules for subtracting one anything from another anything are the same as the rules for adding. You have to be talking about the same thing. You end up with what you're talking about. And the top numbers tell you how many anythings you'll end up with.

Present -1 and number-pair problems.

$$\tfrac{6}{2} - \tfrac{3}{2} =$$

"We're talking about halves so we'll end up with halves. How many? We figure that out by working across the top: 6 minus 3 equals 3. We'll end up with 3 halves."

If the child forgets a subtraction fact, tell him the answer and have him repeat it after you. Don't be afraid to repeat problems that give trouble.

Adding Parts to Make a Whole: This exercise kills a yardful of birds with one stone. It helps the child see why his rules for addition and subtraction are true; it helps him see why there are any number of fractions that are equal to one; and it sets him up for adding and subtracting unknowns in fractions.

Draw a circle on the board. Divide it into 4 parts and shade in 3.

1. Write the fraction on the board. ¾. "Make 4 parts and color 3."

2. Explain, "Each of these colored pieces is a *fourth*, and I have 3 of them. Now, how many fourths would I have to color so that the whole pie is colored? How many pieces aren't colored? . . . 1. So I have to add 1 fourth."

3. Express the operation as an addition fact: ¾ + ¼ = ⁴⁄₄. Refer to the answer. "This fraction says: 'Make 4 parts and color 4. *Color all of them.*'"

Rule for Fractions That Are Equal to One Whole: After the child has worked on adding parts to make a whole for one or two sessions, introduce this rule: When a fraction equals one whole, it always tells you to color every part that you make, so the top number is always just as big as the bottom. Give the child practice in applying the rule to determine whether different fractions are equal to one whole.

⅔   ⅘   ⁶⁄₆   ²⁄₄   ⁹⁄₉

"Remember, if it equals a whole, the top and bottom are the same."

Rule for Fractions That Are More Than One Whole: Present a fraction that is equal to more than one whole.

⁴⁄₃

Diagram the fraction by applying the familiar rule. "The bottom number tells us to make 3 parts, so . . ."

"And the top number tells us to color 4. So . . ."

"Oh, oh. We're in trouble. We've colored the whole thing, but we only colored 3 parts and the fraction told us to color 4. What should we do? Well, we're talking about thirds, so let's make another circle and divide it into thirds, too . . ."

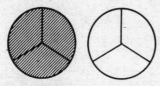

"Now let's color 1 of them . . ."

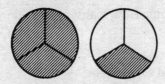

"There, we did what the fraction told us to do. We made pies with 3 parts and we colored 4 parts. This is more than one whole pie, isn't it?" Repeat with several other examples. Then give the rule for telling when a fraction is more than one whole. *"If the top number is bigger than the bottom number, the fraction tells you to color more parts than you make, so when the top number is bigger than the bottom, the fraction is equal to more than one whole."*

Give the child practice with various fractions.

$$\frac{6}{6} \qquad \frac{7}{4} \qquad \frac{6}{7} \qquad \frac{9}{8} \qquad \frac{3}{1} \qquad \frac{2}{2}$$

Approach each fraction with the question: Does it tell me to color more parts than I make? If it does, it's more than a

251

whole. If it tells me to color just as many parts as I make, then it's equal to one whole. And if it tells me to color fewer parts than I make, it's less than one whole. Work on these rules for at least a week, presenting six to eight fractions during each session.

Algebra Problems with Fractions: The child can go from what he knows about fractions to algebra problems in three small jumps.

1. Express the circle-diagram problems as algebraic problems.

"You want the whole pie colored. How many parts must you color? Yes, there is 1 part left to color. Each part is a fourth. Let's write the problem out. How many fourths do you start out with? . . . 3."

$$\frac{3}{4}$$

"Now, you're going to add some parts."

$$\frac{3}{4} +$$

"You're going to end up with fourths . . . 4 fourths."

$$\frac{3}{4} + \quad = \frac{4}{4}$$

"We want to know how many to add. How many *whats?* How many cows? No, *how many fourths.* For 'how many' let's put a D, so we get $^D/_4$. That says 'how many' fourths."

$$^3/_4 + {}^D/_4 = {}^4/_4$$

"Let's read it: 3 fourths plus how many fourths equals 4 fourths. So, 3 plus how many is 4? 3 plus 1. So D equals 1."

Repeat with different circles, always asking the question, "How many parts do you have to add to end up with the whole pie colored?"

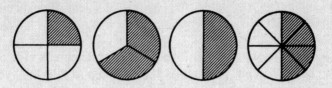

2. Wean the child from the circle diagrams as quickly as possible—perhaps after two sessions. Present problems involving + 1, + 2, and pairs. For example:

$$\begin{array}{ccc} \text{A} & \text{B} & \text{C} \\ {}^{C}/_{4} + {}^{4}/_{4} = {}^{5}/_{4} & {}^{3}/_{3} + {}^{E}/_{3} = {}^{6}/_{3} & {}^{5}/_{A} + {}^{B}/_{A} = {}^{10}/_{A} \end{array}$$

A. "The bottom numbers tell us that the problem is talking about fourths. Add across the top to get the number of fourths. Read the letter C as 'how many?' How many plus 4 is 5? . . . 1 plus 4 is 5. C = 1."

B. "This problem is talking about thirds: 3 plus how many is 6? . . . 3 plus 3. E = 3."

C. "This problem is talking about As. The top tells us how many. We start out with 5 and add how many to get to 10? 5 plus 5 is 10. B = 5."

Put any expression you wish for the bottom number. The same rules apply.

$$^{1}/_{\text{dog}} + {}^{A}/_{\text{dog}} = {}^{3}/_{\text{dog}}$$

In fact, you can even pronounce the fraction as one dogth, if you wish. These problems can be a lot of fun, and they help drive home the point that the bottom merely tells you what you're talking about. It goes through the entire problem unchanged.

3. Introduce algebra problems that involve subtraction. Make them like the addition problems. Use the same approach, the same rules. Let the child work on them for about a week. He should have no trouble, except perhaps in remembering −1 or number-pair facts. When he has trouble, give him the answer and have him repeat it after you. Don't waste a lot of time on lengthy explanations.

DIVISION

Division can be the stickiest operation this side of square root. The big problem is that when you "divide" you're not actually dividing. In a very few cases, it seems as if you are. "A man has 20 apples. He puts them in 5 piles. How many are in each pile?" The solution: "Divide" 20 by 5. The answer is 4: 4 apples. But this is a rather peculiar and misleading example of division. Consider the problem $5\overline{)20}$ without the apples. You probably find yourself saying something like this: "5 goes into 20 how many times? . . . 4 times." Put the problem in a different form—$^{20}/_5$—and you probably find yourself saying the same thing. There's no dividing going on here. You're multiplying. You're saying, "5 times how much is 20?" ($5 \times K = 20; K = 4$)

If you recognize two points about division, you can teach a 4½-year-old a kind of dividing operation in less than half an hour. Point 1: Division is merely a variation of multiplication; Point 2: Division doesn't make much sense when you divorce the operation from fractions.

Consider $^{20}/_5$ again. If you divide it (more appropriately, *reduce* it), you discover how many *wholes* the fraction is equal to. Since $^5/_5$ is equal to one whole, you have one whole every time you count $^5/_5$. So you count by $^5/_5$ until you use up the entire $^{20}/_5$. It turns out that you count four times, so you have 4 wholes, and no parts left over. This approach ties in with the way you presented fractions and multiplication problems involving an unknown. It also clarifies the notion of where remainders come from in a fraction. Consider $^{21}/_5$. You have 4 wholes and 1 left over. But 1 what? Well, the bottom of a fraction, according to the familiar convention, tells you what you're talking about. Since the bottom number of this fraction is 5, the remainder must be $^1/_5$.

1. Introduce the task of division this way. "We're now going to work a new kind of fraction. In these, the top num-

ber is much bigger than the bottom. They are still fractions, and we still read them as we always did, but we have a new way to solve them."

Write the fraction $10/5$ on the board and have the child read it. "See how much larger the top number is than the bottom number. So tell me about this fraction. Is it more than a whole or less than a whole? Yes, it's more than a whole. How many fifths would we need to have one whole? Yes, 5 fifths.

"Let's keep adding $5/5$ until we have $10/5$."

$$5/5 + 5/5 = 10/5$$

"There. And look. We have one whole for each $5/5$. So we have 2 wholes."

Repeat with various small fractions that don't go beyond the child's ability to add: $4/2$, $9/3$, $6/3$, $8/4$, $14/7$, and so forth. Follow this procedure:

(*a*) Figure out what fraction, using the given bottom number, is equal to one whole. Do this by making the top of the fraction as big as the bottom of the fraction. It's not as confusing as it sounds. If the given fraction is $16/8$, then one whole is $8/8$ (make 8 and color 8).

(*b*) Keep adding $8/8$ until the sum is equal to $16/8$.

(*c*) Count the number of wholes you had to add.

2. Next, introduce a shortcut, a faster way of counting the wholes. Present one of the problems the child has already worked.

$$\frac{10}{5}$$

"Point to the bottom number and say, 'Count by fives how many times to get to 10?' "

$$\frac{10}{5}\big)$$

"Five . . . 10. How many times did I count? 2. Then 10 fifths must equal 2 wholes."

$$\frac{10}{5}\big)\quad 2$$

If you want to go further into the question of why this method works, explain, "This is just what we did before: 5 fifths equals 1 whole. So every time we count 5 fifths, we count a whole. We count until we use up all 10 fifths. The number of times we count tells us how many wholes there are."

3. Spend several weeks on division. Give four to six problems during each session, and work for a fast attack. Present any kind of problem that the child can figure out on the multiplication chart.

$$\frac{49}{7} \qquad \frac{56}{8} \qquad \frac{36}{9} \qquad \frac{72}{8} \qquad \frac{16}{2}$$

"How many wholes is $\frac{49}{7}$? Point to the bottom number and say, 'Count by sevens how many times to get to 49? . . . 7, 14, 21, 28, 35, 42, 49 [looking over at the lefthand column of the chart] I counted 7 times. So $\frac{49}{7}$ equals 7 wholes."

The idea of counting by a number how many times to get to a different number is important. It is a fundamental mathematical operation, and the child will use it in many different ways. So make sure he learns it. He may have trouble remembering the statement he's supposed to make in order to divide. On fractions like $\frac{8}{2}$, for instance, he may find himself saying, "Count by twos 8 times" instead of "Count by twos *how many times* to get to 8." If he has this trouble, rig the problems so that the top number is larger than 10.

$$\frac{16}{2}$$

Now he'll be able to catch his mistake. "Count by twos 16 times . . . but I don't know how to count 16 times. My chart only goes to 10. I must have goofed." This mistake is common, but the prevention is rather simple.

MONEY

We strongly advocate rewarding children with money, either after they finish a book in reading, or on a regular allowance basis, starting when they are 4. Until they're 6 years old, it's probably better to reward them for performance. They might as well get the idea early in life that good performances pay off. And if you let them spend their money as they please, without making them feel that they should be saving for their college education, you will give them an appreciation of what money can do, how far it goes, how much candy and comics it can buy. After they learn this, then perhaps saving will mean something.

Introduce money problems when the child is about 4½.

1. Make a chart showing the value of coins. Tape actual coins, and a *dollar*, using clear tape, on pasteboard. Letter with a crayon or felt pen.

5 (P) = 1 (N)

10 (P) = 1 (D)

25 (P) = 1 (Q)

50 (P) = 1 (H D)

100 (P) = 1   Dollar

2. Introduce the basic penny relationships. (How many pennies are in a nickel, dime, quarter, half-dollar and dollar?) Point to the coins on the chart and read the various entries: "5 pennies equal 1 nickel. Your turn . . . *10* pennies equal 1 dime . . . 10 pennies and 1 dime are *worth the same* . . ." And so forth.

The idea that the values of 10 pennies and 1 dime are equal is difficult for the child to grasp. How can any reasonable person say that 10 nice brown pennies are the same as 1 tinkly little dime? The coins are obviously different. Probably the best way to get the value notion across is to explain: "If you had 1 dime and Henry had 10 pennies, who could buy the most bubble gum?" Or, "If you had 25 pennies and Henry had a quarter, who would be able to go on the most pony rides?"

The answer, of course, is, *"1 quarter is worth 25 pennies.* They are equal. So you'd both be able to go on the rides the same number of times. A quarter is just another way of saying 25 pennies."

3. After the child knows the penny relationships (three weeks), introduce coin problems in the daily arithmetic lessons.

First figure out various relationships between coins. "How many nickels are in a dime? Let's figure it out . . . When we ask how many nickels are in a dime, we're really saying, 'Count by nickels how many times to get to a dime?' We can write it like this."

$$N \times ? = D$$

"Now we ask, 'What do I know about a nickel? What's it worth? What's it equal to?' . . . 5 pennies. And what do we know about a dime? It's worth 10 pennies."

$$N = 5$$
$$D = 10$$

"If N is equal to 5, it means we can put a 5 wherever we have an N in the original problem."

$5 \times ? = D$

"And wherever we have a D we can put a . . . 10. That gives us . . ."

$5 \times ? = 10$

"Now we've got a simple algebra problem. Count by fives how many times to get to 10? . . . 2 times. How many nickels are in a dime? 2 nickels."

This is the basic procedure. Use it to figure out such relationships as how many nickels in a quarter, how many dimes in a half-dollar, how many dimes in a dollar. As the child becomes more familiar with the assumptions the problem makes, you will be able to speed up the procedure. "How many dimes in a dollar? A dime is worth 10 . . . and a dollar is worth 100. So we have to count by tens how many times until we reach 100?"

$$10 \times D = 100$$
$$D = 10$$

"There are 10 dimes in a dollar."

4. Use a different approach for quarters and half-dollars. Use the pie approach.

"The word *quarter* means 1 fourth—1 fourth of a whole."

¼

"Now what does this fraction tell us? [Pointing to the bottom of the fraction.] It tells us to make 4 parts and color 1 of them."

"That's a quarter. Now, how many quarters would we need to have *half* a dollar or half of the pie? Let's see. I'll color in this next quarter . . ."

"Yes, that's a half. And how many quarters do we have? Yes, 2 quarters equal 1 half."

$$2 Q = 1 HD$$

Repeat the procedure for finding out how many quarters are in a dollar, and how many half-dollars are in a dollar.

Work coin-value problems several times a month. Emphasize the fact that the child can use what he already knows to figure out the value of various money combinations.

5. After he has been working with coin relationships for two months, introduce story problems that involve familiar operations. Remember to stress the key words in the problem, and if the child gets stuck, explain how these words specify a certain operation. Give the child enough problems of the same form to familiarize him with the ways we go about changing a word situation into a familiar problem pattern. When you present a story problem, write the key numbers on the board. Don't expect the child to remember three numbers. If the problem has to do with a boy that started out with 8 pennies and lost some, ending up with only 4 pennies, write something like this on the board.

$$8 \qquad 4$$

Then show precisely how to fill in the details of the problem. "What did he start out with? . . . 8. And what happened? Did he get more or did he get less? He got less, so we subtract."

$$8 - \qquad 4$$

"*How many* should we subtract? We don't know. So we write 'How many.'"

$$8 - P \qquad 4$$

FOUR YEARS TO FIVE YEARS

"How many did he *end up with?* 4. So . . ."

$$8 - P = 4$$

"And 8 minus how many is 4? . . . 4."

$$8 - P = 4$$
$$P = 4$$

Spend a couple of minutes rehearsing the problems you plan to present. Your presentation will benefit. Here are a few hints:

(a) *Adding:* There are many types of adding problems you can make up with coins. "You have a dime and 6 pennies. How much money—how many cents—do you have?" First convert the dime into 10, then add 6 to it. Another example: "You have 8 cents and somebody gives you a nickel for doing your arithmetic so well. How much money —how many cents—do you have?"

(b) *Adding that involves an unknown:* Make up problems involving quarters, dollars or dimes. Don't convert the coins to cents, because that would make the problems too difficult. "Harry has 6 dimes on Monday and the next day he has 9 dimes. Somebody gave him some dimes. How many?" [Write $6 + B = 9$.] "And we say, '6 plus how many equals 9?'" Point out that you can add because you're talking about dimes in both cases—6 dimes and 9 dimes.

(c) *Subtracting:* Keep these simple (minus 1, minus 2, and pairs). Don't be surprised if the child is rusty on subtraction. Review the operation before proceeding. "If you have 6 pennies and give me 1, how many will you have left?" "If you have 10 pennies and lose 5 of them, how many will you have left?" And so forth.

(d) *Subtracting that involves an unknown:* Keep these simple, involving small numbers and pennies. "You start out to the store with 5 pennies. On the way you lose some of them. You now have 2 pennies left. How many did you lose?"

$$5 - R = 2$$

(Read, "5 minus how many is 2?")

"A man gave away some money. He had 6 cents; now he has 3 cents. How much did he give away?"

$$6 - A = 3$$

(e) *Multiplication:* Limit these problems to those involving nickels or dimes—the numbers by which the child can count. "How many cents would you have if you had 6 nickels? A nickel is 5 cents. So you would count by fives 6 times."

$$5 \times 6 = 30 \text{ cents}$$

"How much money would you have if you had 10 dimes?"

$$10 \times 10 = 100 \text{ cents}$$

"That equals 1 dollar."

(f) *Multiplication that involves an unknown:* Again, use only nickels and dimes. "A man has a handful of nickels. He knows he has 45 cents. He wants to know how many nickels he has. Count by fives. The number of times you count to reach 45 will give you the number of nickels."

$$5 \times C = 45$$

"I give you 80 cents in dimes. How many dimes do I give you?"

COLUMN ADDITION

When the child is about 4½, he should be ready to tackle column addition. The prerequisite is familiarity with +2, number-pairs, and if-then reasoning. Column addition can provide a dramatic demonstration of the continuity and simplicity of the number system, if it is handled properly.

1. First show how in-line problems translate into column form.

$$3 + 1 = 4$$

Explain, "We're going to write this problem in a new way, that you read from top to bottom. Watch . . ."

First move the 3 above the 1 :

$$3$$
$$+1 = 4$$

Then move the 4 below the 1.

$$3$$
$$+1 =$$
$$4$$

"Now we're going to change the equal sign into a line. And we'll put this line just where it belongs, right between the 1 and the 4."

$$3$$
$$\underline{+1}$$
$$4$$

Repeat with several other problems. The purpose of this demonstration is to show that nothing has changed, that every element in the original problem is in the column problem, in the same relative position and performing the same job. It is very important to make this point quite clear.

Give the child practice in reading column addition problems that add up to less than 10.

3	2	5
$\underline{+5}$	$\underline{+2}$	$\underline{+4}$
8	4	9

Read from top to bottom, calling the line beneath the second number "equals."

$$4$$
$$\underline{+2}$$
$$6$$

"We say, '4 plus 2 equals 6.' "

2. Present the basic rule for column addition: "Whatever you have above the line you must have below the line." Apply the rule first to problems in which zero is added to another number.

3	0	9	0	7
$\underline{+0}$	$\underline{+6}$	$\underline{+0}$	$\underline{+4}$	$\underline{+0}$

After the child reads the problem, state the rule as it applies to the problem. "Whatever we have above this line, we must have below this line." Proceed to work the problems. "There's 3 above the line in the first problem, so . . ."

$$\begin{array}{r} 3 \\ +0 \\ \hline 3 \end{array}$$

3. Introduce two-place numbers. Long explanations aren't necessary if you begin with a familiar +0 problem.

$$\begin{array}{r} 0 \\ +3 \\ \hline \end{array}$$

Apply the rule. "We have a 3 above the line, so we must put a 3 below the line. 0 plus 3 equals 3."

$$\begin{array}{r} 0 \\ +3 \\ \hline 3 \end{array}$$

Now add a twenty above the line.

$$\begin{array}{r} 20 \\ +3 \\ \hline 3 \end{array}$$

Don't refer to the number as a 2. It is a 20. "I put a 20 in front of the 0." Make it clear that the 20 goes *in front of* the original number. This explanation will help prevent some serious mistakes later on. Two points: Refer to any number in the left column as a 60 or 40, not as a 6 or 4. And stress that the 60 or 40 goes in front of the other number. Now apply the rule. "Whatever I have above the line I must have below the line. I added a 20 above the line, so I must add a 20 below the line."

$$\begin{array}{r} 20 \\ +3 \\ \hline 23 \end{array}$$

Have the child read the entire problem. "Yes, 20 plus 3 is the same as 23."

Give practice in working similar problems.

$$\begin{array}{cccc} 40 & 5 & 4 & 20 \\ +6 & +70 & +90 & +4 \\ \end{array}$$

Do not present problems that add up to paired numbers (such as 33, 55, 77).

4. Introduce teens during the fifth or sixth column addition session. Adopt the convention of referring to the number in the left column as a "teen" or a "ten." Demonstrate with problems that add up to 13 or more.

$$\begin{array}{r} 3 \\ +0 \\ \hline 3 \end{array}$$

"If I add a teen above the line, I must add a teen below the line."

$$\begin{array}{r} 3 \\ +10 \\ \hline 13 \end{array}$$

"A teen is just another way of saying 'ten,' isn't it?"

5. Next, demonstrate that a number such as 20 or 30 can be added to either of the terms above the line.

$$\begin{array}{r} 0 \\ +5 \\ \hline 5 \end{array} \qquad \begin{array}{r} 0 \\ +5 \\ \hline 5 \end{array}$$

"I'm going to add an 80 above the line in both of these problems. And it doesn't matter where I put it. Watch . . ."

$$\begin{array}{r} 80 \\ +5 \\ \hline 5 \end{array} \qquad \begin{array}{r} 0 \\ +85 \\ \hline 5 \end{array}$$

"We use the same rule for both problems. If I add an 80 above the line, I have to have an 80 below the line."

$$\begin{array}{r} 80 \\ +5 \\ \hline 85 \end{array} \qquad \begin{array}{r} 0 \\ +85 \\ \hline 85 \end{array}$$

"We know that 80 plus 5 is 85, and 0 plus 85 is 85. Does it matter which number I put the 80 in front of? No. I still end up with 85."

6. After the child has worked problem pairs like the one above for several days, introduce a new continuity notion. He already has a vague idea that you can make similar statements about 50, 30 and 80. However, his idea is prob-

ably pretty vague. The continuity exercise will sharpen it up.

"Now remember the rule. If you add something above the line, you have to add it below the line."

$$\begin{array}{r} 0 \\ +3 \\ \hline 3 \end{array}$$

"If 0 plus 3 is 3, 20 plus 3 is . . ."

$$\begin{array}{r} 20 \\ +3 \\ \hline 3 \end{array}$$

"We added a 20 above the line, so we have to add a 20 below the line . . . 20 plus 3 is 23."

$$\begin{array}{r} 20 \\ +3 \\ \hline 23 \end{array}$$

"Let's see how it works with another number. If 0 plus 3 is 3, 40 plus 3 is . . . 43. If 0 plus 3 is 3, 90 plus 3 is . . . 93." And so forth. The child will catch on to the pattern pretty quickly. The point to make is that a number like 93 is made up of a 3 and a 90: "90 plus 3 is the same as 93. Say it . . ."

After the child has worked continuity exercises for two or three sessions, reverse the exercise. "What's another way of saying 93? . . . 90 plus 3. What's another way of saying 45? 40 plus 5 . . ."

Do not present teen problems.

7. Introduce problems that do not involve zero. Start with the problem

$$\begin{array}{r} 3 \\ +1 \\ \hline \end{array}$$

Apply the rule, "Whatever we have above the line, we must have below the line. How much do we have above the line? We have 3 and 1. Three and 1 is 4, so we really have a 4 above the line." Write 4 to the right of the problem.

$$\begin{array}{r} 3 \\ +1 \\ \hline \end{array} \; 4$$

"If we have 4 above the line, we must have 4 below the line."

$$\begin{array}{r} 3 \\ +1 \;\; 4 \\ \hline 4 \end{array}$$

The purpose of this procedure is simply to show the child that he does have 4 above the line.

After you have presented four or five problems of this kind, you can probably discontinue writing the number above the line. However, continue to ask the question, "How much do we have above the line?"

$$\begin{array}{r} 4 \\ +4 \\ \hline \end{array}$$

"We have an 8 above the line, so we have to have an 8 below the line."

Present problems that add up to *less than* 10.

8. Convert simple addition facts into two-place problems. This is a combination exercise. Start with a simple problem that does not involve zero.

$$\begin{array}{r} 4 \\ +1 \\ \hline \end{array}$$

"We have 5 above the line, so there must be 5 below the line."

$$\begin{array}{r} 4 \\ +1 \\ \hline 5 \end{array}$$

Now remind the child of how two-place numbers are formed. "What if I added a 20 in front of this 4? 20 and 4 is . . . 24."

$$\begin{array}{r} 24 \\ +1 \\ \hline 5 \end{array}$$

If the child has trouble with this step, remind him that the 20 has *nothing* in the right column."

$$\begin{array}{r} 20 \\ +4 \\ \hline 24 \end{array}$$

Now apply the rule: "If I add a 20 above the line, I must add a 20 below the line. So . . ."

$$\begin{array}{r} 24 \\ +1 \\ \hline 25 \end{array}$$

"Read the whole thing."

To demonstrate that it doesn't matter which term you tack the 20 onto, write

$$\begin{array}{r} 4 \\ +1 \\ \hline 5 \end{array}$$

next to the first problem, and put the 20 in front of the 1.

$$\begin{array}{r} 4 \\ +21 \\ \hline 5 \end{array}$$

The same rules apply: "20 and 1 is 21. And when you add 20 above the line, you have to add 20 below the line. So . . ."

$$\begin{array}{r} 4 \\ +21 \\ \hline 25 \end{array}$$

"It doesn't matter where we add the 20, does it?"

Repeat with various examples. Make sure that the numbers in the right column add up to less than 10.

9. Present ready-made column problems. Until now, the child has been in on the build-up of problems. These taught him quite a bit about the continuity of our number system. The jump to "ready-made" problems is not great, but it is not trivial. It may confuse the child about *how to attack the problem*. When he approaches the problem

$$\begin{array}{r} 34 \\ +2 \\ \hline \end{array}$$

raw, he may make the mistake of reading the top number as "43" instead of "34." This mistake is perfectly natural. He knows that when you work this kind of problem, you do something backward. You start working on the right side. It seems to follow that you should also read the numbers backward. Anticipate this kind of mistake.

Present problems in which one of the terms is a two-place number. Put arrows over them.

$$\overrightarrow{28} \qquad \overrightarrow{43} \qquad \overrightarrow{71} \qquad \overrightarrow{45} \qquad \overrightarrow{2}$$
$$+ \; 1 \qquad + \; 3 \qquad + \; 3 \qquad + \; 2 \qquad +27$$

"Let's take it a step at a time. First we read the problem. We always read just like we read a book. We start over here and follow the arrow. We read 28. Then we forget about the 20. Let's cover it up. Now what's above the line? An 8 and a 1. That's 9. So we put a 9 below the line."

$$\begin{array}{r} \textcircled{2}8 \\ + \; 1 \\ \hline 9 \end{array}$$

"Now we uncover the 20. If there's 20 above the line, there has to be 20 below the line."

$$\begin{array}{r} 28 \\ +1 \\ \hline 29 \end{array}$$

Treat the 20 as if it were independent of the 8 and 1. Make a note of the "backward" way you work the problem. "We read the problem this way →. But when we work it we go this way ←. That's kind of strange, isn't it?"

10. Next, introduce problems with 2 two-place numbers. Make sure they involve familiar addition facts. Continue to use the arrows if the child becomes confused.

$$\begin{array}{r} 23 \\ +43 \\ \hline \end{array}$$

First figure out how much there is above the line. Cover the 20 and the 40. "What's left? A 3 and a 3. That's 6. So there has to be a 6 below the line."

$$\begin{array}{r} 23 \\ +43 \quad 6 \\ \hline 6 \end{array}$$

Now uncover the 20 and 40 and figure out their total. "Look at these numbers. This is a 20 and this is 40. When we add them up, we say, 'If 2 plus 4 is 6, 20 plus 40 is *60*.' Say it . . . We have a 60 above the line. So we have to have a 60 below the line."

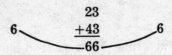

"See? Whatever we have above the line, we have below the line. We have a 60 and a 6 above the line, and look below the line . . . a 60 and a 6."

Present similar problems for about a week. Make sure that they involve only familiar addition facts and that the numbers in either column add up to less than 10.

11. Introduce adding tens. The purpose of this exercise is to familiarize the child with the kind of adding he'll be doing when he carries, which is next on the schedule.

$$\begin{array}{r} 10 \\ +20 \end{array}$$

Approach the problem like any other. Read it; then cover up the 10 and the 20 and add the numbers on the right.

$$\begin{array}{r} 0 \\ +0 \end{array}$$

"Zero plus 0 is 0. Now add 10 and 20. Remember, if 1 plus 2 is 3, 10 plus 20 is 30." The child may have a little trouble with this if-then because of the rough transition from the 1 to the 10. Give him plenty of practice.

12. Then introduce problems that have three parts.

$$\begin{array}{r} 10 \\ 20 \\ +30 \end{array}$$

The 10 should be the top term and the total of all numbers should be less than 100.

"Okay, read it. Now let's cover up the 10 and these other numbers and figure out how much is over on the right: 0, plus 0, plus 0. That's 0. We started out with nothing and we added nothing. Now look in front of those zeros. We've got three numbers above the line: a 10, a 20, and a 30. First, let's add up the 10 and the 20 . . . 10 plus 20 is 30. Let's write it down, and cross out the 10 and 20 to show we've used them up."

$$\begin{array}{r} \cancel{1}0 \\ 3\ \cancel{2}0 \\ +30 \\ \hline 0 \end{array}$$

"Now what do we have above the line? We have a 30 and *another* 30. We know that 30 plus 30 is 60. So we really have 60 above the line."

$$\begin{array}{r} \cancel{1}0 \\ 3\ \cancel{2}0 \\ +30 \\ \hline 60 \end{array}$$

The child should **have a** good idea of how the operation works after three or four sessions. Remind him that he's using a series of familiar rules and show him how. Point out that the 10 row on his multiplication chart shows what the sum is when you add 10 to 20, to 30, to 60 or to any of the other "tens." It's always the next number down. 40 plus 10 is 50, and so forth.

$$\begin{array}{r} 10 \\ 20 \\ 30 \\ \curvearrowright 40 \\ \hookrightarrow 50 \\ 60 \\ 70 \\ 80 \\ 90 \\ 100 \end{array}$$

13. Introduce carrying. Start out with this example:

$$\begin{array}{r} 35 \\ +25 \\ \hline \end{array}$$

"Okay, how much do we have above the line on the right? 5 plus 5? . . . 10."

$$\begin{array}{r} 35 \\ +25 \quad 10 \\ \hline \end{array}$$

"Oh, oh. "We've got *two* numbers here. We've got a 10 and we've got a zero. What are we going to do with them? I know, let's put them where they *belong*. Where does the 10 belong? It belongs out in front with the 30 and the 20. And we'll put the 0 underneath the fives."

"Now, let's add up: 10 plus 30 is 40. Let's write it down."

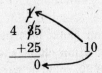

"And 40 plus 20 is . . . well, what's 4 plus 2? 6. So 40 plus 20 is 60."

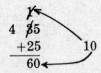

Go through all of the steps noted above during the introduction lesson. Give the child four or five problems. Make sure that the numbers in the right column add up to no more than 18 and that those in the left add up to no more than 90.

During the next lessons, speed up the process. For instance, instead of writing the total for the righthand column above the line, put the 10 above the lefthand column and the righthand number below the line. Give the child four or five carrying problems during each session for about three weeks. After the first three or four sessions, introduce unfamiliar addition facts in the right column, 6 + 8, 5 + 7, 3 + 9, and so forth. Tell him the answers and repeat the problems from time to time so that he becomes familiar with the facts.

14. Introduce problems that add up to more than 100. Begin with the following demonstration:

```
200
 20
  2
```

"The bottom is is *2*. The middle one is *20*. Notice, there is one 0 after the 2. Is the top number called 20? No. It has two zeros after the 2. It's called *two hundred*." Repeat with different series, such as:

```
500      100      800
 50       10       80
  5        1        8
```

After the child can accurately identify the different numbers in series such as these, show how the series can be condensed to form a different kind of three-place number.

```
400
 40
  4
```

"I'm going to take the 40 and put it with the 400. I'm just going to push it up."

```
400      440
 40
  4        4
```

"Now the top number is *four hundred and forty*. Here's the 400 . . . and here's the 40."

Complete the condensing process by merging the 4 with the 440.

```
400        444
 40
  4
```

"This is a new number. Four hundred . . . and forty . . . *four*."

The primary lesson the child should learn from this presentation is that a number such as a 4 changes its name when it occupies different positions in a longer number such as 444.

After several days, the child should be ready to tackle other types of three-place numbers. Use the same basic procedure.

```
400
 20
  3
```

First read the different numbers. Then condense.

```
400        423
 20
  3
```

"Four hundred . . . twenty . . . three. Four hundred and twenty-three. Your turn."

In reading three-place numbers, the child will have trouble with teen numbers (such as 314), with numbers that end in 1 (such as 341), and with numbers that have a zero for the middle number (such as 407). He'll have a tendency to read teen numbers backward, calling 314 "three hundred and forty-one." (Remind him that there's a 10 [or a "teen] in front of the 4.) He'll probably also read numbers that end in 1 as teen numbers. (Remind him that when the number is all the way over on this side → it's a 1, not a teen.) The 407 kind of number is difficult because it departs from the standard three-place–number pattern. To make sense out of the number, the child will probably try to read it as a two-place number, 47. Correct him by pointing out that there's "nothing in the middle at all. So we say four hundred and—we skip over the zero—*seven*." Give him practice with all three patterns. If he has trouble, show how the number builds up. Use number build-up exercises often. They show how addition is related to number formation.

15. Introduce addition problems that total more than 100. Introduce the simplest versions first.

$$
\begin{array}{ccc}
50 & 60 & 80 \\
+50 & +70 & +80 \\
\end{array}
$$

Add up the zeros, and then use an if-then to arrive at the sum of the lefthand column. This is not an easy if-then but it is an important one. It helps the child look at larger numbers as wholes, not as atoms. The first problem: "Let's see how much we have in front here. We have a 50 up here and a 50 down here. 50 plus 50 is . . . well, what's 5 plus 5? . . . 10. *So 50 plus 50 is 100.* We put a 100 out here where it belongs and a 0 to show there's nothing in the middle column."

$$
\begin{array}{c}
50 \\
+50 \\
\hline
100 \\
\end{array}
$$

Next problem: "If 6 plus 7 is 13, 60 plus 70 is 130."

$$
\begin{array}{c}
60 \\
+70 \\
\hline
130 \\
\end{array}
$$

"See, it looks like a 13, but it's really 130, because it's out in front of the 0."

After the child has mastered the basic if-then, introduce more complicated problems.

$$
\begin{array}{cccccc}
56 & 14 & 78 & 66 & 75 & 12 \\
+61 & +86 & +97 & +66 & +76 & +98 \\
\end{array}
$$

If he has trouble with any addition facts, encourage him to figure out the answer with if-thens. "You can always figure out the answer. All you have to do is start out with something you know. If you can't remember what 2 plus 8 is, you say, 'I don't remember what that is, but I do remember what *1* plus 8 is: 1 plus 8 is 9. So 2 plus 8 must be 10.' Always back up or go forward to the nearest 'fact'; then 'if-then.' "

Work on column addition for about two months. Present a variety of problems.

COLUMN SUBTRACTION

Spend about a week on column subtraction. Start out with one-place problems that involve familiar subtraction facts.

8	6	5	9	7	5	3
-2	-3	-1	-4	-1	-3	-2

Work up to problems in which a one-place number is taken away from a two-place number. Make sure the combinations are relatively familiar.

14	18	10	15	10	12
-7	-9	-1	-7	-5	-6

Point out that the top number is formed by adding a 10 in front of the other number. "See? . . . 14 is a 4 with a 10 in front of it." After the child solves the problem, point out the relationship between addition and subtraction.

$$\begin{array}{r} 14 \\ -7 \\ \hline \end{array}$$

"Remember the rule for subtracting. You always start out with the big number and end up with a part. The big number is the one that's below the line when you add. When you subtract, you start out with it, and end up with one of the smaller parts."

The child may have forgotten the rules about the parts and the big number. Review them. Draw a box around the big number.

$$\begin{array}{r} \boxed{14} \\ -7 \\ \hline 7 \end{array} \qquad \begin{array}{r} 7 \\ +7 \\ \hline \boxed{14} \end{array}$$

"When you subtract you start out with a big number and end up with a part. You end up with less than you start out with. When you add, you start out with a part and end up with a big number."

Use the relationship between the big number and the parts to present a rule for subtracting. "Remember, the other two numbers always add up to the top number in a subtraction problem, so if you forget what

$$\begin{array}{r} 12 \\ -6 \\ \hline \end{array}$$

is, point to the 6 and say, 'When you add the other number to 6 you end up with 12.' 6 plus how many is 12? . . . 6 plus *6*. So your answer is 6."

Present a variety of simple column subtraction problems. Don't introduce borrowing or problems that go beyond the child's repertoire of simple addition facts. Stress the idea that subtraction is closely related to addition.

MORE ABOUT THE RELATIONSHIP BETWEEN THE TERMS OF A PROBLEM

The formal relationships between the terms in a problem aren't particularly mystic. By the time your child is about $4\frac{3}{4}$ years old, he should be ready to learn them. Caution: Don't skim over this section.

1. Present the rule for equal. The child already understands that the symbols on the left of an equal sign are somehow the same as those on the right. But he needs a more productive definition. We've already hinted at it. Rule: If A equals 6, it means that wherever there is an A you can put a 6, and wherever there is a 6 you can put an A. The resulting statement will always be true.

$$A = 6$$

"Okay, let's use the rule. Here's an A. If A equals 6, I can put a 6 in place of this A."

$$A = 6$$
$$6 = 6$$

"Is that true? Sure: 6 equals 6, doesn't it? Now, remember, we started out with A equals 6. That means that wherever I have a 6, I can put an A. So I can do this."

$$A = 6$$
$$6 = 6$$
$$6 = A$$

"Is that true? Sure. Now let's try the rule one more time. Wherever I have a 6, I can put an A. Okay, I'm going to put an A where the 6 is in the bottom equation."

$$A = 6$$
$$6 = 6$$
$$6 = A$$
$$A = A$$

"Does A equal A? Sure it does. The rule holds. If A equals 6 you can put an A wherever you have a 6 and a 6 wherever you have an A."

Give the child two or three simple equations, such as $B = 9$, $R = 1$, $M = 6$, each day for a week. Show how the rule applies. This is a powerful demonstration. It is ridiculously simple, but it makes the fundamental point that when two things are equal you can *substitute* one for the other. *Substitution is the key to success in mathematics.*

2. Introduce more complicated types of substitution. The first of these is a direct extension of the form just presented.

$$A = 6 + B$$

If A and $6 + B$ are equal, you can put an A wherever you have a $6 + B$ and you can put a $6 + B$ wherever you have an A. So—

$$A = 6 + B$$
$$6 + B = 6 + B$$
$$6 + B = A$$
$$A = A$$

Present problems like these for about a week. Stress the idea that $6 + B = A$ is the same as $A = 6 + B$.

The next type of substitution problem is more difficult.

$$A = 20$$
$$B = A$$
$$B =$$

"The top equation tells you that A and 20 are equal. What does that mean? Yes, we can put a 20 wherever we have an A and an A wherever we have a 20. Now, look at the second equation. Does it have a 20? No. Does it have an A? Yes. So let's use the rule and put a 20 in place of the A."

$$A = 20$$
$$B = \cancel{A} \quad 20$$
$$B =$$

"Look. We've already solved the problem. B equals 20."

The secret to working these problems is to take them a step at a time. Apply the rule to the top equation. Then apply it to the second. That will give the answer.

Work on these double-substitution problems for about a week.

3. Introduce the egg diagram to show the relationship between the big number and the parts. The child already knows the rules: When you add, you start out with a part and end up with the big number. When you subtract, you always start out with the big number and end up with the part. Before he proceeds into problems that have *no* numbers, however, he should have a firm understanding of why the rules work. That's where the egg diagram comes in.

Write a familiar problem on the board:

$$3 + 2 = \boxed{5}$$

Draw a box around the big number, the 5. Then explain that you're going to diagram the problem. Draw an egg on the chalkboard, with a jagged line separating the top half from the bottom. Stick a box on the right side of the egg and put the 5 in it. Label the halves "3" and "2."

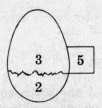

Explain, "This egg shows the two parts and the big number. The big number stands for the whole egg, the parts are 3 and 2." After the child understands the diagram, continue: "Now let's look at the problem."

$$3 + 2 = \boxed{5}$$

"It says to start out with 3. So we'll color the 3 part of the egg . . ."

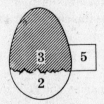

"The problem says start out with 3 and *add 2*. Let's do that by coloring in the 2 part . . ."

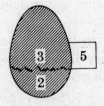

"The problem says that if you start out with 3 and add 2, you'll end up with the 5. If that's true, we should have the whole egg colored . . . and we do."

Present four or five problems like the one above. Emphasize the idea that the 3 and 2 *together* are the same as the 5. "When you take 3 and add 2, you already have 5."

280

Next, introduce subtraction.

$$3 + 2 = \boxed{5}$$
$$\boxed{5} - 3 = 2$$

"When we subtract, we *start out* with the big number and end up with a part. Let's see how that works with the egg diagram. The problem says that we start out with the big number, so we must have the whole egg colored."

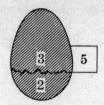

"Now it says that we take away 3. Let's just erase the 3 part."

"What's left? The 2 part. Well, isn't that just what the problem says?"

$$\boxed{5} - 3 = 2$$

"If you start out with a big number and take one of the parts away, you'll end up with the other part."

Repeat with four or five problems.

4. Diagram the rule: One part plus the other part equals the big number. Draw an egg and label it.

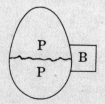

And write the equation P + P = B. "One part plus the other part equals the big number. We start out with one P colored in. Then we color in the other P. And we end up with the whole egg colored, the big number."

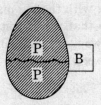

Now subtract, using the completed P + P = B diagram as your starting point.

$$\boxed{B} - P = P$$

"We start out with the big number, with the whole egg colored. Now it says to take away one of the Ps. Which one? It doesn't matter. Which one do you want to take away? Okay. And when we take that P away, what's left? The other P."

Show that by substituting any big number and any parts for the letters P, P and B, it is possible to diagram any familiar addition fact. Write three or four familiar facts next to the egg diagram.

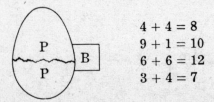

4 + 4 = 8
9 + 1 = 10
6 + 6 = 12
3 + 4 = 7

Now, substitute the parts in each problem (in turn) for the letters P and P; the big number in each problem for the letter B. Make the point that the P–P–B arrangement is true of any addition or subtraction fact.

Next, introduce a more precise rule for determining which term to start out with and which to end up with. Rule (and a very important one): You always end up with the term that is all alone, set off by the equal sign. In the problem $9 = 4 + 5$, you always end up with the 9 because it's alone, set off by the equal sign. By using the rule for substitution, you can help the child understand the convention.

$$4 + 5 = 9$$

If 9 and $4 + 5$ are equal, you can put a 9 wherever there is a $4 + 5$ and a $4 + 5$ wherever there is a 9.

$$4 + 5 = 9$$
$$9 = 4 + 5$$

In the original equation, you ended up with 9. Since the idea of "ending up" has a special meaning in the way it has been presented, you're "ending up" with 9 in the bottom equation also. The term that is alone, set off by the equal sign, is the one you end up with.

How do you find the number you *start out with?* First locate the number you end up with. Then look at the other two numbers. Read them this way →. *The number you read first is the number you start out with.*

In the problem $9 = 4 + 5$, you end up with 9 *and start out with 4.* You can make the process a great deal easier for the child to comprehend by drawing an arrow to indicate the way to attack a reverse-order problem.

$$9 = 4 + 5$$

Present both regular and reverse-order problems and ask the child to tell which term you start out with and which term you end up with. Demonstrate that reverse-order problems can be converted to the regular order without changing the problem. Remind him of the substitution rule. If $6 = 5 + 1$, you can put a $5 + 1$ wherever there's a 6. So $5 + 1 = 6$ and $6 = 5 + 1$.

5. Have the child punctuate problems.

7 6 1

"Oh, oh. Look at these three numbers. They go together. One is the big number and the others are parts. You can see which one the big number is, can't you? Okay, let's put the signs in this problem. Now think hard. *If we were adding,* how would this problem look? Where would the plus sign go and where would the equal sign go?"

To work the problem, start with the rule for addition. "When you add you always start out with a part and end up with the big number. Which is the big number? *So we end up with 7.* That means 7 must be all alone, set off by the equal sign."

$7 = 6 \quad 1$

"The rest is easy: 6 and 1 are parts. We have to add them together to get the big number."

$7 = 6 + 1$

"Now let's erase the signs and see what this problem would look like if we were subtracting."

7 6 1

"We start with the rule. When you subtract you always start out with the big number and end with a part. Which is the big number? 7. So we start out with 7. That means *we must end up with 1,* and 1 must be all alone, set off by the equal sign."

$7 \quad 6 = 1$

"We're subtracting. So . . ."

$7 - 6 = 1$

"There it is."

Work on problems like these for about a week.

6. Introduce a procedure for solving equations. The reason we have labored over the reverse-order problems is because of a potentially confusing convention used in mathematics. When you solve for 5 in the equation $4 + 5 = 9$, you don't normally begin the conversion this way, _____ $= 5$, and then ask what you'd have to do with 9 and 4 to end up with 5. Obviously, if this were the conventional way of handling conversions, many people would be a lot less confused about algebra.

According to the usual convention, if you want to solve for 5, you begin with a reverse-order equation.

$$4 + 5 = \boxed{9}$$
$$5 = \underline{\hspace{2cm}}$$

This convention is not at all confusing if you recognize that the 5 *is the number you end up with*. The rest follows. You've got a 9 and a 4. What do you have to do with them to end up with 5? Subtract.

$$4 + 5 = \boxed{9}$$
$$5 = \underline{\boxed{9} - 4}$$

Translate this convention into the framework you've already built for the child by applying the rule, "When you want to find out what 5 equals, it means that you want to end up with 5. So we write . . ."

$$4 + 5 = \boxed{9}$$
$$5 =$$

Then proceed a step at a time. "Ask yourself what you know about 5. Is it a part or a big number? It's a part. So you want to end up with a part. How do you do that? Do you add or do you subtract? You subtract, don't you?"

$$4 + 5 = \boxed{9}$$
$$5 = \quad -$$

"And when you subtract, what do you start out with? A part or the big number? The big number, which is 9."

$$4 + 5 = \boxed{9}$$
$$5 = \boxed{9} -$$

"Take the other part away, and there we are . . ."

$$4 + 5 = \boxed{9}$$
$$5 = \boxed{9} - 4$$

Obviously, both teacher and child must understand the rules very well to make these conversions. Actually the process is not as difficult as it seems at first.

7. Introduce conversions with letter problems. The procedure is exactly the same as that used with number problems. The big difference is that when the problem involves only letters, *the child cannot see that the big number is actually bigger than the others*. The only way he can locate the big number now is by using the rules for addition and subtraction.

$$A = B + C$$

Take it a step at a time.

Step 1. "What are we doing? Adding."

Step 2. "What's the rule for adding? When you add, you always start out with a part and end up with the big number."

Step 3. "Which term am I ending up with? The A. So A must be the big number. Box it."

$$\boxed{A} = B + C$$

Step 4. "What if I want to end up with C? I write . . ."

$$\boxed{A} = B + C$$
$$C =$$

Step 5. "Now I ask, 'What do I know about C?' Look at the original equation. Is C the big number? No, C is a part."

Step 6. "How do I end up with a part? By subtracting. Write down the minus sign."

$$\boxed{A} = B + C$$
$$C = \quad -$$

Step 7. "Now what's the rule for subtracting? What do I start out with? The big number. So I start out with A."

$$\boxed{A} = B + C$$
$$C = \boxed{A} -$$

Step 8. "And what do I take away? The other part."

$$\boxed{A} = B + C$$
$$C = \boxed{A} - B$$

Make up fun-type problems such as,

$$\tfrac{1}{2}M + dog = B$$

Point out that the rules hold for any kind of problem. "It tells us to start out with ½M and add a dog. What will we end up with? Yes, B, whatever that is. What are we doing? Adding. So which is the big number? B. Now what if I want to end up with *dog*? What do I write? Dog equals."

$$\tfrac{1}{2}M + dog = \boxed{B}$$
$$dog =$$

"What do we know about dog?"

$$\tfrac{1}{2}M + dog = \boxed{B}$$
$$dog = \boxed{B} - \tfrac{1}{2}M$$

Set some of the problems up so that the term you end up with is on the right side.

$$B = A + R$$
$$\quad = R$$
$$\quad = A$$

The approach remains unchanged.

8. Present punctuation problems.

A   B   C

The big difference between these problems and the ones with numbers you presented earlier is that there is no way of telling by inspection which is the big number. During the first exercises, indicate that the left term is the big number.

$\boxed{A}$ B   C

Have the child indicate how the problem would look if you were adding and if you were subtracting. First, adding:

Step 1. "What's the rule for adding? We end up with the big number, A."

$\boxed{A} = B$ C

Step 2. "Since we're adding, we'd better put a plus sign in the equation."

$\boxed{A} = B + C$

Next, subtracting:

$\boxed{A}$ B   C

Step 1. "What's the rule for subtracting? We start out with the big number, A, and end up with C."

$\boxed{A}$ B $= C$

Step 2. "Put in the sign for subtracting."

$\boxed{A} - B = C$

The child should find these problems fairly easy. If you wish, you can diagram a few of them to show that they are logically the same as the number problems.

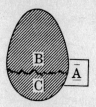

"Start out with the whole egg, the big number A. And take away the B part. And look what's left . . ."

    $\boxed{A} - B = C$

Don't overdo the diagrams, however. They are useful in demonstrating what addition and subtraction are all about. They are good for keeping a problem in perspective. But after these diagrams make the point that all addition and subtraction problems are basically the same, they cease to be of much value. And the child should be weaned from them as quickly as possible.

After the child has worked on punctuation problems in which the first term is the big number, have him punctuate problems in which the middle, or the last term is the big number.

Present four to six conversions a day for several weeks.

MULTIPLICATION AND DIVISION

Multiplication and division parallel addition and subtraction. The rules are similar.

Use variations of familiar diagrams and exercises to present multiplication-division. The child will learn these operations in only a fraction of the time he spent on addition-subtraction.

1. Establish the parallel. Rule: "Multiplication works just like addition; division works just like subtraction."

2. Introduce a new way of expressing division. The child knows division only as a way of working top-heavy fractions, $^{15}\!/_5 = 3$. With some misgivings, we suggest teaching

the child that there's another way to write fractions. "We can write a subtraction problem two ways:

$$4 - 1 = 3 \text{ and } \begin{array}{r} 4 \\ -1 \\ \hline 3 \end{array}$$

We can write division problems two ways, too:

$$15/5 = 3 \text{ and } 15 \div 5 = 3$$

They both say the same thing. Fifteen fifths. Another way of reading them is, '15 *divided by* 5 is 3. The / in the fraction and the $\div$ sign say, *divided by*.' "

Give the child practice in reading division problems. Make the point that every mark in the problem has a function.

3. Specify the operation for handling in-line problems.

$$10 \div 2$$

"That says, 'Start out with 10 and divide it by 2.' To figure out the answer, we have to remember that *this is really a fraction*, with 10 on the top and 2 on the bottom. So we point to the 2 and say, 'Count by twos how many times to get to 10?' Five times. So if we start out with 10 and divide it by 2, we'll *end up* with 5. We can write it like this":

$$10 \div 2 = 5$$

"Or like this":

$$5 = 10 \div 2$$

Unfortunately, the procedure is awkward. But don't get involved in lengthy explanations. "When we want to figure out what the problem is telling us to do, we treat it just like a subtraction problem. But when we *work it*, we remember that it's really a fraction."

4. Present the rule for multiplication. It has a very familiar ring: When you multiply, you always start out with a part and end up with the big number.

$$5 \times 2 = 10$$

Step 1. "Which is the big number? The 10."

$$5 \times 2 = \boxed{10}$$

Step 2. "So 5 and 2 are the parts."

Step 3. "Can we write the problem another way? Yes."

$$\boxed{10} = 5 \times 2$$

Step 4. "Which term are we starting out with? The 5. Which one are we ending up with? The 10."

Step 5. Multiplication works just like addition.

You can use the egg diagram to show how the problem works.

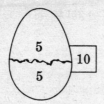

It says to count by fives 2 times and you'll end up with the big number. "We count one time on the top, another time on the bottom. And it's true. We end up with the whole egg colored."

Give the child practice with simple (easily diagrammed) problems. He should have no trouble with them.

5. Introduce the rule for division. It, too, has a familiar ring: When you divide you always start out with the big number and end up with a part.

$$20 \div 5 = 4$$

Step 1. "Which is the big number? The 20."

$$\boxed{20} \div 5 = 4$$

Step 2. "Therefore, 5 and 4 are the parts."

Step 3. "Can we write the problem another way? Sure."

$$4 = \boxed{20} \div 5$$

Step 4. "Which term are we starting out with? The 20. Which one are we ending up with? The 4."

Step 5. "Division is just like subtraction. You start out with the big number and end up with a part."

Diagram the problem, if you wish.

$$20 \div 5 = 4$$

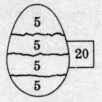

"Count by fives how many times to get to 20?"

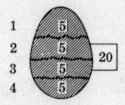

"You count 4 times."

6. Introduce conversion problems. Point out that multiplication conversions work just like addition conversions, while division conversions work just like those of subtraction—with one important exception. Multiplication goes with division. Addition goes with subtraction. If the original problem involves multiplication, you can convert only to division, not to subtraction.

In other words, *division and multiplication go together; addition and subtraction go together*.

$$\boxed{A} = B + C \qquad \boxed{A} = B \times C$$
$$B = \boxed{A} - C \qquad B = \boxed{A} \div C$$
$$C = \boxed{A} - B \qquad C = \boxed{A} \div B$$

The conversion on the right parallels the familiar addition-subtraction conversion on the left, except that the $\times$ sign is substituted for the $+$ and the $\div$ substituted for the −. Teach this parallel by having the child first work out an addition-subtraction conversion of *letter problems*. Then have him work the parallel multiplication-division conversion.

$$D + A = \boxed{C}$$

"Solve for D."

$$D + A = \boxed{C}$$
$$D = \boxed{C} - A$$

"Now work this problem. Remember, addition and subtraction go together; multiplication and division go together."

$$D + A = \boxed{C} \qquad D \times A = \boxed{C}$$
$$D = \boxed{C} - A \qquad D = \boxed{C} \div A$$

7. When the child is able to model multiplication-division conversions after addition-subtraction conversions, have him solve multiplication-division problems for different terms, using the rules. Note: We suggest working from the more abstract letter-type problems, such as $A \div B = C$, to the number problems, such as $6 \times 2 = 12$. We do this for several reasons. The child will probably get the idea that addition and subtraction go together while multiplication and division go together if he works from the more abstract problems. Also, his repertoire of multiplication facts is limited. The demonstration with numbers will not have the intuitive value it had with addition-subtraction. Present series such as these:

$A \times 24V = M$	$Dog = A \times R$	$P \div M = T$
$A =$	$A =$	$P =$
$24V =$	$R =$	$M =$

Also have the child figure out how to punctuate sets of terms for both multiplying and dividing.

GIVE YOUR CHILD A SUPERIOR MIND

$\boxed{A}$ B C

8. Introduce substitution exercises. Begin these after the child has worked on numberless problems for about a month. Start out with the pattern

$$\boxed{A} = B \times C$$
$$B = \boxed{A} \div C$$
$$C = \boxed{A} \div B$$

Now take any multiplication fact and put it in the form of

$$\boxed{A} = B \times C$$

$$\boxed{A} = B \times C$$
$$16 = 8 \times 2$$

To see if the other relations hold ($B = A \div C$ and $C = A \div B$) you simply substitute. Wherever a B is called for, put 8; wherever a C is called for, put 2; wherever an A is called for, put 16.

$$B = \boxed{A} \div C \qquad C = \boxed{A} \div B$$
$$8 = \boxed{16} \div 2 \qquad 2 = \boxed{16} \div 8$$

All statements are true.

Use this kind of demonstration whenever the child has trouble with a conversion. Remind him: "If you get stuck with a letter problem, think of a number problem and see how it works. If it's true that $D \times J = M$, it has to be true for every big number and its parts. So it has to be true for $6 \times 2 = 12$, $9 \times 1 = 9$, $4 \times 5 = 20$, or any other multiplication fact."

Combination Problems: As the child approaches his fifth birthday, introduce combination problems such as $4A \div 2 = 8$. The solution involves two steps. First, find out what 4A equals. Then find out what 1A equals. Point out, "We want to find out what 1A equals, but first we'd better find out what 4A equals. So we write . . ."

$$4A \div 2 = 8$$
$$4A =$$

"We want to end up with 4A. What do we know about 4A? It's the big number. So we want to end up with the big number. That means we multiply."

$$\boxed{4A} \div 2 = 8$$
$$\boxed{4A} = 2 \times 8$$

"If we want to end up with 4A, we have to count by twos 8 times."

$$\boxed{4A} \div 2 = 8$$
$$\boxed{4A} = 2 \times 8$$
$$\boxed{4A} = 16$$

"4A is another way of saying 4 *times* A. We can put a little times sign between the 4 and the A to show that we're really multiplying."

$$4 \cdot A = 16$$

"It's so small, it looks like a dot, doesn't it? Now the problem tells us to count by 4 how many times to get to 16? Let's figure it out: 4 . . . 8 . . . 12 . . . 16. I counted 4 times, so A equals 4."

$$\boxed{4A} \div 2 = 8$$
$$\boxed{4A} = 2 \times 8$$
$$\boxed{4 \cdot A} = 16$$
$$A = 4$$

To make up combination problems, find a number that can be reached by counting by more than two numbers. We know that 24 can be reached by counting by eights, sixes, fours (also twos and ones). Therefore, you can make up a series of combination problems involving 24. And 30 can be reached by counting by threes, fives, sixes and tens; so you can make up combination problems involving 30, such as,

$$3 \times 5A = 30$$

ARITHMETIC REVIEW

When the child is about $4\frac{3}{4}$, begin a systematic review of addition, multiplication, fractions and algebra. Stress the rules, and present familiar problems. The child will have forgotten how to apply some of the rules and will have forgotten some of the "familiar" facts. For instance, he may have forgotten that $7 + 7 = 14$. Mistakes of this kind are quite natural. They can be reduced—and in many cases avoided—by presenting the review material in a familiar *set*. In reviewing number pairs, for instance, present them in a continuity sequence, starting with $1 + 1$ and $2 + 2$. In reviewing fractions, go over the rules for making fractions, the rules that explain the function of the bottom number and the top number. Try to jog the child's memory by giving the review some meaning. He'll get much more out of the review if you do.

Another point to keep in mind when reviewing: the child knows more than one way to solve simple algebra problems. He originally learned to solve the problem $2 + B = 4$ by treating the B as a "how many" and saying, "2 plus how many is 4?" More recently he has learned to solve algebra problems by analyzing them in terms of their parts and big number. This approach can be used to solve $2 + B = 4$. Here, 4 is the big number.

$$B = \boxed{4} - 2$$

Have the child work simple algebra problems both ways.

Spend about fifteen minutes a day on the review, as part of the regular arithmetic lesson. Spend time on areas that give the child trouble. By the time he's 5, he should have a fairly good grasp of the different operations and rules he has studied.

SPATIAL RELATIONS, INFERENCES, AND PRACTICE

SPATIAL RELATIONS

The type of reasoning necessary to play chess is reasonably—but not completely—independent of other reasoning patterns.

The 4- to 5-year-old child is ready to learn new forms of spatial reasoning. But remember that these patterns are not a direct extension of what he already knows. So don't expect him to learn spatial tasks as rapidly as he learns verbal tasks. He'll be quite unsophisticated at first, quite slow.

Here are the spatial-reasoning activities that should be presented during the fifth year: playing spatial games, judging distances, learning directions, and interpreting maps.

Playing Spatial Games: There are several good spatial games. Chinese checkers is particularly good. It requires various strategies, but always leads to a certain amount of success. Even if the child doesn't win, you can point out that the child managed to move four or five "men" all the way across the board. "That's very good."

Simple jigsaw puzzles prompt the kind of spatial strategies that are quite relevant to mechanical aptitude. Simple jigsaw puzzles, composed of perhaps five large pieces, are the easiest introduction. Even if the child is fairly facile with these, you can play games that have important instructional value. "Let's see how fast we can put the puzzle together . . . I'll bet I can beat the best time that you had the other day . . ."

You can introduce variations of the game in which the pieces are piled up far from the puzzle, or in which you perform with your eyes closed.

Electronic games provide an interesting variety of visual-spatial activities. Some of these games require the learner to track, to remember paths that an object took, or to manipulate buttons in time with the progress of an object. All activities build useful skills.

In addition to these games, you can design simple visual-spatial games that are both fun and that help the child develop a very useful system for organizing information. At the University of Oregon, we have conducted experiments involving visual-spatial displays and have found that children who use them as a basis for organizing information are able to learn more information in less time than children who do not receive the displays. For the simplest game, make up a display of three or four pictures and several letters. Present the display on the chalkboard. Point to each entity as the child identifies it.

Tell the child, "Close your eyes and see if you can tell me the things I erase." Erase some of the letters and pictures. (Or remove them if they are attached to the chalkboard.) Point to the space each occupied. "What went here?"

You will probably be surprised at how fast children become facile at this game. After playing perhaps a dozen times, you should be able to make up a new display of perhaps ten entities (letters, pictures) and remove six of them as the child waits with eyes closed. The child will probably correctly identify each empty space.

Checkers: You can introduce checkers when the child is about four-and-a-half. He will encounter two problems with the game. The first is that of manipulating the pieces. The other is the problem of orientation. He somehow has to orient himself so that he knows which way his men are supposed to be moving. You can help him out by putting

298

a strip on either side of the board on which you have drawn large arrows that show the direction he should be going.

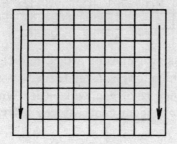

After he has played the game for about three months, you can remove the strips. But expect the child to get confused from time to time even after he's played for a year.

When you play with the child:

1. Set up a lot of jumps for him. Take a fall. Let him win most of the time, *but not all of the time*. If he asks, tell him that you're letting him win.

2. Point out some of your if-then choices. "Oh, oh. If I move here, you'll jump this other man. But if I don't move, you'll jump both of them."

3. Don't make a habit of correcting the child's play, but point out flagrant errors. Do it gracefully. "Yes, that might work, but think big. Do you have another move, a better one? It's hard to see, but I bet if you try hard you can find it."

4. Play on the red squares one time and on the blacks another. The purpose of this convention is to force the child to formulate rules of space, not of color.

Tic-tac-toe: 1. Teach a basic pattern for winning. Rule: If you go first, try to get to three corners and try to keep your opponent from lining up down the middle.

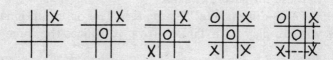

The X side wins because it has two lines of attack and the O side can only stop one attack. Another example:

Again the X side has two lines of attack and the O side has only one move in which to try to stop them.

Using the three-corner rule, you will either win or tie. There is no way your opponent can beat you (if you move first).

2. Point out the basic strategy of the three-corner play. Actually what you're doing is *using one of your men twice.* He works as a pivot point for two other men. In order to see the man in both roles, you have to re-orient yourself. You have to see him first one way, and then another. This is not easy, especially for a child. To get him used to the double role of the pivot figure, take a pencil and lay it on the tic-tac-toe problem so that it shows one of the possible courses.

"See? They're lined up, aren't they?"

Then rotate your pencil to indicate the other course.

Play tic-tac-toe once or twice a month, starting when the child is about 4½. Point out strategy in if-then propositions, but play the game primarily for the practice it gives in establishing double roles. Don't expect the child to catch on to these for several weeks.

Three-dimensional Tic-tac-toe: This is an optional game you can play with Tinker Toys. It utilizes the same double-role used in regular tic-tac-toe, but it involves a great deal more visual reorganization because the double role is framed in a three—not a two—dimensional setting. Construct a gizmo that looks like this:

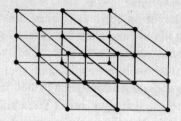

Show where a man is by sticking a red or blue peg in the appropriate hub. To win, you must be the first to line up three consecutive pegs forming a straight row in any direction. The straight row may be formed on a vertical face of the model or a horizontal face. Or it may cut diagonally through the maze. To get an idea of how many combinations are possible, imagine a peg on the middle hub of the center member. You can start a row by using it *and any other hub on the board.* Because the game is more complex than regular tic-tac-toe, the child needs a slightly different approach for making winning combinations.

1. Put the first two men anywhere on the board.

2. Then find a hub that will work for both of them (that will serve as the pivotal point). There is at least one such hub for any two hubs on the board, but some of these are not easy to see.

3. The opponent is then in the position of having to stop two lines of attack with one move, which is impossible.

Use a rod or pencil to show the child the direction his attack is taking and to find the "pivot man." Play three-dimensional tic-tac-toe on a once-in-a-while basis after the child has mastered regular tic-tac-toe.

Chess: When the child is about 4¾, you can introduce chess. His experience with Fascination Checkers will make him quite handy with the knight; his tic-tac-toe experience will make him handy at the visual reorganizations that are necessary to manipulate the pieces capable of pivoting in more than one direction. His if-then experience will provide him with a good game strategy.

Judging Distances: Before a child can judge distances, he has to know something about how they are measured. Teach him the three fundamental units—inch, foot, yard—when he's about $4\frac{1}{2}$. Use a ruler to show him how long an inch is. Then play a game, seeing how close he can come to holding up his fingers for 1 inch, 2 inches, 3 inches, etc. (The child's index finger from the knuckle to the first joint is about an inch.)

Next, introduce a foot. Tell him, "A foot is 12 inches." Then give him practice in holding up his hands for 1 foot, 2 feet, 3 feet.

Introduce a yard in the same manner. "A yard is 3 feet, or 36 inches." Show him how big a yard is. Ask him how many feet and how many inches it is. After he becomes fairly good at estimating yards, feet and inches, let him guess how far it is across the room. Then measure it off. Repeat in different rooms and other places. Let him guess how high the house is and so forth.

Before long, the child will be very proficient at judging distances. This is one task that seems to come much easier for younger children than for adolescents or adults, probably because younger children haven't learned to think in great distances on the horizontal, small distances on the vertical. (Look down from the top of a 60-foot tree; then stand next to the top of that same tree after it's felled. Does the distance seem as great now as it did when the tree was standing?)

Practice distance judging when you're walking with the child. Remember, few trees are taller than 60 feet; single-story houses are rarely higher than 18 feet.

Directions: The notion of directions is a little staggering to the 4-year-old. It is not at all easy for him to grasp the idea of fixing himself in space according to some absolute, invisible lines. His natural tendency is to fix himself according to the surroundings. If he learns directions in the living room, he remembers that the wall with the windows is *east*, the one leading to the kitchen is *south*, and so forth. You can work with him in this room until his performance is perfect. But when he tries to find east in a different room of the house, even an adjoining room, he'll probably fail miserably. He doesn't understand that he was to take the notion of direction with him wherever he went. He left it in the living room.

The best way to overcome this tendency is to define directions in a way that forces the child to take them with him.

1. Teach east-west first. Rule: East is where the sun comes up in the morning. West is where the sun sets at night. When you face east, west is in back of you. When you face west, east is in back of you.

Start out in the yard. Show the child where the sun comes up. Stress the idea that "this is always east, no matter where you are in the world." Then play a game. Have the child close his eyes and turn him around a few times. "Now when I count to three, I want you to face where the sun comes up; I want you to face east. One . . . two . . . three."

2. Repeat the same procedure in different rooms of the house. Demonstrate that the direction you call east inside the house is the same direction you called east outdoors. Have the child face east in a room. "Okay, you just keep facing east and come along with me. Don't turn, now." Take him outdoors, to about the place he stood when he was first introduced to east. "See? You're facing the same way you did the other day. See, there's Tommy's house. And the sun comes up right over there."

3. After he has the idea of east-west, introduce north-south. Draw the four directions on a mat about 2 feet by

2 feet (a shopping bag works nicely; an old towel works better).

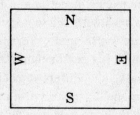

Put it on the floor so that the directions on the mat correspond to the actual directions. Have the child stand in the middle of the mat. Explain what the letters stand for. Then give him a method for finding north. *"Face east and put your left hand straight out to the side . . . that's north."* After a few trials, the child should be able to find north. Move the mat to different rooms in the house, demonstrating that the rule for north holds, no matter where you are. Point out landmarks that will help him remember north. "When you stand here, Maple Street is north. See Jimmy's house? That's north."

4. Once the child is reasonably familiar with north, present the rule for south. "When you face north, *south is behind you.*"

5. Introduce the confusing notion that directions are absolute only as far as you are concerned. You are in the center of four lines that go east, west, north and south, and you are the only fixed element in this grid. Everything else changes. As you take the grid with you on a walk, houses that were "east" become "west"; things that were "south" become "north." Take the mat with you on a walk. "See, you're always in the center, but everything else changes." Take a walk past a friend's house and set the mat up again. "Oh, oh. Is this house still north? No, it's *south.*" Make the point, *"Every place you go, you have four invisible lines sticking out of you, one going north, one going south, one going east and one going west."* Encourage the child to use his knowl-

edge of directions when he explains things. Ask him about the directions in which you're traveling when you take a drive.

Interpreting Maps: Take it in seven steps:

1. Introduce the basic orientation for reading maps. "Spread your wings and fly with me—high above the world. Now look down. Way down there. I see a room. And look—in that room is a boy named Tommy and his mother. They are standing next to the table, in front of the chalkboard. See them?"

2. Demonstrate that you can make a map out of what you see. "Let's pick up that whole room down there and put it on the chalkboard." Pretend to pick it up, so that the wall of the room you are facing is on the top of the map. Draw circles to indicate the people in the room. Draw in furniture and other reference points.

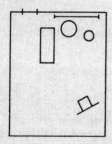

Point out that the reference points on the map correspond to the points in the room. "See? The big blob is me and the little blob is you. We're looking down, down on ourselves, aren't we? See the table next to us? Here it is over here, just as on the map. And the chair is behind us—just as on the map." Ask the child to add details to the map. "Where would the door be? It's in that corner of the room. Can you find that corner on the map? Good."

3. Introduce the convention that north is always at the top of the map. Place the child's direction mat in the middle of the room. Have him stand on it. "Okay, now fly with me,

305

and I'll teach you a rule about reading regular maps. To read a regular map, you must always face *north*. Do it. Now look at the room. This is the way you must imagine the room." Pick up the child's mat so that north is at the top and place it on the wall in front of him. Demonstrate that you can place it on any wall of the room and north will still be on the top.

Draw a map on the chalkboard and put letters in for the different directions. Present the verbal rule, "North is on the top and south is on the bottom. East on this side; west on this side." Singsong the pattern and slap the chalkboard as you name each direction. Go over this rote pattern until the child has learned it thoroughly.

4. Teach a rule for telling the direction in which you're going. Draw a map on the board. Label it, and put a mark on it.

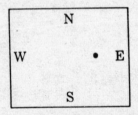

"That's *you*. You're standing still. In a minute you're going to start walking and we have to figure out which way you're going. I'll draw an arrow to show the way you go."

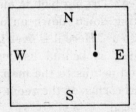

"If the arrow points north, you are going north. The direction the arrow points is the direction you're going." This rule is not as trivial as it may seem. It is just as reasonable to suppose that motion on a map is like a wind, which is named according to where it has been, not where it is going.

5. Present a rule for figuring out relative directions. The rule: "If you want to know whether a point on the map is east, west, north or south of another point, ask yourself, 'How do I get there?' If you go east, the point is east. If you go south, the point is south." Put two points on a map. Label them A and B.

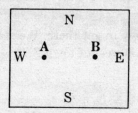

"These are houses. Here's house A, and here's house B. Let's pretend that we're at house B and we want to get to house A. *We put our finger on house A and say, 'How do I get here?'* Let's figure it out. We start at B and go . . ."

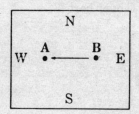

"west. So house A is *west* of house B."

After the child has worked a variety of two-point problems, introduce three-point problems. Put the center point on the board first.

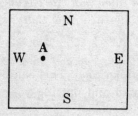

"Is that town east, west, north or south? We don't know, because we don't know *how we get there.*"

Add another point.

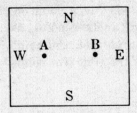

"Now we can figure out how to get there. We start out at town B and we go west. So A is west of town B."

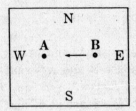

"Now what if we put town C over here?"

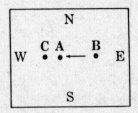

"If we start out at C and go to town A, we'll have to go . . . east. So town A is *east of town C,* but west of the other town. *It all depends on which town you start from.* You ask yourself," 'How do you get there?' *And that depends on where you start out.*"

Give different examples.

6. Make a map of the neighborhood. This can be a lot of fun. Begin by labeling the map and putting your house or

apartment in its proper relation to the street. Then let the child figure out where the other houses, apartments or landmarks should go. "Is the Dennis house on the same side of the street as we are? Is it? Go look out the window and see. It's across the street, so it goes here." After the map is finished, hang it up and refer to it from time to time.

7. Introduce road maps. When you go on a trip, pencil the route on a road map and point out how the map works and how it is like the maps the child is familiar with.

INFERENCES FROM STATEMENTS

The 4-year-old child should have the basic idea that a statement such as, "Dogs have four legs," generates questions such as, "Do dogs have four legs?" and, "How many legs do dogs have?" He has also learned that the statement implies the answers to the questions.

> Dogs have four legs.
> Do dogs have four legs?
> Yes, dogs have four legs.

At 4, the child can begin to take his knowledge of statements a step further by answering some of the more difficult questions that are inferred by statements.

1. The I-don't-know question: Basically, we have two patterns of deductive reasoning. One deals with opposites and concepts that are defined so that there are only two possible choices. "If the stove is not hot it is . . ." "If this side of the seesaw is down, the other side is . . ." The second pattern deals with concepts that are defined so that there are more than two possibilities. "If the glove is not blue it is . . ." I don't know. "If an animal is not a horse, it is . . ." I don't know.

Present various statements that generate I-don't-know answers.

> There are more than four boys in the room.
> Are there five boys in the room?
> I don't know. All I know is that there are more than four.
>
> Many children were in the water.
> Were some of them girls?
> Were all of them girls?
> I don't know.
>
> A boy picked pretty flowers.
> Were some of these flowers yellow?
> I don't know. I only know they were pretty.

2. Identification questions. The child has learned to answer basic questions implied by statements with yes-no answers. But *a statement also implies questions that have parts of the original statement as their answer*. Every statement has at least two of these questions, one for the subject and one for the predicate.

> Animals breathe.
> What do animals do? Breathe.
> What breathes? Animals.

Play statement games starting with such statements as, *The king wears a crown on his head.*

Then ask the questions it implies.

> Who wears a crown?
> What does a king wear on his head?
> Where does a king wear a crown?
> If you saw a man with a crown on his head, what would you know about him?
> How would you know a king if you saw one?

3. Later, extend the game to questions implied by nonsense statements. Construct these so that they deal with *and, or, if-then, since, because, only.*

> Glips eat beans and grasshoppers.
> Do glips eat beans?
> Do glips eat grasshoppers?
> Can you name something that eats both beans and grasshoppers?

And so forth.

Nonsense statements of this kind are very useful in helping the child see the basic reasoning patterns we expect him to see. Play nonsense-statement games at least several times a month from the time the child is 4½.

Put it in your own words: Once the child gets used to the idea that a given statement generates questions and answers, he's ready to take the next step, that of putting stories into his own words. *This is an extremely difficult task.* To be successful at it, the child must first ask the *important questions* about the original story. If you're tempted to think that this is an easy task, remember that a single three-minute story generates about two hundred questions. To put the story in your own words, you have to select the most important ones, not all of them. The important questions that must be answered are: "Who is the hero? What was he doing? What happened then? What was the outcome?"

Give the child practice in rephrasing stories. Make them simple, and make the questions obvious. "Jimmy's mother told him not to get dirty. And Jimmy tried. But all the other boys on the block were jumping across a big mud hole. Jimmy jumped across it, too. Splat! He fell right in the mud. His mother gave him a spanking. . . . Now it's your turn. Tell the same story." At first, he'll probably try to remember the story by rote. You can help him over this hurdle by asking appropriate questions. "Okay, so Jimmy tried not to get dirty. Did he do it? Did he go back home with nice clean pants? . . . No? Well, what happened? . . ."

As the child approaches his fifth birthday, begin pointing out that *he* should begin asking the questions. "Ask yourself, 'What did the bear do then? What happened?' . . ."

The child will probably be only a fair storyteller by the time he's 5. But he'll have a good idea of what he should be doing. During the next year he'll use this knowledge and show great improvement.

Complete the story: This is a game that's fun and at the same time gives the child practice in using language assumptions. Begin telling a story. When you get to a crucial point, stop and let the child continue. "Once there was a fishing bear named Joe. He was the best fishing bear in the whole woods. When all the other bears couldn't catch anything, Joe always had a big, full tummy. Well, one day, Joe went down to the stream to catch a fish. He saw something flash under the water, so he took a fast swipe at it. He pulled it out of the water, and *he stopped cold.* He hadn't caught a fish at all. It was a great, big . . . Your turn." Play the game from time to time. It is an excellent occupier on long trips.

PRACTICE IN SKILLS ALREADY MASTERED

Don't neglect the skills the child has already learned. Continue to teach visual inferences through comic strips. The 4½-year-old child is old enough to handle simple comic books. Go through them once with him and let him browse through them during leisure time. Remind the child of right-left from time to time. And continue to teach facts about the world. Each fact the child learns increases the "surface area" of his knowledge. Therefore, *each fact increases his learning potential.* Use a procedure similar to the one you used to teach the planets and dinosaurs. Work from a well illustrated children's book that deals with the subject you wish to present. Require the child to learn key facts, but make your presentation less mechanical than you did last year. The child knows what's expected of him, and he's worked out the basic rules for learning groups of related facts. So the task can be presented in a more interesting fashion.

One body of knowledge should be required—facts about

the human body (the name of bones and muscles, the functioning of the various body systems). Optional subjects range from early American history to the study of construction equipment. Present these facts on a semi-regular basis. Try to have at least two fact sessions a week, preferably more.

TASK SCHEDULE FROM 4 YEARS TO 5 YEARS

AGE (IN MONTHS) FOR WORKING ON TASKS

TASK	PAGE REFERENCE
Reading	188-192
Reading, Printing and Spelling	192-193
Addition Problems	197-203
Algebra Problems	203-207
If-Then, Addition	207-213
Continuity Game (Addition)	213-214
Subtraction	214-222
Multiplication	222-233
Area	233-237
Telling Time	237-244
Fractions	244-253
Division	254-256
Money	256-262
Column Addition	262-276
Column Subtraction	276-277
Formal Relationships	277-294
Combination Problems	294-296
Fascination Checkers	298
Regular Checkers	298-299
Tic-tac-toe	299-301
Chess	301-302
Judging Distances	302
Directions	302-305
Interpreting Maps	305-309
Inferences from Statements	309-312

Age scale (in months): 48, 49, 50, 51, 52, 53, 54, 55, 56, 57, 58, 59, 60

EPILOGUE: PAST FIVE

THE CHILD'S CAPACITY TO LEARN and understand is always predictable in one sense, because it is always related to his position on the ladder of abstraction. If you know where the child stands, you can predict at least some of the concepts he is ready to learn. You can also list many of those he is not ready to learn. It follows that the more he knows, the more he is ready to learn. To get an idea of why this is true, consider two pans sitting out in an open field during a steady rain. Say that one has a much larger surface area than the other. Just as the larger pan will obviously collect more water, so it is with learning. The environment issues a steady rain of concepts on the child. But only those that fall on his "collecting surface" have any meaning to him. The greater the surface area, the more he will collect.

The program we have outlined in this book is a systematic attempt to increase the size of the child's collecting surface, and the child who is taught by this program will be gifted by the time he is 5 years old.

We end our blow-by-blow program at age 5 for the following reasons:

1. The child's surface area is so large by the time he's 5 that a detailed account of his 5- to 6-year program would require a book at least as large as this one.

2. The manner of presentation is less crucial as the child ascends the ladder of abstraction. On the lower levels, the manner of presentation was quite rigid and "rote" because

it had to be geared to a small surface area. Now, things are different. The child understands the fundamental assumptions of language; he knows which elements of his environment are irrelevant; he knows how to mobilize different operations; he knows how to classify and cross-classify. He therefore stands a far greater chance of collecting any given raindrop that falls in his direction. If he doesn't catch it in the center of the pan, he'll probably catch it out near the rim.

3. You're probably a very good teacher by now. You have worked with the child since birth. You understand him better than anyone else in the world. You have become adept at presenting difficult concepts.

4. Teaching is probably no longer drudgery. The majority of teachers prefer teaching gifted children. They give a variety of reasons, but the primary one—although rarely stated—is obvious. Teaching gifted children is easy. They're quick, and they're usually interested (because the material is easy for them and makes sense). Also, they can be witty. A typical example: Not long ago, we were working with a 6-year-old on physical skills. "Remember," the instructor said as he prepared the child for his chin-ups, "you've got to tell yourself that you can succeed. You've got to get your mind in gear and tell your muscles to *work*." He pressed his index finger against the boy's forehead. "Remember, ninety per cent of all exercises are done *right here!*"

The boy frowned and pressed his index finger against his bicep. "Yeah," he said. "But the hardest ten per cent has to be done *right here!*"

The subjects we have suggested for the child's preschool education have been mostly of the scientific and factual variety, with little emphasis on art, music and other important dimensions of human thought. We have emphasized the scientific subject material because it best teaches the reasoning and classification patterns that are most important in handling the kinds of inference, analogy and fact-collecting skills the child will use throughout his academic life.

The child's formal preschool education in these subjects should never consume more than one to one and a half hours a day—maximum—which means there is a great deal of time for other types of broadening experiences. If you feel that he should learn something about literature or history, teach him. Don't neglect art and music. And, as we have said several times before, don't neglect the physical and social side of the child's education.

Try to make learning a challenging part of life. In addition to the gift of a superior mind, give your child the desire to use his gift. Set the example and he'll follow your lead. The easiest way to do this is to teach him about the things that interest *you*. Whether you like rock collecting or knitting, teach him, not as a schoolmarm, but as someone who wants to share a view from a special window.

THE AUTHORS

Siegfried Engelmann is a professor of education at the University of Oregon. He has worked at all levels of instruction—from preschool to graduate programs—and has worked with virtually every type of child, from retarded and autistic to gifted. Engelmann has developed over fifty instructional programs, including the renowned DISTAR programs. He has also been extensively involved in research and demonstrations of the skills that children can learn. He has directed studies in which preschoolers learned mental operations not typically learned until adolescence, in which deaf children actually learned to hear through tactual vibration, and in which disadvantaged preschool children outperformed their middle-class peers. The most extensive study involved over ten thousand disadvantaged children in Project Follow Through. The model that Engelmann developed, the "direct instruction" model, brought disadvantaged children in grades kindergarten through third grade nearly to the achievement level of their middle-class peers, a feat that has been accomplished by no other large-scale implementation. Engelmann has written a dozen books and manuals on teaching, as well as many chapters and professional articles.

Therese Engelmann, who has degrees in psychology and law, worked with Siegfried Engelmann in developing the program outlined in *Give Your Child A Superior Mind*. She taught preschoolers and was largely responsible for the scope and the direction of the program. Today, she is a practicing attorney, a strong supporter of women's rights, and a grandmother.